The Tokyo Rose Case

LANDMARK LAW CASES

AMERICAN SOCIETY

Peter Charles Hoffer
N. E. H. Hull
Series Editors

For a complete list of titles in the series go to www.kansaspress.ku.edu

YASUHIDE KAWASHIMA

The Tokyo Rose Case

Treason on Trial

UNIVERSITY PRESS OF KANSAS

Published by the University Press of Kansas (Lawrence, Kansas 66045), which was
organized by the Kansas Board of Regents and is operated and funded by Emporia State
University, Fort Hays State University, Kansas State University, Pittsburg State University,
the University of Kansas, and Wichita State University

Library of Congress Cataloging-in-Publication Data
Kawashima, Yasuhide, 1931–
The Tokyo Rose case : treason on trial / Yasuhide Kawashima.
pages cm.—(Landmark law cases & American society)
Includes bibliographical references and index.
ISBN 978-0-7006-1904-7 (cloth : alk. paper) —ISBN 978-0-7006-1905-4
(paperback : alk. paper) 1. Tokyo Rose, 1916–2006—Trials, litigation, etc.
2. Trials (Treason)—California—San Francisco. I. Title.
KF224.T63K39 2013
345.73'0231—dc23
2012049234

British Library Cataloguing-in-Publication Data is available.
Printed in the United States of America
10 9 8 7 6 5 4 3 2 1

The paper used in this publication is recycled and contains 30 percent postconsumer waste.
It is acid free and meets the minimum requirements of the American National Standard for
Permanence of Paper for Printed Library Materials Z39.48-1992.

For A. Russell Buchanan

Alexander DeConde

Wilbur R. Jacobs

Otey M. Scruggs

CONTENTS

EDITORS' PREFACE

Stories of palpable injustice, particularly when the victim is sympathetic, have the power to both move our emotions and rouse our indignation. The trials of Iva Ikuko Toguri d'Aquino in Japan, as an American citizen trapped during World War II, and in the United States, after she returned, fit this description. A woman of valor mistreated by both of the warring nations during and after—long after—the conflict was over, is now shown in her true colors by Yasuhide Kawashima. "Tokyo Rose," the name that Americans gave her, never really fit, but when she finally departed Tokyo, she found that American justice was no fairer to her than Japanese officialdom.

Kawashima's account is deeply rooted in the Japanese language sources, to which he had unparalleled access, the American legal sources, which he fully exploited, and the cultures of both nations. Because of his multicultural heritage, his thorough research, and his abiding commitment to justice in this case, he pulls no punches. There are heroes and villains aplenty, in both the United States and Japan: prosecutors who sought to build careers on her conviction for voluntarily betraying her country, defense counsel who braved public censure to prove her innocence of treason, and above all ordinary men and women who befriended her because of her personal qualities.

In 1977, Iva was finally pardoned by President Gerald Ford, an act of belated grace for which both houses of the California legislature and the city governments of San Francisco and Los Angeles, among others, had pleaded. Los Angeles's act was especially moving, in light of the city's 1948 resolution that she not be allowed to return from Japan. Interwoven in Iva's story are larger ones—of the internment of thousands of loyal Japanese Americans during the war; of the meaning of citizenship and the nation's commitment to the ideal of fair trial; and of the place that tabloid journalism has in our culture. Yet first and foremost, Iva's story is hers—a story that Yasuhide Kawashima has been waiting to tell for many years. No one will read it and come away unimpressed.

PREFACE AND ACKNOWLEDGMENTS

Iva Ikuko Toguri d'Aquino, American-born but infamously identified in history books as the traitorous "Tokyo Rose," found herself living in Tokyo during World War II, arguably the worst period of the city's history. I had a similar experience, living through both the war and early postwar period, first in Nagasaki and then in Tokyo. When the atomic bomb was dropped on Nagasaki, I and many other teenagers were working in the mountains only thirty miles from the city, tapping resin (*matsuyani*) from pine trees for conversion into turpentine. The Japanese government was making desperate efforts to convert such fluids into airplane fuel, and we were responding to the order of government officials who had a vise-grip on our lives in the service of the Emperor.

Word spread immediately after the bomb struck Nagasaki, but I did not go back to the city until four months later. When I did I was appalled by the extent of the destruction this lone "new-style bomb" had inflicted. Although the B-29 had actually missed its target, thus destroying only half of the city, it left in its wake desolate ruins. The devastation was so complete that very little remained; the heights where charming school buildings and houses had once stood had in an instant turned into bare hills, and the sections that formerly contained hospitals and other public buildings and busy, prosperous streets had become darkened, empty fields. Nothing seemed to have been spared. On top of that, the radiation damage, we were told, would be incalculable while remaining at the same time insidiously invisible to us.

I was in the second year of middle school when the war ended, just old enough to read newspapers seriously. Among the news items that stood out to me and my classmates were the stories about "Tokyo Rose" and her alleged propaganda broadcasting activities on behalf of the Japanese government during the war. We thought it odd that two enterprising American correspondents had targeted Iva and tried to purchase the exclusive rights to her story, and that Iva had agreed and thereby implicated herself in ways that later led to her arrest, imprisonment, and trial. (And we were indignant when we found out that the journalists had used her story but not actually paid her.)

Iva had already left for San Francisco for trial and been found guilty of treason and imprisoned by the time I went to college in Tokyo. The capital city at that time still languished amid the enormous physical destruction caused by American bombings during the war—from the Dolittle air raid of 1942 through the terrible fire-bombings late in the war. General Curtis LeMay's systematic destruction of Tokyo by the explosive and incendiary bombs in early 1945 paralyzed the city, destroying over 65 percent of all residences. Yet, due to the selectiveness of the American bombing policies—quite in contrast to the sweeping, indiscriminate destruction wrought by the atomic bombs—Tokyo's financial and business district went largely undamaged and the railroads still functioned effectively throughout the country. Thus in the midst of immense physical devastation, much of the necessary infrastructure and social order remained intact, with national, prefectural, and local governments all functioning nearly normally throughout the period. The Radio Tokyo building, the place of Iva's employment, was one of the survivors. Unfortunately for Iva, its survival also served as a marker for her alleged traitorous broadcasts, which came to occupy (some might say "preoccupy") the military and civilian investigators and prosecutors who relentlessly pursued her case. In the pages that follow, I focus on how that case emerged, evolved, and concluded; what legal and constitutional issues were at stake; and the degree to which justice was ultimately served. By the end of the book, I think the reader will likely detect that Iva's case has an ongoing resonance for our own time.

———

I would like to express my deep appreciation for all the help I have received during the long period of time this project has been in preparation. Indispensable were many comments and suggestions provided by Yuma Totani, of the University of Hawaii at Manoa, who carefully went over the manuscript with a fine-tooth comb, which helped to improve the book greatly. I also thank Roger Daniels and the other reviewer, who read my copyedited manuscript and made many useful comments. I owe a special debt of thanks to Peter C. Hoffer, one of the editors of the Landmark Law Cases and American Society series, for his careful reading of my manuscript and various suggestions that have substantially enhanced the quality of the book.

The University Press of Kansas has done an excellent job transforming my manuscript into a decent book. As always, Michael Briggs, editor-in-chief, has performed superb work. My repeated delays in finishing the book, however, made even Mike, an ideal editor known for his patience, understanding, and ability to elicit the best out of an author, almost lose his patience. In addition, I appreciated his specific suggestions on the Tokyo Rose case, in which he has a deep interest. Thanks also to the entire University Press of Kansas publishing team, and I am particularly grateful to Susan Schott (assistant director and marketing manager), Kelly Chrisman Jacques (production editor), and Martha Whitt (copyeditor) for their superb work.

This book is written as a chapter in American history, and I am deeply indebted to several professors at the University of California, Santa Barbara, who taught me various fields of American history, which cover this topic in one way or another. It is to them I gratefully dedicate this book. Tokyo Rose and her activities during World War II have long attracted the attention of many writers, both scholarly and popular, and the debts I owe to them are acknowledged in the bibliographical essay, but I should specifically mention here the pioneers, Masayo Duus, Rex B. Gunn, John Juji Hada, Russell W. Howe, and Stanley I. Kutler.

I also thank my brother, Takehide Kawashima, professor emeritus of Nihon University, Tokyo, who not only helped arrange all my research in Japan, including at the Japanese Diet Library and the NHK Library, both in Tokyo, and the Yamanashi Prefectural Library in Kofu, but also guided my visit to the Kofu Prefectural High School and Kagami Nakajo in Yamanashi Prefecture, where Iva's father came from.

For personal information about Thomas E. DeWolfe, the main prosecutor, which has been obscure, I am grateful to Elizabeth Torres, reference librarian at the University of Texas at El Paso, who uncovered some rare accounts about him. For all kinds of computer problems I encountered, I heavily relied on the expertise of my good friend, John K. Fahey, director of the Liberal Arts Center for Institutional Technology at the University of Texas at El Paso, to whom I am deeply grateful. This book was written during a period when I was carrying a full teaching load, and my teaching assistants helped me admirably in easing my teaching. I am especially grateful to Craig J. Cummings, Gary Kieffner, Mark Kirkland, and Dana K. Teasley.

Over the years, I have discussed Tokyo Rose with my family, relatives, and close friends on various occasions. Ancy Morse and Robert Morse, former Minnesota district judge and retired Mayo psychiatrist, respectively, who have a strong interest in the subject, talked with me about it over many lunches and dinners and gave me some useful suggestions. And finally, my wife, Ruth Tone Kawashima, has my deepest appreciation for research assistance, criticism of the manuscript, proofreading, and keeping me clear from all kinds of interruption and disturbance.

The Tokyo Rose Case

Guilty!

*Treason against the United States, shall consist only in levying
War against them, or in adhering to their Enemies, giving them Aid and Comfort.
No person shall be convicted of Treason unless on the Testimony of two
Witnesses to the same overt Act, or on Confession in open Court. . . .*

*The Congress shall have Power to declare the Punishment of Treason,
but no Attainder of Treason shall work Corruption of Blood, or
Forfeiture except during the Life of the Person attained.*

U.S. CONSTITUTION, ARTICLE III, SECTION 3

On September 29, 1949, at 6:04 p.m., the jury that had been deliberating for over seventy-eight hours, instead of going to dinner as the judge had suggested, filed back into the courtroom just thirty-three minutes after they had left.

Judge Michael J. Roche of the federal district court for the Northern District of California in San Francisco, who had presided over the trial for almost three months, asked, "Has the jury arrived at a verdict?" "We have, your Honor," replied the foreman of the jury, John Mann, and handed the verdict to the court clerk, James Welch, who in turn passed it on to Judge Roche. He read it without expression and handed it back to the clerk.

The defendant, Iva Ikuko Toguri d'Aquino, stood in front of the defense table facing the judge, flanked by her lawyers. She was wearing the same plaid two-piece suit that she had taken to Japan eight years previously and had been wearing every day throughout the trial, ironing it every night in her cell. She was a slender, "birdlike," and alert Japanese American woman. Her beautiful shoulder-length, raven-black hair (*midori no kurokami*, the kind of hair the Japanese admire) was, as Masayo Duus describes it, "neatly bobbed and swept back by a band."

In the hushed room Clerk Welch announced in a clear voice: "Guilty."

As a moan of disappointment arose from the courtroom audience, Iva slumped into her chair, staring at her hands. Her face clearly revealed expressions of shock and incredulity. The verdict, however, was guilty only on one count but not guilty on the other seven counts.

A week later, Judge Roche sentenced Iva to ten years in prison and fined her $10,000, in accordance with the U.S. statute stipulating that "a person convicted of Treason shall suffer death, or shall be imprisoned not less than 5 years and fined not less than $10,000 and shall be incapable of holding any office under the United States." She was ordered imprisoned in the Federal Reformatory for Women at Alderson, West Virginia, where Iva's German counterpart, Mildred ("Axis Sally") Gillars, had already been serving her time and where, more recently, Martha Stewart served for five months.

What exactly had Iva T. d'Aquino, a Japanese *nisei* woman, who went to Japan just before the Japanese attack on Pearl Harbor, done to have been declared guilty of such a crime as treason, the "gravest of all crimes"? She was accused of having broadcast propaganda from Tokyo to the American GIs fighting in the Pacific, saying things like "Give up fighting" and "Now, you fellows have lost all your ships. . . . How do you think you will ever get home?" How could anyone, let alone a college graduate, not understand that making such announcements over the enemy radio was a grievous betrayal of country?

What specific work did d'Aquino really do that would constitute a treasonable act? Or was she convinced that whatever she was doing was not treason because she was either doing her broadcasting under duress or making only innocuous announcements?

————

Under Anglo-American law, as in other legal systems, treason has been considered one of the most serious crimes. The essence of treason is the violation of the duty of allegiance owed by a citizen or subject to the sovereign. In English law, however, treason was construed broadly and often used for political purposes, to punish and eliminate political enemies or those who criticized and challenged the monarchical authorities. It was the American Revolution that forced the colonists to seriously reconsider the problem of treason. The colonists who declared independence and challenged the British Empire were, in British eyes, traitors and rebels, guilty of treason. At the same time, they had to deal with the internal enemy within the colonies.

In accordance with the recommendation of the Continental Congress in 1776, most of the states enacted their treason statutes, some of which were harsh and even abusive. These laws were frequently enforced without trial by jury and other basic rules, and there were executions for treason during the war. One Philadelphian, for example, was executed for treason for passing counterfeit money.

When they won the war and achieved independence, the Americans reevaluated the problem of treason and thoroughly reformed, not just revised, the law of treason. The Constitution, drafted in 1787 and coming into effect in 1789, in the words of the leading American legal historian Lawrence M. Friedman, turned treason, "the king of crime," into "a constitutional monarch," defining it narrowly to "a naked essence." Treason was now to be considered only in "levying War against the United States, or adhering to their Enemies, giving them Aid and Comfort." This eliminated a large number of English traditional definitions of treason, such as counterfeiting and killing a judge.

The Constitution also placed procedural restrictions on trials for treason. No one could be convicted of this crime "unless on the Testimony of two Witnesses to the same overt Act, or on Confession in open Court." Congress was given the power to declare the punishment of treason, but the punishment could not include "Corruption of the Blood, or Forfeiture except during the Life of the Person attained." Accordingly, in 1790, Congress passed a law providing the death penalty for anyone convicted of treason.

Together with murder, treason has continued to be one of the most serious crimes in the United States, although due to the reform discussed above, the conviction rates were not as great as they had been in the previous decades. The leader of the 1794 Whisky Rebellion became the first American traitor sentenced to death, but he was pardoned by President George Washington.

The first major American treason case was that of Aaron Burr, whose trials took place in 1807. Burr escaped being convicted of treason because the case did not have the required two witnesses to the same overt act. He was tried by a U.S. circuit court, over which Supreme Court Chief Justice John Marshall, riding that circuit, and a district court judge, Cyrus Griffin, sitting in the circuit, presided.

Reaffirming the significant role Marshall played in the treason case, American legal history expert Peter Hoffer points out that Marshall insisted that the constitutional definition of treason required the actual levying of war, not participating in or conspiring to levy war. As "the dress rehearsal" for the Burr case, Hoffer examines two Supreme Court decisions, *Bollman v. U.S.* (1807) and *Swartwout v. U.S.* (1807), and argues that it was in these cases that the Supreme Court for the first time explored the nature of treason, though only incidentally, as the main issue was the issuance of a habeas corpus.

While sitting as the chief justice of the Supreme Court, Samuel Chase wrote the opinion for the court in these cases, implying that there could be treason by conspiring rather than by act. On the testimony of the main witness, General James Wilkinson, commander of U.S. forces in the Mississippi Valley, Hoffer asserts that Chase "had to swallow hard and work harder to get around this point in his opinion on the admissibility of Wilkinson's evidence in the Burr trial." It was Marshall's view that the Constitution demanded the levying of war, not just participation in a conspiracy ("one had to perform a traitorous act") that prevailed.

John Brown of Harpers Ferry was indicted for treason against the state of Virginia and tried in a Virginia court, not in a federal court, and was convicted and hanged. When the Civil War started in 1861, the treason law of 1790 had still been in force. The unique nature and extent of the war, however, made it difficult for the North to enforce not only this law but the subsequent acts, the Seditious Conspiracy Act of 1861 and Second Confiscation Act of 1862, against Confederate leaders and the disloyal Northerners. No one was convicted of treason, and even Jefferson Davis, president of the Confederacy, though charged after the war with treason, was reprieved and never tried.

During World War I, treason again became an important issue, but there were no civil convictions for treason in the United States. World War II produced several important treason cases. For example, Max Stephan, a Detroit restaurateur, was convicted in 1942 of assisting an escaped German POW and was sentenced to hang, but the sentence was commuted to life imprisonment by President Franklin D. Roosevelt one day before the scheduled execution.

A landmark case is *Cramer v. United States* (1943–1945). Anthony Cramer was convicted of treason for safekeeping the money of the German saboteurs who landed on Long Island from a submarine, but the case was appealed to the Supreme Court, where the original conviction was overturned. It was in this case, J. Woodford Howard, Jr., convincingly argues, that the Supreme Court for the first time tackled the whole host of the constitutional issues such as meanings of "treason," "overt act," and "aiding the enemy" and the requirement that the overt act be proved by testimony of two witnesses.

The government, before the Supreme Court, insisted that the traitorous character is inherently embodied in "an overt act of aid and comfort," and thus need not be specifically proven ("any overt act must be an act of treason"). The defense, on the other hand, argued that a traitorous intent must independently be proven for such an overt act. The Supreme Court upheld the defense contention and established a significant precedent. In the opinion for the Court, Justice Robert Jackson stated that the framers of the Constitution were "aware of the misuse that a partisan executive might make of treason and imposed 'every limitation' possible." "Overt acts," Jackson insisted, taking language directly out of Marshall's earlier opinion, as Hoffer points out, "must be so visible that two witnesses to each act could clearly testify to the nature of the act as well as the participants in it." Jackson further declared that if "there is no adherence to the enemy," even in "the actions which do aid and comfort the enemy," and if "there is no intent to betray, there is no treason"—lines, as Hoffer noted, "Marshall would have been proud to have written himself." The action requires proof by two witnesses not only of the overt act but all elements of the crime. "No one should be branded a traitor and perhaps executed," Richard T. Davis, a member of the defense team headed by Harold R. Medina emphatically asserted later, "on the testimony of two witnesses for acts lacking 'essential traitorous purpose or effect.'"

The *Cramer* case, Howard insists, is a milestone in American Constitutional law because the Supreme Court defended civil liberties against claimed war power by "stiffening the Constitution," sticking to what the Constitution meant when it said: acts of adherence that aided the enemy on the oaths of two witnesses. The ruling, however, did not stop further prosecutions, although the frequency of treason charges was reduced. After the war, many were indicted for treason, some of whom were involved in broadcasting enemy propaganda. Nine convictions for aiding the enemy during World War II were upheld on appeal.

The Tokyo Rose case, known officially as *United States vs. Iva Ikuko Toguri d'Aquino* (1949), is one of the earliest treason cases in the postwar era. To what extent did Iva's case follow the precedent established by the

Cramer case? Announcing from the enemy radio to American soldiers might certainly have been unethical or even illegal, but, as will be elaborated later, not necessarily treasonous, unless the content was detrimental and was broadcast with the specific intention to betray the country.

This is the first book-length legal history of the Tokyo Rose case, treating all aspects of Iva Toguri d'Aquino's activities fully from the legal point of view. The chapters that follow will recount the life story of the defendant of the Tokyo Rose case, closely scrutinizing her wartime broadcasts in Japan and analyzing her trial in San Francisco. The main objective of the book is to ascertain, through the court's findings, whether Iva did indeed broadcast to the American servicemen with clear traitorous intent (a required element in the establishment of her guilt) and to assess the significance of this landmark case in the context of American law and legal history.

CHAPTER I

Born on the Fourth of July

Our family home was located in a typical American community. I went to the
neighborhood grammar school and attended church in the neighborhood. I took part in
normal activities at school and at church. . . . There was some Japanese spoken in our
family until we started to attend public school; thereafter English dominated.

We followed both American and Japanese customs at home. We had both
Japanese and American cooking in the home. My parents tried to raise us
according to American customs. We celebrated all the national holidays, all
Christian holidays . . . anniversaries, birthdays, etc.

IVA TOGURI D'AQUINO STATEMENT, *issued through Wayne M. Collins, September 1948,*
quoted in Masayo Duus, Tokyo Rose: Orphan of the Pacific *(1979), 42*

In the beautiful foothills of the massive Japan Alps in Yamanashi-ken
(prefecture), there was a small farm village (*mura*), Kagami Nakajo, part
of the town of Wakakusa-machi, noted for orchards of delicious peaches.
It was in this village Iva's father, Jun Toguri, was born in 1882. In 1959 this
village, together with neighboring towns and villages, was merged and re-
organized into a city, Minami Arupusu-shi (South Alps). Toguri was one
of the dominant surnames in the village, and Jun grew up surrounded by
family members and relatives who all bore the same surname.

After graduating from the Kagami Nakajo Elementary School in 1894,
he apparently attended the Kofu Middle School (now Kofu High School)
in Kofu, the prefectural capital, some eight miles away, commuting by bi-
cycle with neighboring friends. There is no record of his graduating from
the school nor of how many years he attended.

In 1899, at the age of seventeen, Jun immigrated to the United States,
landing in Seattle, and was admitted to permanent residency, although he
could not then get American citizenship. He moved to Southern California, where he tried working at many jobs, although nothing turned out to
be very successful. By the time he reached twenty-one, he had become
financially stable and independent. He also managed to get Canadian

citizenship, a procedure followed at the time by many Japanese Americans who could not get American citizenship but frequently went back to Japan for visits. This enabled them to come back to the United States by way of Canada, circumventing any possible restrictions imposed on Japanese coming directly from Japan.

In June 1907, when he was twenty-five, Jun returned to Japan and married a nineteen-year-old woman, Fumi Iimura, from his prefecture, Yamanashi. The wedding took place in Yokohama. Jun could not afford to bring his bride with him back to America and instead frequently visited Japan to see her. Their son, Fred, was born in 1910 and baptized in a Japanese Christian church. In 1913, six years after their marriage, Jun was able to bring his wife and their three-year-old son to America. Jun met them in San Francisco where they landed.

The Toguri family was finally reunited. Iva's parents and brother, who had been born in Japan, all became permanent residents of the United States, but none of them were able to become naturalized citizens until after the McCarran Walter Act passed in 1952, when Jun was already seventy, his wife dead, and Fred, forty-two.

Iva Ikuko Toguri was born on July 4, 1916, in Watts in South Central Los Angeles, the area where the first major black riot erupted in the mid-sixties. At the time of Iva's birth, the area was a working-class neighborhood dominated by whites. The Toguri family moved around a lot in Southern California, but mainly in the Los Angeles area. Iva was the first American citizen in the family.

In September, two months after Iva's birth, Jun entered her name in the Family Register (*Koseki*) of his ancestral family at his native village, Kagami Nakajo, in Yamanashi, Japan. Customary at the time among the Japanese in America, this procedure gave Iva citizenship rights in Japan, but she lost her dual citizenship in 1932 when she was nearly sixteen because her father had the registration canceled. The 1930s were a strenuous period for Japanese Americans. As Japan invaded Manchuria in 1931 and eventually made it Manchu-ko ("the country of Manchu"), anti-Japanese sentiment grew stronger in the United States. In order to dispel any suspicions attendant on "dual nationality," many Japanese Americans deleted the names of their *nisei* (second-generation Japanese American) children from the Japanese family registry to make them fully American. Iva's father did not register her with the Canadian government, so she lost any eligibility for Canadian citizenship rights. Thus by the time she reached sixteen, Iva Toguri was a citizen of the United States only.

Jun, like many other industrious Japanese immigrants, worked hard while trying various jobs. In 1921, when Iva was four years old, her father took the family to Calexico on the Mexican border to grow cotton. By then the infamous Alien Land Law of 1913 that had originally permitted leasing but in 1920 made it illegal for noncitizens to own or lease agricultural land made Jun's enterprise unprofitable. After a third child, June, was born there, the family moved to San Diego, where their third daughter, Inez, was born. Finally, in 1927, when his recent series of business ventures proved unsuccessful, Jun Toguri decided to take his family back to Los Angeles. He started a small import business that slowly but surely prospered. It developed into a retail grocery and variety store, specializing in goods from Japan. It was a family operation in which everybody pitched in. Fred was his father's chief helper, and the daughters helped after school, tending the shop.

After returning to Los Angeles, the family moved several times. They first settled on East 38th Street and then moved to the 1700 block of Wilmington Avenue, a block from their store, Wilmington Avenue Market. Then they moved to 11718 Bandera Avenue, and in 1938, to 11630 Bandera Avenue.

Although Jun's store sold Japanese groceries and other goods and profited from having a solid Japanese American clientele, the Toguris did not socialize much with Japanese Americans. Throughout the course of the family's many moves, Jun was not only very careful in selecting a house in a non-Japanese area but was determined to see his children become fully Americanized. The Toguris rarely went to Japanese American festivals, gatherings, and events, and Jun tried to limit their association with other Japanese. Since Jun always tried to find a house in a neighborhood where there were many Caucasians, Iva's playmates and friends were mainly Caucasians.

English was the primary language spoken at home, and the family belonged to the Methodist Church. The Toguri children were discouraged from speaking Japanese, except to their mother until she learned enough English to communicate with them. This was not the age of diversity in the United States, and the Toguris did indeed become a typical American family. Like many other Japanese American families on the Pacific coast in the thirties, forties, and fifties, the Toguri family was Americanized, pro-American, and independent, believing in Americanism and the American system.

Because Fumi Toguri suffered from diabetes and high blood pressure, Iva, as oldest daughter, took over much of the household responsibility, including looking after her younger sisters. Like most Americans at the time, the Toguris valued self-sufficiency; everybody in the family willingly did the family chores and was self-reliant, unwilling to accept any outside help and support.

Iva was a responsible, competitive, disciplined, and reliable person. While attending public schools, she joined the Girl Scouts, took piano lessons and became an accomplished pianist, and also became a skilled typist. She was active in many sports, including playing tennis on the school team.

Because her family moved around in Southern California, Iva attended many different schools. She went to Hoffman Grammar School in Calexico and Lincoln Heights Grammar School in San Diego. In Los Angeles, she attended the Ascot Avenue Grammar School and McKinley Junior High School. Finally she ended up at Compton Union High School, from which she graduated in 1933. During her high school years, she also attended Compton Japanese Language School on Saturdays as did most *nisei* children. After graduating from Compton High, Iva attended Compton Junior College for half a year until the winter of 1934. She then transferred to UCLA in the fall of 1935.

During all her childhood and student years she had very little contact with Japanese civilization and tradition. Her strong sense of loyalty to the United States, moreover, somehow forced her to disregard traditional Japanese culture. She had many talents, but in order to become a genuine and true American, Iva seemed to have come to despise everything Japanese, including Japanese foods, especially rice. The Toguri family, though consisting only of *issei* (first-generation Japanese American) and *nisei* members, did indeed become the "typical" all-American family.

At UCLA, as a premed student, Iva chose zoology as her major, hoping that it would prepare her better to get into a medical school. Iva's college life was just like that of other students: she went to football games, dated (usually Japanese American students), and played tennis. She continued to help her father in his business, and during the summer she even helped him drive on long business trips. However, in spite of an upbringing that valued hard work and carrying out one's obligations, it took nearly eight years for her to complete her bachelor's degree after her graduation from high school, perhaps because she procrastinated in doing the required schoolwork. In addition, there were many distractions. A ruptured appendix and the resultant complications, for example, forced her to drop out of school for two years.

According to former fellow students of Iva's, who Masayo Duus interviewed in 1976, Iva was "a lively and lighthearted person, no different from the other American girl students." She had "an extroverted, outgoing personality" and was "full of energy." Iva was also remembered to have "a good sense of humor, always kidding and making jokes." One student got the impression that "she did not have any interest in Japan at all." "She was more mature and more relaxed," another recalled, "perhaps because she was older." Iva was "a completely average American girl," still another commented and added that he "never got the slightest impression that there was anything particularly Japanese about her." "She never used strong words," a conscientious objector student remembered, "but she never budged from the idea that if it were she, she would go and fight for the country, America."

Upon graduating from UCLA with a bachelor of science in zoology in June 1941, Iva's wish was to go to a medical school, as her mother also wished her to do. Her undergraduate GPAs, however, might not have been sufficiently high enough for her to be admitted to an American medical school. She excused herself saying that it was difficult for her to get in an American medical school because she was "a Japanese and woman." One former classmate remembered her talking about going to Japan to study medicine since "she had relatives there who were in the medical field," though she sometimes expressed her feeling that she had no interest in Japan and things Japanese. This might have been just wishful thinking, however, because Iva's knowledge of the Japanese language was too poor to pass the entrance examinations of Japanese medical schools or to carry on the regular medical course work. During the summer of 1941, she was therefore contemplating pursuing graduate work in some other field, although nothing specific materialized.

CHAPTER 2

"Aunt Shizu Is Sick"

She could still see them in her mind's eye as they had been that summer morning—
the receding figure of her mother, the cause of the trip. Fumi Toguri had been
suffering from diabetes and high blood pressure. Her mother's figure had held
Iva's gaze until the details had became blurred, and Iva could see only the small
figure with raised arm flanked by her brother, Fred, her father, and her two sisters,
June and Inez. It had occurred to Iva then that she might not see her mother anymore.

IVA TOGURI *on the deck of the Japanese ship* Arabia Maru, *pulling away from San Pedro,*
California, on July 5, 1941, Rex Gunn, They Called Her Tokyo Rose *(1977), 9*

Sometime during June 1941, Iva's mother, Fumi, received a letter from her
brother-in-law, Hajime Hattori, stating that his wife, Shizu, Fumi's twin
sister, was seriously ill with diabetes and high blood pressure and probably on the verge of death, and, therefore, Shizu very much wanted her
sister to come and see her before it was too late.

Fumi was in no condition to travel to Japan; she, too, was bedridden
with diabetes and high blood pressure. Jun was too busy in his business,
in which Fred, who once hoped to become a lawyer, was now heavily involved. Iva's two sisters were still in school and too young to travel on their
own. Iva, it seemed to her parents, was the only family member available
to make the trip. After graduating from UCLA, Iva was still pondering her
next academic pursuit and doing nothing for the time being except helping her father in the store. So it was natural that her parents would ask Iva
to go in her mother's place. She did not want to go to Japan but reluctantly
agreed to visit Aunt Shizu and her family as the family representative.

Was the parents' decision to send Iva to Japan to inquire after Shizu,
in lieu of Fumi, a crucial decision in retrospect, and was it reasonable and
well thought-out? The Tokyo Rose case was contingent solely upon the
decision Iva's parents had made. Were there any other options? If someone
else or no one went to Japan, Iva would have never encountered her future
problems. While Shizu would no doubt be delighted to meet a niece who
had traveled all the way from America, especially during the time she was

bedridden, it was not that urgent. It was Fumi she was desperate to see, not having seen her twin since Fumi left for America twenty-eight years ago. Did the Hattori family (husband Hajime, daughter Rinko, and two sons) need any additional help in caring for the ailing Shizu?

Nevertheless, because the Toguris thought the matter pressing, Iva had to leave promptly. The only available transportation then was by ship, which took at least two weeks; airline passenger service to Japan did not start until 1947.

Iva took with her twenty-eight pieces of luggage, a third of which were presents for her aunt's family. Every item was carefully selected by Jun. The most important items, of course, were all kinds of medicine for Aunt Shizu, including insulin and aspirin, which were considered better than the Japanese products. Iva also took many gifts for the entire family: fruits, chocolate, and other American foods. A sewing machine was for cousin Rinko, who was a year younger than Iva.

Jun Toguri, who was concerned about Iva's aversion to Japanese food, had also packed American foods for her personal use during her stay: sugar, coffee, cocoa, jam, canned meat, tomato paste, chocolate, and, perhaps most important, flour and baking powder, so that she could make her own bread instead of rice, which she hated. There were also yams, soap, and a typewriter for her use.

As a passport would take too long to obtain, her father secured for her a certificate of identification. On July 5, 1941, one day after her twenty-fifth birthday, Iva set sail from San Pedro to Yokohama on the *Arabia Maru* of the Osaka Shipping Company. Iva's father simultaneously applied for a passport for her, which, he was informed, Iva would be able to receive at the American Consulate General in Yokohama when she reached Japan. It was, however, not just because the matter was urgent that she traveled only with a certificate of identification, instead of waiting to secure a passport. It was common for Japanese Americans to travel to Japan without much difficulty using only the certificate of identification, and they could usually return to the States easily. In fact, Jun had traveled to Japan and back many times that way.

Iva had a traveling companion, Chieko Ito, an eighteen-year-old girl whom Iva had known since childhood. When they heard about Iva's going to Japan, Chieko's parents decided to send Chieko to visit her uncle in Tokyo. Both were *nisei* girls leaving the country without a passport. As always for first-time ocean voyagers, the early days of the trip were miserable for

Iva and Chieko because of seasickness, but they were gradually able to overcome it.

As American legal history authority Stanley Kutler points out, the certificate of identification signed by Iva Ikuko Toguri on July 1, 1941, was not an official, State Department–issued document. Iva's certificate, prepared by a Japanese American notary public, stated that "Miss Toguri was born in Los Angeles on the Fourth of July, 1916, that she currently resided in the city, that she was temporarily leaving the United States on July 5 on the *Arabia Maru* for Yokohama, that she intended to visit her aunt who was 'eagerly awaiting her,' and that she intended to return to the United States in six months." The certificate was duly signed by Iva Toguri, witnessed and sealed by the notary public, with Iva's photograph attached and her fingerprints affixed.

Iva's document, as Kutler insists, was substantially valid, and proof of citizenship was adequate for leaving and reentering. According to a law enacted on May 22, 1918, however, "in time of war or national emergency," citizens would need passports to enter or depart.

As it turned out, it was a doomed crossing from which Iva could not return home for a long, long time. The summer of 1941 was the beginning of the period when diplomatic relations between the United States and Japan were rapidly deteriorating to the final brink. Yet, the American people, the Toguris among them, were generally optimistic for various reasons and tried to go about living their daily lives as normally as possible including their outside activities like international travels and dealing with overseas friends and relatives.

While Iva was preparing for her trip to Japan, Japanese troops, following the decision the Japanese government made on July 2, 1941, formally occupied French Indochina, moving first to northern Indochina and then into southern Indochina, clearly as the first step to invading British Malaya and the Dutch East Indies. Within three weeks, the United States, responding to the Japanese southward thrust, declared an immediate freeze on all Japanese assets in the United States and imposed an embargo on trade with Japan.

During the period of growing tension between the two countries, all reports of Japanese Americans traveling to Japan were now seen as suspect, and Jun Toguri's application for a passport for his daughter was handled with deliberate slowness. By the time she left, Iva had only a certificate of identification and the instructions from the Immigration and Natural-ization Service in Los Angeles to collect her passport at the American Consulate General in Yokohama. Upon arriving in Japan, she went to the consulate general, but to her surprise, nothing had been done about her passport application.

On July 24, two days before President Roosevelt declared an American embargo against Japan, the *Arabia Maru* arrived in Yokohama after taking nineteen days to cross the Pacific. Iva and Chieko could not disembark on that day because they, as American citizens, needed a proper passport or visa. Jun Toguri, who took care of Iva's immigration matters, seemed to have overlooked the problem Iva had to face: Iva as an American citizen needed an American passport in order to get a visa in Japan. Since Jun was still a Japanese citizen carrying a Japanese passport, the only thing he needed was a certificate of identification, a situation totally different from that of an American citizen like Iva.

On the following day, Iva and Chieko were given temporary visas for six months and were finally able to disembark. When she arrived, Iva had $300 in her possession, just enough for her return passage. As she left the ship, Iva found on the pier her uncle and cousins waiting for her, who had had to come back again that day because she could not leave the ship on the previous day. It was wonderful to see the relatives, whom she had never met before. They took Iva to a Western lunch at the New Grand Hotel in Yokohama. It was quite a surprise for Iva, who had never expected to eat such food in Japan. They then went to their home in Setagaya-ku in To-kyo by train. Iva was stifled by midsummer heat and humidity. Like most American visitors, Iva was shocked by the fact that everybody in Japan was a Japanese!

Aunt Shizu, though she could not come to see her at the port, was in better health than Iva expected. Her mother's twin sister looked like her and even her voice sounded exactly like her mother's. Iva's cousin, Rinko, looked very much like Iva herself. In Japan everything was different and strange to Iva, and Aunt Shizu and Rinko did their best to teach her all the daily customs and manners. Because her Japanese was poor, she had to take Rinko with her everywhere as an interpreter. Determined to become more independent, in September she began to attend every morning the Matsumiya Nihongo Bunka Gakko (Japanese Language Culture School) in Shiba-ku. In August, after a few weeks of getting acquainted with relatives she had never met before, she rushed to the U.S. Consulate in To-kyo to apply for an American passport. She presented her birth certificate and certificate of identification, but any person of Asian ancestry claiming U.S. citizenship found considerable difficulty because this was during the period of total prohibition of Asian immigration under the provisions of the Immigration Act of 1924. Moreover, the situation between the United States and Japan was becoming more critical. On September 6, a Japanese Imperial Conference stipulated that if a reversal of the American embargo was not achieved through diplomatic means by early October, Japan should launch her very ambitious "southern campaign" to secure the oil of the Dutch East Indies. Prime Minister Fumimaro Konoye, a moderate, tried to meet personally with President Roosevelt to prevent war, but when his proposal collapsed, he was forced to resign. General Hideki Tojo took over as prime minister on October 16.

Unable to read the Japanese papers or to understand much of the news on the radio, Iva was slow in realizing how bad relations had become between Washington and Tokyo. As her August 1941 passport application had not yet produced a passport by October, she became progressively nervous over the increasing war rumors in Japan. In his letter dated December 1, 1941, the U.S. Consul informed Iva that her application had never been processed.

On top of that, in addition to the oppressively hot and humid summer climate, Iva also suffered from culture shock. She was finding out that she was not really comfortable at Aunt Shizu's house. Uncle Hajime, who operated a large tailoring shop with thirty employees nearby, was nice enough to take care of Iva, but things were, she felt, not working out well. Such an outlook and attitude were reflected in the letters she wrote home.

In a long letter she wrote home in mid-October, which, due to the deteriorating communication across the Pacific, she asked her *nisei* friend who was returning home under a proper passport to mail for her in the States, she had a lot to say to every member of the family. "I have finally gotten around," she told her parents, "to eating rice three times a day. It's killing me, but what can I do?" She was delighted when her uncle managed to get her ration changed from rice to bread. "I can't buy an oven to bake any bread, and since I didn't bring one," she bitterly complained, "the flour which I brought just sits in the kitchen." That huge amount of flour still sitting in the kitchen did not have to get wasted. She could have used a *seiro* (steaming basket), a necessary device nearly every Japanese household owned at that time. The Hattoris would surely have helped her to make all kinds of delicious bread and *manju* (buns).

She told her parents, who had been born in Japan and had lived most of their early lives there, not to come to Japan because of Japan's terribly hot and humid weather and "the kind of living you have to put up with here." "Fred," she wrote to her brother, "settle down and get married and do the best you can with the business and be content and never think of coming to Japan." "June and Inez," Iva advised her sisters, "you both do the same. Eventually settle down and get married, and plan to live and die in the country which can give you so much."

Finally, Iva ended the letter with a more hopeful note. "I have gotten used to many of the things over here," she was trying to assure her parents, "and I think that in a few more months that I will be able to say that I don't mind living in Japan. It has been very hard and discouraging at times but from now on it will be all right, I'm sure."

Although Iva did not have accurate information on U.S.-Japan relations, she had a general sense of the situation changing from bad to worse. On November 26, Secretary of State Cordell Hull handed the Japanese ambassadors, Kichisaburo Nomura and Saburo Kurusu, a ten-point statement of the American position. It insisted on Japan's withdrawal from China and demanded its abandonment of the Southeast Asian adventure. When Iva became sufficiently frightened by the crisis, she decided to make an unusual and expensive telephone call to her father, saying that she wanted to come home right away. Four days later, her father cabled her to take a third-class passage on the *Tatsuta Maru*, which would leave Yokohama on December 2. Since the telegram took two days to reach her, she had only one day to make arrangements.

Iva and Uncle Hajime were able to collect the two papers, which she was told were necessary. When they went to the Yokohama office of the Nippon Yusen Kaisha (Japan Steamship Company) to get a ticket on the *Tatsuta Maru*, they were told of another problem at the last minute: Iva would have to have a complete clearance from the Japanese Finance Ministry before she could book passage to the United States. What she specifically needed to do was to secure a Ministry of Finance certificate, proving that she was not leaving the country with more money than she had brought. The strict clearance had been put into effect because the United States had frozen Japanese assets and the Japanese were eager to lay hands on any American gold and silver they might find. This, she was told, would take three or four days. The *Tatsuta Maru* left without her. Although she missed the boat, she went on to clear the Finance Ministry requirements so that she might be able to get on the next ship.

On November 14, 1941, however, eighteen days before Iva tried desperately to get on the *Tatsuta Maru*, President Roosevelt issued a proclamation declaring the existence of a national emergency. This means, Professor Kutler argues, that all Americans, citizens and legal residents, would now be required to possess a passport for foreign travels. Those who had already been out of the country might not necessarily be able to come back to the United States. For Iva, therefore, even if she had managed to get passage on the *Tatsuta Maru*, there was no guarantee that she would be able to disembark in the United States without a passport.

All the same, the *Tatsuta Maru* did not make it to the United States.

Six days later, Japan attacked Pearl Harbor, war began, and the ship turned back. Iva, however, had no way of knowing that the ship had to turn back. Ironically, it was this Japanese steamer bound for Honolulu and Japan, Louis Fisher points out, that several German Americans, who were later caught and convicted of their planned sabotage in the United States, took from Long Beach to Yokohama in early 1941, when they decided to return to their fatherland. These future Nazi saboteurs then continued their "arduous journeys" home through Russia.

The Japanese attack on Pearl Harbor was certainly a surprise attack for the American people, but it was also a big surprise for the Japanese, since the plan had been developed in complete secrecy. The ensuing war in the Pacific devastated Iva's life in two significant ways. First, the war totally destroyed the chance of her returning to the United States, and, second, she was alienated from her aunt's family, the very family to whom she had come to visit as her sole purpose in traveling to Japan.

A Dozen Roses

*Under normal circumstances I should be called a "bad girl" but there were
so many complicated cobwebs during the war years. I was one who had to find a
way to survive this war. I was one with a United States citizenship in a foreign
country and was one who was under close surveillance by the civilian and military police
and although being cornered managed to come out alive. I was in a similar position as the
prisoners of war and had little chance in choosing a way to survive.*

FROM IVA TOGURI D'AQUINO'S LETTER TO WALTER WINCHELL,
April 14, 1948, Tokyo, Japan

On December 8, 1941, the day the Pacific war began, two policemen from
the Setagaya Police Station came to see Iva at her uncle's house. They informed her that Mr. Fujiwara of the Japanese Special Military Police (*kempei
-tai*) was interested to know what she was going to do. On the following
day, Fujiwara himself came to the house and interrogated Iva, demanding
that she renounce her American citizenship and apply for Japanese citizenship — or else life in Japan would be "very, very inconvenient."

When the war began, there were about 10,000 young Japanese American men and women stranded in Japan. Some, like Iva and Chieko Ito,
were in Japan visiting relatives, but most were there to attend Japanese
schools and colleges or to work for Japanese firms. Due to severe employment discrimination in the United States, some Japanese American
children were sent to Japan for part of their education. Most Japanese
Americans who graduated from American universities found that the only
decent jobs available for them were in Japan.

Two such American college graduates working in Japan, in fact,
later became the key prosecution witnesses against Iva. George Nakamoto Mitsushio was born in San Francisco and attended the University
of California, Berkeley, and Columbia University. He worked briefly for
the *Raufu Shinpo*, a local Japanese-language newspaper in Los Angeles.
He went to Japan in 1940 and became chief of the Overseas Section at
Radio Tokyo. Kenkichi Oki, born in Sacramento, California, attended St.

Mary's College, Moraga, California, and later transferred and graduated from New York University. Since he could not find a decent job in the United States, he went to Japan in 1939 and started to work for the Overseas Section in 1940, becoming one of the wartime production supervisors of Radio Tokyo's "Zero Hour," the English-language program for which Iva became an announcer.

Fujiwara explained that to become a Japanese citizen was very simple for the *nisei* caught by the war in Japan. They could do it just by registering in the *koseki* (Japanese family registers). Iva, as mentioned earlier, had been registered in her family *koseki* by relatives in Yamanashi-ken at the request of her father on September 13, 1916, when she was only two months old. Her name had been stricken out of the *koseki*, again by her father's request, on January 13, 1932, when she was soon to be sixteen.

The only thing Iva could do to regain full Japanese citizenship, Fujiwara told her, was to have her name written back in the *koseki*. If she would do that, there would be no more trips to the police station as an alien, no more visits of *kempei*, no more worry about travel visas and special ration cards, thus it would ensure peace with her relations, and the end of neighbors' suspicions. Many American *nisei* stranded in Japan, in fact most of them, were doing exactly that. Fujiwara came every other day and persistently demanded that she become a Japanese citizen. "A person born and raised in America," Iva flatly refused, "doesn't give up his citizenship for a piece of paper." Even her aunt and uncle, who were trying to interpret for her, were appalled by Iva's firm position.

The threats of the police and *kempei-tai* were immediate. She soon learned that she was classified as an enemy alien, and her movements came to be restricted. She was denied food rations and was constantly harassed by the civilian and military authorities.

More damaging to her, although she did not at that time realize it, was her citizenship status and passport issue. As the situation in the United States was moving from "national emergency" to "time of war," American foreign travelers became deeply affected. Iva Toguri's fate, "with nothing more than the certificate of identification in hand," Stanley Kutler argues, "as of December 7, 1941, was for all purposes sealed for the duration of the war." Iva, who seemed almost completely ignorant about the situation in the United States, continued her efforts in vain to get passage on an evacuation ship home.

Two months after the outbreak of the war, in February 1942, Iva saw an announcement in the *Mainichi* newspaper that the Swiss legation in Tokyo representing the United States was accepting applicants for evacuees to the United States. This was based upon the Japanese American agreement allowing repatriation through neutral nations. The ship was the USS *Gripsholm*. Iva applied immediately, but without a passport she was told that her citizenship must be confirmed by the American consulate. Iva asked the Swiss consulate to telegraph the State Department at her expense to establish her American citizenship. The reply from Washington a few days later indicated that there were some doubts about her citizenship. The State Department's doubts were indeed curious since Iva had been born and reared in the United States: she had never set foot outside the country before the age of twenty-five.

On April 4, 1942, the American consular staff, themselves awaiting repatriation on the *Gripsholm*, at long last processed her August 1941 passport application by attaching a notation stating that her U.S. citizenship was "not proved." She was also told that she would get the same treatment as other nonresident *nisei* at the end of the war. It was not just her American citizenship that was in doubt, she was informed, but the status of all Japanese Americans, including those in the United States, was in doubt.

But Iva did not know exactly what it meant because she had not been aware of what was happening in the United States. As soon as the war started, the Japanese Americans on the West Coast were classified as the "enemy race" and were forcefully removed to inland relocation camps. If, in fact, she had succeeded in returning to California then, she would have had to share the fate of all Japanese and been interned.

Sometime in April 1942, the *Gripsholm* set sail for the United States. Although on board were Ambassador Joseph Grew and his party and several hundred other Americans, Iva had to suffer another setback, as she was refused the passage on the ship.

At the Hattori home, moreover, the situation became progressively worse. Iva continued to argue with the family members saying things like, "Japan had started the war," "Japan will lose," and "the Americans will win, and, I hope, it would be quickly." In addition, Iva never contributed to the Japanese food and clothing drives. The members of the Hattori family were also constantly harassed by the neighbors "for harboring an enemy." Police agents of the *kempei-tai*, who had been coming to the Hattori house regularly, now started to go to the neighbors to ask them questions about Iva. The neighbors were frightened and became more angry at Hajime.

On the street, neighborhood children insulted Iva, saying she was a *horyo* (captured enemy) and sometimes threw stones at her.

By June 1942, life became so intolerable that the Hattoris wished they could ask Iva to leave and live elsewhere. But they didn't: they fully understood their obligation to treat her decently for what she had done and to protect her from the hostile environment she had inadvertently jumped into.

Finally, it was Iva who asked whether it would be all right for her to move out. Hajime and Shizu were embarrassed at the awkwardness of it, and "abashed at the thought of making her go," but there was no choice for Iva. "I didn't think badly of my uncle and aunt," Duus remembers Iva recalling later, "I decided to leave myself. It was awful for them."

Her money situation was becoming tighter even before she moved out. By the end of March, she decided to look for a real job. She had been giving the Hattoris 50 yen a month for food, and her transportation expenses were not small. She tried to conserve the $300 she had for return passage as much as possible, but it gradually dwindled away. She sold some of the wool yarn and cotton socks she had brought with her.

Kazuya Matsumiya, the principal of the Japanese Language School that she had been attending since she was still at the Hattoris' house, decided to let her earn her tuition, when Iva asked him to reduce it, by doing some work for him. He asked her to type an English translation of a grammar book he had written and to give piano lessons to his son and daughter and to some of their friends. However, these efforts netted only 20 yen a month.

When she left her aunt's house in June, armed with an introduction from Matsumiya, she moved into the Onarikin ("new big rich") House in Shiba-ku, Tokyo. This boardinghouse cost 65 yen a month for a room and two meals a day and was run by Mrs. Furuya, who became a close and trusted friend and supporter of Iva.

Since she could not read or write Japanese or "converse coherently" in it, she could not do any interpreting or translating. Later that month, a fellow tenant of the boardinghouse found her a part-time typist-monitor job at the Atagoyama listening outpost of the Domei News Agency (Domei Tsushin Sha) in Tokyo. Her job was to monitor American and Allied shortwave broadcasts for five hours a day (late at night), five days a week, at a salary of 110 yen (82 yen after taxes) a month. The job at Domei enabled her to listen to shortwave war news from Hawaii, San Francisco, New York, and London.

She also learned, through the International Red Cross, of her family's having been incarcerated in Gila River Relocation Camp in Arizona. She could not get much detailed information, but what actually was happening to the Japanese Americans was shocking. Already in the spring of 1942, 120,000 Japanese Americans, two-thirds of whom were American citizens, living on the Pacific Coast were forcibly removed, as the "enemy race," from the region designated as "military areas," based on "military necessity." They were imprisoned en masse in the deserts in eastern California, Idaho, Arizona, Utah, Wyoming, Colorado, and Arkansas. The U.S. government called them "relocation centers," but they were "concentration camps," as the leading scholar on the subject, Roger Daniels, calls them; the facilities were actually mass detention camps, complete with barbed wire and guard towers.

Iva did not know until the end of the war the full extent of the ordeal endured by her parents, brother, and sisters, who were sent with many fellow Japanese Americans to Gila River. Her mother died on her way to the camp at one of the assembly centers in California, one of many makeshift facilities, in a converted racetrack stable that still retained the smell of animals.

Anti-Japanese sentiment in California was not a sudden development. As Roger Daniels points out, as early as the first two decades of the twentieth century, James D. Phelan, San Francisco mayor and later U.S. senator, clearly enunciated the first strong anti-Asian (especially anti-Japanese) sentiment. He became fully convinced of the view that "the native Japanese are as undesirable as the imported." Making the crude, unabashed observation that "a Jap's a Jap," he declared that the Japanese had "to be excluded," since they could not "be treated as the negro."

Such a strong anti-Japanese campaign prevailing in California throughout the first four decades of the century gained a great momentum when the Pacific War started. The vital moving force behind the Japanese relocation program included men such as General John L. DeWitt, commander of the Western Defense Command; Colonel Karl R. Bendetsen; Assistant Secretary of War John J. McClory; U.S. Attorney General Francis Biddle; and California Attorney General Earl Warren. Echoing what Phelan had remarked a few decades earlier, they advocated that "all persons of

Japanese ancestry" be rounded up and removed from the West Coast, a "combat zone," and put in remote camps because "the Japanese race is an enemy race" whose racial traits are "undiluted." They declared that "a Jap's a Jap" and that the Japanese were all enemies "whether they were born in the United States or in Japan." The Japanese, as Warren put it, were "qualitatively different from other prospective 'enemies'"—branding them, in essence, as disloyal without proof.

As soon as she learned of the "relocation," Iva tried to write her family, but she heard nothing. She wondered what had happened to her father's prosperous business in Los Angeles. It was only in late 1945 in Sugamo Prison in Tokyo that she learned that her mother had died in May 1942.

It was also at Domei where Iva in late July 1942 met Filipe d'Aquino, who started to work as a linotypist a month after she did. Filipe was three-fourths Japanese, but a Portuguese citizen, following the paternal line of ancestry under the laws of Portugal. His Portuguese grandfather married a Japanese woman, and their son, Filipe's father, married a Japanese. He was then twenty-one years old, five years younger than Iva. Filipe attended Catholic mission schools from primary school through junior college. He was fluent in English, spoke Japanese but didn't read it or write it well, and knew no Portuguese. Iva and Filipe became fast friends and eventually married. They shared the pro-American view, and Filipe deeply disliked the militaristic and suppressive atmosphere of wartime Japan.

In late August 1942, Iva received a notice from the Swiss legation advising her that the second and final repatriation ship was to leave in September. Since most of the diplomats and other supposedly important Americans had already left on the first ship, she thought her chances of getting aboard were good. She and Chieko tried at once to get aboard. For both of them, returning home to a prison camp seemed better than staying in Japan. She was informed that she needed $425 as fare. Could she raise the necessary money? Unfortunately, she had no savings (her 110 yen per month salary at Domei was used for bare survival), had not received any support from her relatives in Japan, and had no means for contacting her parents in America. In fact, her parents not only were barred under the provisions of the Trading with the Enemy Act from advancing any such fare but also were helpless to assist her, by reason of their detention in the Gila Relocation Center. Realizing that she had no way of raising the passage money, she had to cancel her application. Some may wonder whether she withdrew her application for the passage on the expatriation ship because she might not wish to return to the United States just to be put into a relocation camp. Iva firmly asserted later at trial that her sole reason was lack of fare.

As the war went on, at Domei frequent, heated arguments on such issues as the battles of the Midway and of the Coral Sea arose between Iva and Filipe, both of whom took a strong pro-American view, and the majority of the other workers, who were strongly pro-Japanese. "Maybe you think the Americans are winning," an angry Japanese named Nagamoto accused Iva, "because you want them to win." Iva retorted, "I am saying that we are getting the truth from the Allied news sources and not from the Japanese reports." "Maybe somebody should tell the *kempei-tai*," he threatened, "that you know more about the war than they do."

One day in February 1943, a few months after she canceled her application for the last repatriation ship, Iva came home from work to find the three agents of the *kempei-tai*, who had been regular visitors, in her room. She immediately feared that this was the result of some Domei worker having reported her to the police. Nagamoto, after all, might not have been bluffing when he said someone should report Iva to the military police. Her recent cancellation of her application to sail on the last ship might have also triggered their visit.

Iva found her room had been searched thoroughly, turned upside down and inside out. "What reason is there now to keep you from becoming a Japanese citizen?" one of them asked. "The same reason," she firmly responded. They had searched through her books, trunk, and papers without restoring them back in order. "Why are you doing this?" she protested. "We are looking for things about the Japanese government written in English," another *kempei* replied. "We better not find anything against the Japanese government here or you will be sorry."

Iva decided to leave Domei. She knew it wouldn't be easy to get another job, but she worked hard; she visited all foreign legations in Tokyo. The Danish consul, Lars Tillitse, told her that he expected an opening within a year. It was not until December 1943 that Iva quit Domei, after she learned that she could begin work at the Danish legation as a secretary in January 1944. (The new job put her to work "in pleasant and congenial surroundings" for the first time since she had come to Japan. Lars Tillitse was very much interested in the United States, and he seemed to have hired Iva because she was an American. Her salary started at 150 yen a month but soon increased to 160 yen. She did not have much work to do. Beside two maids, she was the only employee at the legation.)

Meanwhile, by June 1943, Iva was suffering from malnutrition, beriberi, and a sinus infection and had to be hospitalized at Amano Hospital for six weeks. She was treated by Dr. K. W. Amano, a Japanese national and specialist of eye, throat, nose, and ear ailments who had studied medicine in Japan, the United States, and many European countries; he and his wife, who was also a physician and surgeon, had treated foreign diplomats and their dependents, missionaries, and businesspersons in Tokyo since 1934.

After Iva regained her health and strength, she found an employment ad for a typist job in the business office at Radio Tokyo. She took a competitive examination and passed. She began working there on August 23, 1943, in the third-floor business office under Shigechika Takano. She was a temporary, part-time worker (*rinji shokutaku*) and was to work only two or three hours a day, six days a week. The job paid 100 yen a month. If she could keep the Domei job, she thought, she could double her income.

Radio Tokyo, the Broadcasting Corporation of Japan (*Nihon Hoso Kyokai*—NHK), was a large corporation in a modern building on Uchi-saiwai-cho in a fashionable section of Tokyo. She could lose herself in this large office with many typists, she felt, during the duration of the war. She resolved that she should stay out of mischief by avoiding conversations about "who started the war" or "who was winning."

The situation suddenly changed on her second day of work. In the afternoon of August 24, 1943, when she was talking to one of the staff announcers, Ruth S. Hayakawa, an *issei* who once lived in Los Angeles, three men, two white and one Asian, escorted by two guards, entered the overseas section through the business office. They were all underweight, in dirty and shabby clothes, and looked like scarecrows. "Who are they?" Iva asked. Ruth Hayakawa replied in a low voice that they were Allied POWs who had been captured in Southeast Asia and brought to Tokyo to take part in broadcasts from Radio Tokyo. When Iva told Ruth that she would like to meet the prisoners, Ruth asked her why. "I would like to meet with them and talk with them if I can," Iva replied. "I just feel sorry for them." "Don't ever say that at Radio Tokyo," Ruth warned her, "because there are too many plainclothes *kempeis*." Ruth promised to arrange for Iva to meet the prisoners if she really wanted to. The next day, August 25, 1943, Iva took the first opportunity to introduce herself and talk to them.

The three prisoners of war had been experienced radio broadcasters prior to their capture, and they had been assigned to work on the English-language "Zero Hour" since March 1943. They were Major Charles Cousens, an Australian captured in Singapore; Captain Wallace E. (Ted) Ince, an American captured in Corregidor; and Lieutenant Norman Reyes, a Filipino, captured in Bataan.

Iva spent much of her meager funds to purchase food, medicine, and tobacco and at considerable risk to herself secretly gave the supplies to the POW broadcasters and other prisoners of the Bunka POW camp in Surugadai, Kanda-ku, Tokyo. Her association with the three POW broadcasters became a turning point in her life in Japan.

———

When the Pacific war began, the Japanese military felt the need of intensifying its propaganda campaign. The Japanese overseas broadcasts in English had been weak and ineffective mostly because of the poor knowledge of English among the Japanese engaging in the radio work. They suffered from lack of talented personnel, especially script writers.

Since there were few professionally trained English-speaking announcers in Japan, many of the NHK broadcasters had been recruited from American *nisei* who had come to Japan in the hope of finding better jobs. Although none of them were formally trained, some of them had become very competent broadcasters. There had been more than a dozen such female English-speaking announcers stationed at Radio Tokyo in Tokyo. They were, to name the most popular ones, June Y. Suyama, a Canadian *issei* (born in Japan but reared in Canada), working at NHK since before the war and regarded as the most exciting announcer, with "good vocal range and control"; Ruth Hayakawa, an American *issei* (born in Japan but lived in the United States until she graduated from a Los Angeles junior college) with "a very low, resonant voice"; and Fumy Saisho, a Japanese citizen, "distinctly feminine with a broad range of expression."

Beside the Tokyo station, Radio Tokyo used English-speaking women broadcasters on thirteen other Japanese-controlled radio stations: Arai, Bondung, Bangkok, Hsinking, Seoul, Manila, Nanking, Rangoon, Saigon, Shanghai, Singapore, Soerabaja, and Taipei. It is, therefore, erroneous to assume that there had been only one "Tokyo Rose."

No one knows exactly who invented the term and when and to whom it specifically referred. It was a figment of the American GIs' imagination and was a vague and generic term. It was one of several terms that the ingenious American fighting men in the Pacific had coined; others included "victory disease," the "Cactus Air Force," the "Tokyo Express," and "Turkey Shot."

No Japanese or Japanese American announcers at Radio Tokyo had ever used the name "Tokyo Rose" when they broadcast from Tokyo or any other stations scattered throughout Southeast Asia and the western Pacific. Nor did any American monitoring centers that had recorded the Japanese broadcasts extensively ever hear the name. Any female announcers broadcasting from Tokyo or any other Japanese station in Asia, therefore, must have been, to the American GIs in the Pacific, "Tokyo Rose." The notion that Tokyo Rose was a single individual, nevertheless, persisted and took on a new momentum as the war progressed.

It was not the broadcasting but the script writing that had posed the major problem for the overseas radio program. There were few good *nisei* script writers, and the English of most native Japanese simply was not adequate for the task. Their direct translations were often unintelligible, and their pronunciation inaccurate and misleading. In order to combat this inherent problem, the army headquarters came up with the idea of recruiting radio professionals from among the Allied POWs captured in the early phases of the war. The orders were sent to the front line, and all the military officers were on the lookout for any radio specialists among the enemy. By late 1942, three were already working at Radio Tokyo.

The most important was Charles H. Cousens. British-born and a graduate of Sandhurst, the British West Point, he served briefly in India before resigning his commission and emigrating to Australia, where he had tried many jobs. He became a sportswriter and joined the Sydney Radio Station, where he became the chief announcer and eventually the best-known voice of the Australian Broadcasting Corporation, whom Russell W. Howe dubs the Walter Cronkite of Australia.

When all the British Commonwealth nations went to war, Cousens, along with many Australians, joined the Australian army. Now thirty-seven years old with a wife and two sons, he became a captain and commanded an infantry battalion against the Japanese invasion of Malaya. Two days after his promotion to major, he participated in the surrender ceremonies of Singapore as it fell into Japanese hands. When the Japanese forced him to reveal his prewar profession, he said only that he had been a "journalist," but they quickly found out his real identity. As Howe recounts the story, he was ordered to Tokyo, but when he refused, he was thrown into solitary confinement. When that did not work, he was sent on to the labor battalions in Burma, where the new bridge was being constructed by the infamous POW labor camp later depicted in the movie *The Bridge on the River Kwai*.

Cousens, however, was suddenly brought back to Singapore, where he was finally persuaded to do limited work: to broadcast only POW messages to families and an appeal to the International Red Cross for food and other aid. It was in June 1942, four months after the fall of Singapore, that Cousens was flown to Tokyo, instead of taken by boat. When he landed at Haneda airport on a summer night, he was immediately taken to the office of Major Shigetsugu Tsuneishi.

Tsuneishi, through his interpreter, said, "I learn you famous man in Australia. Best man on radio. Very fine. Now you write news and speak news in English on Nippon Hoso Kyokai (NHK), Japan Radio Corporation."

"Impossible, sir." Cousens said firmly. "Against my orders as an Australian officer." "Not impossible," the Japanese major barked at him and added, "Not against orders I received." Cousens protested that he had agreed only to broadcast prisoners' messages and an appeal to the International Red Cross, but Tsuneishi said he couldn't answer for the consequences if Cousens resisted orders. After various kinds of intimidations and threats, Cousens agreed to do as Tsuneishi asked, resolving at the same time to sabotage Japan's overseas radio program from within. He was then taken to the Dai-ichi Hotel, given a room with clean futons on the *tatami*, and allowed to shave.

The next morning, he was taken to the NHK studio and handed a script to read. It was a vicious attack on President Roosevelt. Cousens protested and insisted that he as a prisoner of war could be made to do menial work but could not be forced to participate in the war effort of his enemies, to no avail. Cousens was assigned to the NHK Overseas Broadcasting Bureau, under Tsuneishi, a clear violation of the Geneva Convention. The Japanese major summoned all senior members of the English division and explained the problem they were facing with Cousens. If he remained defiant, Tsuneishi declared that he would execute Cousens then and there.

Tsuneishi confronted Cousens with all kinds of verbal abuses, but the Australian calmly decided to stick to his original plan to sabotage the Japanese program from within. He tried various strategies such as reading scripts in a way peculiar to Japanese speaking English. Some Japanese, of course, detected what he was doing and became angry with him. He sometimes pretended he was very sick and read scripts in a way a very sick man would read.

About two and a half months after Cousens arrived, Wallace Ince and Norman Reyes came from the Philippines, also in direct response to Tsuneishi's "requests." Ince, a thirty-year-old American army captain, came from Corregidor, where he had been in charge of the propaganda program the "Voice of Freedom," under General Jonathan Wainwright, who replaced General Douglas MacArthur. Reyes, a Filipino lieutenant, not yet twenty, came from Manila, where he had been serving on Ince's staff.

Upon arrival, they met Tsuneishi, who told them that "you will regard orders from the Overseas Bureau as orders from the Army." He continued, "If you do not follow these orders, I do not think I need to explain to you what will happen."

At first Reyes and Ince were put to work correcting and rewriting news scripts written by the Japanese. They soon discovered that it was more time-consuming to correct them than write their own scripts from scratch, so before long they were writing their own scripts.

Since August 25, 1943, when Iva met these three POWs, she visited them almost every day in their small room on the second floor from her business office on the third floor without attracting much attention. During the first month, Iva felt that they were apprehensive, limiting themselves to brief greetings. Iva was naturally the one who did the talking. She told them about herself, her time at UCLA, her favorite sport, football, her unlikely trip to Japan, her difficulty in getting out, her hatred of Japanese militarism, and her persistent refusal to accept Japanese citizenship.

They gradually opened up to Iva and started to ask her for medicine, food, and tobacco. She began to make daily deliveries of such things as medicine, aspirin, and lemons, hiding them in her purse and clothes. Sometime in mid-October, Cousens began telling her about his encounter with Major Tsuneishi, the army boss of Radio Tokyo, and how ruthless he had been in forcing Cousens to do his bidding. "With Tsuneishi, you do just what you are told," Cousens said to her, but it seemed he was not just warning her but indoctrinating her in a specific "state of mind." "Eventually," he added, "you do just what you are told or you die." Using their long experience in radio broadcasting, the POWs seemed determined to take advantage of the relative inexperience and inability of the administration.

"We've got this operation going just about the way we want it," Cousens told Iva shortly after the first of November. "As propaganda, it's a laugh." He explained to her various ways they had been subverting the Japanese efforts.

He, for example, not only repeated "key propaganda words until they fell on the ear with ludicrous effect" but also "spoke cheerfully where a solemn tone would have served the scrapped Japanese purpose." Ince added to the damage by reading the news as fast as 200 words a minute so that it was unintelligible, by scraping needles across records, and by leaving microphone switches open so that studio noises distorted the program. Indeed, Iva must have thought, they ran "the gamut of operational errors" insofar as they dared. It was like the work of a "resistance group" operating under the strict enemy occupation.

The golden opportunity for the POWs to implement their idea came when Nakamoto, one of the supervisors of the "Zero Hour," brought to them an Imperial Army order to expand the program and presented a plan. Ince took a look at the sketch and said, "The hell with it."

"All right," said Cousens to Nakamoto, pointing at the proposals he had brought. "Get out of here and we'll see what we can do. It won't be like them."

Nakamoto left, and Cousens turned to Ince and Reyes and said, "I think this is our chance to make a complete shambles of the Zero Hour."

"How?" Ince asked inquisitively.

"We'll use a woman," Cousens responded.

"Who?"

"One we can trust. Iva Toguri."

"You're crazy." Ince shook his head. Then he thought about it, and he began to laugh. "Do you think we can get away with it?"

They talked it over. Cousens finished his plan, and then took it to Nakamoto. The POWs knew that plenty of experienced female announcers were available at Radio Tokyo, like June Suyama, Ruth Hayakawa, Fumy Saisho, and Mieko Furuya, but they were all proven pro-Japanese, thus not qualified for this purpose.

When Cousens named Iva Toguri as his choice, Nakamoto protested, "Her voice is all wrong. She's the wrong person."

"She's the one I want," said Cousens. "If it is your neck as well as mine, stay out of the way."

"I had in mind of making a complete burlesque of the program," Cousens later remarked about Iva's raspy voice. It was "the comedy voice," "rough, almost masculine, nothing of a femininely seductive voice, that I needed for the particular job."

On November 10, the order was given to the head of the personnel section, Shigechika Takano, who informed Iva that she must take a voice test that afternoon. Iva was completely taken aback. She objected vehemently, and she was still protesting when she went down to a ground-floor studio. Cousens took her aside, out of Nakamoto's hearing, and said:

> Now, listen. This is a straight out entertainment program. I have written it and I know what I'm doing. All you have to do is look upon yourself as a soldier under my orders. Do exactly what you are told. . . . Don't try to do anything for yourself and you will do nothing that you do not want to. You will do nothing against your own people. I will guarantee that personally because I have written the script and I know what I'm doing.

At 6 o'clock that night, Iva sat before a microphone looking into the control booth where Reyes spun a Boston Pops recording of "Strike up the Band" to open the show. Cousens read a few minutes of POW messages. She heard him say the prearranged cue.

"Here comes your music."

The "on the air" panel lit up and she was talking. She read announcements between records for 15 or 20 minutes and then her part was over. Ince followed with "Home Front News," items selected from broadcasts monitored in the United States. Then Reyes took over with his announced "Original Zero Hour"—jazz records. Iva followed Cousens into the POW room.

"This is crazy," she said. "I can't do this. I'm no good at it."

"You are just what we want," Cousens assured her. "We don't want an experienced announcer. We want a Yankee voice with a certain personality in it—a little touch of a WAC officer and a lot of cheer. I'll coach you to read the scripts the way I want them, so don't worry. You are just what we want."

He coached her daily after that on how to read the scripts, which he wrote in longhand. "Put yourself among the GIs in the South Pacific," he said. "You are with them to sing-along with our records. Always be cheerful. Always laugh when you say 'enemy.'" Cousens gave Iva the broadcasting name "Orphan Ann" and began writing it into the script. For the first time in the war Iva felt useful, doing something for the American war effort under the very noses of the Japanese. Like the Norwegian "resistance group" trying to overthrow German rule in occupied Norway, Cousens, Ince, Reyes, and Iva were all conducting subversive activities undermining the radio war propaganda.

About the time she went to work at the Danish legation, the POWs at the Bunka camp in Surugadai, Kanda-ku, begged her to make an all-out effort to help not just Cousens, Ince, and Reyes, who had already moved back to Bunka, but all twenty-seven POWs. At the time the food was getting ever more scarce and foraging was becoming increasingly difficult, but she was able to collect a variety of goods. She got fruits and vegetables from Filipe's grandmother's place in Atsugi; eggs, flour, rice, bread, and oatmeal from farmers and neighbors; sugar, matches, and soap from the Danish minister; and salt from a friend's father who owned a bakery. Medicine, including quinine, aspirin, vitamin pills, and yeast oil tablets, she acquired from drugstores and from her doctor, Dr. Amano, and she got tobacco by lining up for her turn and from the black market.

Meanwhile, Iva's broadcast was becoming more popular and more famous. Because of Cousens's coaching she was enjoying her broadcast more and more. She felt lucky to learn the trade from a real pro and was even considering going into radio announcing in California after the war.

Iva's broadcast lasted a little more than a year. It was a twenty-minute entertainment segment on an hour program. It was Iva who made the transition from "Tokyo Rose" news commentator to sing-along disc jockey. The following excerpts from Ann's "Zero Hour," dated from February to May 1944, depict the nature of her announcements that became very popular among the GIs in the Pacific:

2/22/44

Hello, there, enemies . . . how's tricks? This is Ann of Radio Tokyo, and we're just going to begin our regular program of music . . . news and the Zero Hour for our friends . . . I mean, our enemies! . . . in Australia and the South Pacific. . . . So, be on your guard, and mind the children don't hear! All set? O.K., here's the first blow at your morale . . . the Boston Pops . . . playing "Strike Up the Band"!

3/27/44

Thank you . . . thank you . . . Greetings, everybody! This is your little playmate, I mean your bitter enemy, Ann, with a program of dangerous and wicked propaganda for my victims in Australia and the

South Pacific. . . . Stand by! You unlucky creatures. . . . Here I go! . . . Peter Dawson singing "Ol' Man River."

[OL' MAN RIVER]

See what I mean? . . . dangerous stuff that . . . and it's habit forming, before you know where you are you're singing, too . . . and then where are you?

Doggone it! . . . there's a war on isn't there? . . . so none of this singing nonsense.

Sergeant!

5/11/44

Who, me? . . . That's not a smile, my shoe's hurting! Hello Everybody! . . . this is your little playmate Ann of Radio Tokyo, presenting our usual nightly program for our Friends in Australia and parts adjoining. . . . How d'you like that? . . . "Parts adjoining" . . . sounds kind of professional, doesn't it? And after all what's a few hundred miles between friends? O.K. I heard you the first time! . . . but it's no good complaining now, Honorable boneheads, so let's be cheerful and have some music.

[STRIKE UP THE BAND]

That's better! . . . now let's have more of that close harmony work from the "New Guinea Nightingales," and other chapters of the Pacific Orphans Choir. Here's some more Stephen Foster for you, so sing nicely little ones . . . Jeep, Jeep!

Rex B. Gunn, a GI war correspondent in the Pacific, said that Orphan Ann had become the most widely known "enemy" personality in the Pacific. Men speculated constantly about who she might be. By the fall of 1944, however, the listeners detected a change in Orphan Ann. She began to call her "boneheads" "your fighting GIs," and when she said it she didn't laugh. Gunn noticed there was a consistent undertone of friendship, projecting herself as one of her listeners.

As the new "Tokyo Rose," Iva had a vast audience, which was getting bigger all the time, stretching from the Aleutians through the Pacific to northern New Guinea. But just when Orphan Ann's popularity reached its peak, Charles Cousens left Radio Tokyo after suffering a heart attack. Without his scripts, the quality of the program had gone down. Iva absented herself from the station more frequently.

{ *Chapter 3* }

Beginning in November 1944, as the B-29 bombing intensified in Tokyo and Radio Tokyo's activities slowed down, Iva used the air raids, which often disrupted transportation, as her new excuse for absences. Iva was on her extended absence through all of March and April 1945, during which time she married Filipe and became a Portuguese citizen, still retaining her American citizenship.

During her absence, Mieko Furuya, June Suyama, Mary Ishii, and others substituted for her, but the entire operation, entertainment or propaganda, became pointless in the midst of destruction. Tokyo was devastated by the terrible incendiary raids on May 25 and 26.

By then, Tsuneishi, now promoted to colonel, left Tokyo for the homeland defense. The Danish legation closed down, ending Iva's job there. Radio Tokyo shut down on August 15, the day of the Japanese surrender, and Operation Zero Hour was finished.

———

The woman known as "Orphan Ann" of "Zero Hour" was almost as much a mystery at Radio Tokyo as she was to her GI listeners in the South Pacific. From the time she started her broadcasting in November 1943, she spent only about thirty minutes at the radio station each day, arriving at ten of six, then leaving immediately after her broadcast at 6:15 or 6:20. She had no friends and acquaintances at work, except Cousens. Iva herself said that she didn't have even one friend at Radio Tokyo.

Nor did her colleagues, though very few in number, have particularly warm feelings toward her. Many resented her short working hours and high salary. While the best of the woman announcers with the top pay, June Suyama, got only 150 yen for a day's work, Iva got 100 yen for working less than an hour. Combined with her salary from the Danish legation, she was fairly well off, indeed. Some coworkers also disliked her frequent absences. Since Major Tsuneishi considered her role in the "Zero Hour" program indispensable, they were not openly critical, but they did not like her remoteness toward *nisei* workers, especially her snobbish attitude toward those who had given up their American citizenship.

One person, however, knew about Iva's daily life very well. He was Master Sergeant Katsuo Okada of the Thought Control Section of the military police, who was charged with keeping Iva under close surveillance and left a remarkable piece of information on her life during the latter half of the war. His report, though never submitted anywhere formally or used as evidence in her trial, was nevertheless fully exploited by Rex Gunn, vividly revealing Iva's daily activities and her strong patriotic attitude toward the United States.

According to Okada, each weekend, Iva, disguised as a teenager wearing blue jeans and American oxfords, went out foraging for food, which she bartered for with scarce goods including woolen clothing, soap, sugar, and salt (all virtually unobtainable in the stores in Tokyo). Every Saturday morning, she would begin her journey, walking ten to fifteen miles, to the farmhouses. On Sunday night, she might be seen lugging some combination of vegetables, fruit, eggs, flour, rice, and oatmeal back to the city. From the look of her she ate very little herself.

On weekdays, she was a totally different person. Wearing her hair waved, dressed in oxfords and a suit, she would leave her room in the boardinghouse in Setagaya and walk to the Danish legation, where she worked as receptionist and personal secretary to the minister, from 8:30 to 4:30. When she left the legation, she would take a bus downtown, getting off in front of Radio Tokyo. After half an hour or 45 minutes, she returned to the street.

In the evening, she could be found standing in line for hours at a tobacconist or drug store, searching for large quantities of cigarettes, vitamin tablets, yeast oil tablets, quinine, whale oil, and aspirin. She also went to the black market for those supplies. All that she collected vanished as quickly as she got it. Despite her weekly forage supply, sufficient for a large family, the girl remained as thin as ever and had to be treated for malnutrition, pellagra, and beriberi.

In the neighborhood where Iva lived, the *kempei-tai* and the Tokyo Metropolitan Police had watched the girl. They had talked not only to Iva's landlady, Mrs. Kido, but to the neighbor women. The girl bought no war bonds, gave no clothing, old jewels, or old metals to the neighborhood organization for helping the war effort, refused to change her citizenship from American to Japanese, and could be heard speaking English most of the time to the small man named Filipe, also a foreigner, whose father had been interned as a dangerous enemy alien.

Master Sergeant Okada, who had ready access to all this talk among the neighbors, was the nephew of Mrs. Kido, whose husband was in the Japanese army in Manchuria. Mrs. Kido had sought his advice before allowing the American girl to move in. "You will have trouble," he told his aunt, "because she is known as pro-American, but if you caution her to be careful and are, yourself, careful, it will be all right."

For Okada, the investigation of the girl became a simple matter. The neighbors rushed in to tell him their tales. "The girl was seen on the bus," one told Okada, "as it passed the emperor's palace, and she refused to bow, and when another passenger told her to bow, she just got off the bus at the next corner." It was also a neighbor who found out about the Christmas tree that Iva brought into her room and was decorating. The neighbor, who could see "the twinkling tree through Iva's window," realized that it was "an American ceremony" and spread the news all through the neighborhood, causing Mrs. Kido to order her to take the tree down. It was against the law to have a Christmas tree, she was told. Iva refused, but her friend Filipe took it down.

Okada said to Iva one day that he could arrest her at any time for one of the three things she had been doing. For one, she had been disposing of her food supplies at Radio Tokyo for the POWs. Okada also said that Iva was supplying the POWs with war news through Domei listening posts, a clear violation of the law. Finally, Okada said that he could arrest her for "her habit of saying that Japan would lose the war." If she thought so, then she could at least keep it to herself, but she had said it even to Okada! He warned her:

> You as a person who had long residence in the United States know the strength of the United States well. So it is probably correct that you say America is going to win the war. But I don't want to think that Japan will lose. For you to talk about that is violating Japanese law, and I caution you that you better not talk about this to outsiders. If you talk about such things to people other than myself you will be investigated by the *kempei* gendarmes and the Metropolitan Police. I am a *kempei*, but I am also your friend. I don't want to accuse you of the crime, but I am going to caution you of this as a friend.

As Gunn's account reveals, Master Sergeant Okada counted Iva no less a war prisoner than the men with whom she was broadcasting on the "Zero Hour." He was certain that Iva would extend her resistance to the Japanese war effort beyond her aid to the prisoners. Though he couldn't have realized it, Iva had already begun doing just that, the struggle she continued until the end of the war.

CHAPTER 4

The American Paparazzi

Two American correspondents have offered $2,000 for your exclusive story as Tokyo Rose,
and they will be waiting for you with the money at the Imperial Hotel in the morning.

LESLIE SATORU NAKASHIMA TO IVA TOGURI, *August 31, 1945*

On August 30, 1945, a day before the advance party of General Mac-Arthur arrived in Japan, Clark Lee of International News Service and Harry Brundidge, associate editor of *Cosmopolitan Magazine*, both part of the Hearst publishing empire, were sitting on the rock wall at the entrance to an ancient burial tomb in Okinawa, bathing in the yellow light of a tropical moon. They had been buddies together around the world for a long, long time. Back in 1939–1940, these war correspondents had followed the Japanese army throughout North, Central, and South China.

Brundidge said to Lee, "Want to make a deal?" "Sure," Lee answered. "What kind of a deal?" "Well," Brundidge went on, "we've lived in Japan. We know something about the people. We know that when Hirohito told 'em to quit, they quit. I feel certain that most of the armed forces, and all of the civilian population, have folded, and that it would be perfectly safe for us to dash to Tokyo the minute we land in Japan. The hottest story in Japan today is: Who is Tokyo Rose? Let's find out and get her. Our old Japanese friends will help us." "Okay," said Lee, "it's a deal."

As soon as the advance party arrived at Atsugi, two of the group, Brundidge and Lee, hitched a ride and rushed to Tokyo, forty miles away, to find Tokyo Rose before anyone else. They contacted Leslie S. Nakashima, a Hawaiian *nisei*, who had been a Domei News Agency writer. When asked about Tokyo Rose, Nakashima said that there was no person named Tokyo Rose, but there were several women at Radio Tokyo who might fit the description. The American newspapermen insisted that Nakashima locate any Tokyo Rose. Because of his prewar obligation yet to be repaid to them, Nakashima reluctantly agreed to help them find one.

He took the Americans to the Oversea Broadcasting Bureau of NHK, but no one there could identify Tokyo Rose. The reporters then promised

Nakashima $500 (a substantial amount in Japan then) if he could find her. Nakashima later went back to NHK and spoke to production supervisor Kenkichi Oki, but he was evasive, saying that no female announcers had ever used that name and that there were several female announcers on the "Zero Hour" broadcasts. Nakashima asked for their names, but Oki, though he earlier identified Hayakawa as Tokyo Rose, now became very reluctant to name any regular members of Radio Tokyo, including Hayakawa and especially his bride, Miyeko Furuya Oki. After thinking for a while, Oki finally suggested, in order to protect the regular, full-timers, one name, that of the outsider on the staff, Iva Toguri d'Aquino.

Late in the afternoon, Nakashima came rushing into the Imperial Hotel and found Lee and Brundidge in the lobby. He told them that he had found "a Tokyo Rose." Brundidge told Nakashima to tell Tokyo Rose that if she agreed to an exclusive interview, *Cosmopolitan* magazine would pay her a fee of $2,000. He also suggested that the interview should take place, if possible, on the following day, September 1, at 9:30 a.m. at the Imperial Hotel. Nakashima promised that he would convey the Hearst reporters' message to Iva.

For the past two weeks, following the last broadcast at Radio Tokyo on August 14, Iva was anxiously waiting for the American occupation of Tokyo, sitting in her tiny room in the burnt ruins of the city. Her feelings must have been far different from those of her neighbors. Her side had won, and she could not wait to celebrate the victory with other Americans.

The opportunity came much sooner and in a different way than she had expected. On the evening of August 31, one of Filipe's friends at Domei, Nakashima, called on the d'Aquinos with exciting news. Two American correspondents, he said, had offered $2,000 for Iva's exclusive story as Tokyo Rose, and they would be waiting for her with the money at the Imperial Hotel in the morning.

Iva protested, saying that she wasn't Tokyo Rose, only one of a dozen announcers. But the money was tempting; it was a substantial amount, especially due to the unfavorable exchange rate (360 yen to 1 dollar). Filipe also pointed out that if the deal would keep the other reporters away, it was worth accepting. And she would have a chance to tell her story of how the war prisoners and Orphan Ann had sabotaged Japanese propaganda right under their captors' noses. They finally agreed to meet Lee and Brundidge at the Imperial Hotel.

These two war correspondents with whom Iva unfortunately had to deal turned out to be perhaps among the worst kind of journalists. They were fame-driven, selfish, and ruthless go-getters, who had no professional integrity as journalists.

How much did they know about Tokyo Rose in the United States at the end of the war? The U.S. Navy, for example, on August 7, 1945, a week before the war ended, issued a citation to Tokyo Rose for her morale-building efforts. The citation said that Tokyo Rose "has persistently entertained them [U.S. armed forces] during those long nights in fox holes and on board ship, by bringing them excellent States-side music, laughter and news about home." The broadcasts "have inspired them to a greater determination than ever to get the war over quickly," it concluded, "so that soon they will be able to thank Tokyo Rose in person."

Yet the identity of Tokyo Rose had never been determined. Shortly before the Japanese surrender, the Office of War Information, which had already been investigating the phenomenon, had come to a conclusion. The OWI said: "There is no Tokyo Rose, the name is strictly a GI invention. The name has been applied to at least two lilting Japanese voices on the Japanese radio. . . . Government monitors listening in twenty-four hours a day have never heard the words Tokyo Rose over a Japanese-controlled Far Eastern radio."

The rumors, nevertheless, persisted. On September 1, 1945, American papers carried an Associated Press story about the "frustration" of U.S. troops in Japan at finding out that Tokyo Rose was a figment of their own imagination and did not exist. These stories vividly demonstrate that Tokyo Rose did not exist or, if she existed, she was doing something beneficial for the American GIs. The Tokyo Rose story should have ended right then and there. It did not end, however.

As if they hadn't paid any attention to all these new developments, some reporters, not just less serious ones but those who aggressively wanted to exploit Tokyo Rose for their own interests, were still determined to search for her. In fact, on the very day the Associated Press story appeared, Lee and Brundidge were meeting Iva Toguri.

Early that morning, Iva dressed as she had for her weekend foraging trips into the countryside. She put on slacks, a blouse, and a leather jacket, and she braided her hair in pigtails, tying them with a red ribbon. Then she, Filipe, and Nakashima hurried to the American reporters' room at the Imperial Hotel. When she entered the room, she was shocked by the fact that these men were wearing officers' uniforms and pistols, though it was the style for American correspondents in World War II.

Both men seem to have been disappointed. They never expected Tokyo Rose to look like an innocent, pigtailed high school girl, though she was twenty-nine. Lee, dark-haired, handsome, and trim, soon took out his portable typewriter and prepared to do the interview straight onto the machine. Brundidge, who was drinking bourbon, was smaller, plumper, older, and red-faced with an imperial mustache; he was ready to listen intently. But, first, Brundidge gave Iva a contract to sign.

Nervous, Iva sat down and read a one-page contract. The room had all the curtains drawn and "the air of secrecy and the presence of the revolver." The Brundidge contract said:

Tokyo, Japan

September first, 1945

This contract, entered into at the Imperial Hotel, in Tokyo, Japan, on the above date, between Cosmopolitan Magazine, party of the first part, and Iva Ikuko Toguri, known as "Tokyo Rose," the party of the second part, sets forth and agrees to the following:

That Iva Ikuko is the one and original "Tokyo Rose" who broadcast from Radio Tokyo;

That she had no feminine assistants or substitutes;

That the story she has related for publication is to be exclusive for first publication in *Cosmopolitan*, with subsequent syndicate rights for King Features of International News Service, is her own true story, told for the first time, and not to be repeated to anyone for publication.

Cosmopolitan Magazine, represented by Harry T. Brundidge, agrees to pay Iva Ikuko Toguri $2,000 (American dollars) for the above described rights. It is also agreed and understood that any additional monies which might accrue from motion picture rights, publication by Reader's Digest, or any other source, shall be turned over to Iva Ikuko Toguri.

Iva signed as Iva Ikuko Toguri, Brundidge for Hearst, and three persons (Clark Lee, INS; Leslie Nakashima, Domei; and Filipe d'Aquino, Radio Tokyo—though he had never worked there) signed as witnesses. Iva made the foolish and serious mistake of signing it and identifying herself as the "original Rose." Some say Iva acted from "greed," not truth.

This document, drafted by a nonlawyer, contains a number of contradictions and loopholes to the Hearst reporters' advantage. It lacks specifics as to payment arrangements, kinds and nature of publication, breach of contract, and the like.

The contract reveals that Iva knew the statement was not entirely true, but the false statement was endorsed by the witnesses. After all signed the one-page contract, Nakashima left. Iva should have asked Lee and Brundidge to show her money. If they wouldn't, she should have ended or postponed the interview until they showed the money. Iva, however, was ready to talk about her broadcasting activities.

She explained freely about how the war prisoners had made a mockery out of the "Zero Hour" propaganda. As she talked steadily, Lee typed. When she said she started broadcasting in November 1943, Lee paused and wondered about the time sequence. Lee remembered some soldiers talking about Tokyo Rose on Bataan in 1942, a year and a half before Iva's first broadcast. It should not have concerned him much because Lee, Brundidge, Iva, and Filipe all knew that the story making Iva out to be the one and only Tokyo Rose was a fake.

They had lunch in the room and continued working until the afternoon. By about three o'clock, Lee had seventeen pages of double-spaced notes. His impression was that he had just heard what Rex Gunn termed "one of the war's biggest cock-and-bull stories." Lee simply could not believe Iva's stories about the POWs getting her to broadcast and about her supplying the prisoners with food, drugs, Allied news, and tobacco under the noses of the secret police.

Totally unsuspicious of Lee's intention, Iva left the interview still hoping that she could soon return home and reunite with her family. "It never entered my mind . . . that my conduct would be in any way interpreted as wrong," she later commented. "I was not aware of any need for a lawyer," Iva continued, adding, "I answered all of their questions. . . . I had never made statements referring to troop and ship movements and 4Fs out with soldiers' girls." She left the room "with no sense of uneasiness. If I had been impressed with some threat growing out of this interview, I would have contacted a lawyer. I didn't."

Iva, however, really needed a lawyer during her entire interview. If guilty suspects need lawyers, more so with innocent people. "Lawyers," to borrow Justice Hugo Black's famous words, in *Gideon v. Wainwright* (1963), "are necessities, not luxuries," and this is applicable to all human activities, not just criminal affairs. With a lawyer representing her in the interview, she could very well have prevented what was going to happen. On the following day, Iva was appalled to see Lee's article in the *Los Angeles Examiner.*

As soon as Iva had left, Lee wrote his story and sent it to California via cable that night. The next day, Iva Toguri as Tokyo Rose was on page one.

"TRAITOR'S PAY — TOKYO ROSE GOT 100 YEN A MO . . . $ 6.60"
by Clark Lee
(Staff correspondent for INS)

Tokyo, Japan (Delayed) — The one and only "Tokyo Rose," a Los Angeles born American of Japanese ancestry, is "willing to take her medicine."

But Iva Ikuko Toguri . . . does not feel that she was a traitor to the U.S.

For the job of trying to make American troops homesick she was paid a miserable 100 yen monthly — $6.60 at the present exchange rate.

In an exclusive interview with this correspondent, Iva admitted she did not think it through when she took the job, nor did she consider the possibilities of being adjudged a traitor to her country.

She said she believed Americans would enjoy her music and laugh at her propaganda. . . . (From the *Los Angeles Examiner*, Sept. 3, 1945)

This article, though brief, contains a number of false and inaccurate statements. Iva, for example, did not admit "she did not think it through," nor did she ever broadcast "propaganda." The article clearly reveals that Lee had already fixed the story in advance, completely ignoring the real and much more fascinating story of survival in wartime Tokyo and of how Iva and Major Cousens had conspired to undermine the Japanese radio program.

Lee's piece was a fabricated account, making Iva guilty without evidence. So was Brundidge's. He designed his 5,000-word story for *Cosmopolitan* as a first-person confession of treason, as told by Iva Toguri to Harry Brundidge. He cabled his story to Frances Whiting, editor of the magazine in New York. The next morning, he received shocking news. A cablegram informed him that Whiting had rejected his article, the exclusive confession of Tokyo Rose, stating that she would not glorify a traitor and refused to pay the $2,000 that Brundidge had promised Iva. Moreover, a copy of her cablegram had been posted on a bulletin board at Atsugi Air Base so that all 300 of Brundidge's rival correspondents might enjoy it. If Brundidge had got the true story, turning the Tokyo Rose legend upside down and making her a hero, some have speculated, Whiting would probably have been very happy to pay.

Whiting's rejection outraged Brundidge. Exploding and turning into a madman, he decided to do two things. First, he rushed to the office of Brigadier General Elliot R. Thorpe, head of the Eighth Army Counter Intelligence Corps (CIC), and urged the arrest of Iva Toguri as Tokyo Rose. "She's a traitor," he said, "and here's her confession," offering the seventeen pages of notes typed by Lee. Second, in order to release himself from the obligation to pay Iva the promised $2,000, Brundidge persuaded the army to hold a mass news conference with Iva. In actuality, he had already breached the contract by being unable to pay Iva.

On the next day, September 3, an Eighth Army officer and a sergeant came to Iva's house in a jeep, arrested her, and drove her to the Bund Hotel in Yokohama. Dale Kramer of *Yank* magazine persuaded her to give an interview, which turned out to be a more professional job than Lee's. The readers of *Yank* said that Toguri had convinced them that her role in "Zero Hour" was innocuous and that the "only untrue portions of it or the only part that could be construed as enemy propaganda were contained in the news items which were read by another announcer into the program from time to time."

Kramer, in fact, was the first reporter who had gotten hold of Iva's whereabouts from Oki and rushed to her home to conduct an interview with her. Finding that Iva was not at home, he left without waiting. "It was a big mistake," he later deplored. He missed the opportunity of writing an article for *Yank* that would have been favorable to her, and one that, by preempting the Brundidge-Lee interview and ensuing events, could have saved Iva from her eventual fate.

At the press conference held at the Bund Hotel on the following day, the reporters, over a hundred of them, all wearing officer uniforms, were friendly. When they heard Iva's voice, several of the American and Australian reporters stated that she was not the broadcaster whom they had heard making questionable statements about the activities of wives and girlfriends back home or other incendiary remarks.

The *New York Times* quoted Iva as telling reporters that she was "one of four Tokyo Roses" and that "I didn't think I was doing anything disloyal to America." The paper noted that she had "merely announced record programs, from Bach to jive," and quoted her as saying that she had "never, never broadcast any propaganda" or "mentioned wayward wives or sweethearts." Asked who the other Tokyo Roses were, she had mentioned Ruth Hayakawa and June Suyama.

After the press conference, Sergeant Merrit Page of the CIC asked the d'Aquinos to meet General Thorpe, a meeting that was arranged for the following morning. Iva and Filipe stayed overnight at the Grand Hotel as General Thorpe's guests. As soon as the investigation started the next morning in the Grand Hotel, where the CIC headquarters had been located, General Thorpe decided that Iva's case was a minor one to be handled by Sergeant Page.

Page's interrogation continued until midafternoon. It was a light and "untroubling encounter." Officers and enlisted men entered the room constantly for a look at "Tokyo Rose." At one point, General Robert Eichelberger, the Eighth Army Commander, telephoned Iva and asked her to come to his office for a picture. They had "a picture taken together like old friends." The commander thanked her for her music, which he said his soldiers had appreciated. He asked if she had received the package of wartime hits that he had had parachuted over Tokyo and addressed to Tokyo Rose. It was revealed later that the general's gift did reach the ground but was in no playable condition.

At two-thirty, she was fingerprinted and released "into your husband's custody." The CIC announced that it was uncertain of her citizenship, but that when it became certain that Iva was an American, she would be rearrested. The army sent the d'Aquinos home to Tokyo in a jeep. The *New York Times* on September 6 reported Iva's conference and subsequent arrest and noted that it was "uncertain whether charges would be filed against her for broadcasting sweet music and sour propaganda on the enemy radio. First it must be determined if she is still a United States citizen." At the end of the second week of September apparently the potential charge against Iva seems to have been dropped.

During the interview with Brundidge and Lee, Iva tried to present her story as honestly and accurately as possible, but these reporters were not willing to have any of it. If a lawyer had been present on her behalf, she could have insisted on the kind of articles she wanted them to write and on a contract more beneficial to her. More important, Brundidge and Lee might not have been able to take advantage of Iva so easily if her lawyer was present. The contract was already void because of the reporters' nonperformance, thus they had no right to publish any article about Iva based upon the "confession." Yet all kinds of problems resulting from the interview would end up following her for a long time.

Lee soon lost interest in Iva after 1947, except for the time he appeared in court in 1949 as a prosecution witness. Harry Brundidge, on the other hand, continued for the next several years to insist and promote his narrow, stubborn, and dogmatic ideas and position. Lee and Brundidge's manner of dealing with Iva clearly exhibits their coldhearted approach and vicious treatment of others whose views and interests might not conform to theirs.

———

Although the investigation of Iva instigated by Harry Brundidge was just about running its course and the Eighth Army CIC was ready to release her, it was not sure whether she was completely clear of the accusation because of the uncertainty of her citizenship status. Upon her release, the army announced that she would be rearrested if she were proven to be an American citizen. By the end of the second week of September, however, it seemed increasingly likely that this charge against Iva would not be made.

The decision to rearrest Iva came from an entirely different place: Southern California, where an ambitious U.S. attorney, Charles C. Carr (later a judge), announced that Iva d'Aquino would be arrested and tried in Los Angeles for "spreading discontent and dissension among American troops." This sudden change was not the result of new information. On October 17, 1945, she was rearrested at her apartment and was taken to the Yokohama Military Stockade. She was told to bring a toothbrush, but she was held in prison for a year.

There was one technical problem involved in Iva's arrest. Could the U.S. Army legally arrest a citizen of the United States living in a foreign country, even though that country was under American military occupation? Quite different from Germany, which surrendered after the Allies' invasion and thus its civil government had to be reconstructed by the Allied powers, Japan surrendered before any Allied soldiers ever set foot on Japanese soil. The Japanese government and civil society were functioning without interruption even in the wake of defeat, and the democratization of Japan was left to the Japanese themselves. Although they could intervene whenever necessary, the American occupation forces under the Supreme Commander of the Allied Powers did not rule Japan directly, except, for example, in the drafting of the new constitution. They simply superimposed themselves over the Japanese government. The U.S. military, therefore, though it did have the power to override the relationship of indirect rule with the Japanese government, did not exercise this power directly, except for specifically designated areas such as military bases.

Japan, though it was under the military occupation of the United States, was not entirely controlled by the United States. American civilians living in ordinary Japanese civilian communities, like Iva, whether they were American citizens or legal residents, were treated just like Japanese citizens with the full protection of the Japanese government and society. They were entitled to the rights, privileges, and duties regular Japanese were entitled to, no less, no more. It should, therefore, be an abuse of power for the American army to go into a Japanese civilian community and arrest a person living there, even though the person was an American citizen, particularly when the U.S. government was disputing the American citizenship status of an individual like Iva. In order to do so, the Eighth Army had to go through the proper channels of Japanese authorities.

After being incarcerated in the Yokohama prison for less than a month, Iva was transferred to Sugamo Prison in Tokyo, the prison where Japanese military and political leaders accused of war crimes had been held, seven of whom, including former prime minister Hideki Tojo, were eventually hanged in 1948. During her twelve months of imprisonment, Iva was illegally detained; was never informed of the charges against her; was denied legal counsel; was denied a speedy trial; and was forbidden spousal visits, sending and receiving mail, and changing her own clothes. She was held totally incommunicado for over two months until her husband was allowed a Christmas visit. Thereafter, her husband, the only person permitted to visit, was allowed just one twenty-minute session per month.

Therefore, at the same time the Japanese were beginning to enjoy basic political, individual, and legal rights as part of the democratization of Japan by the American Occupation forces, the fundamental legal rights that Iva was supposedly fully entitled to as an American citizen came to be flagrantly violated.

While Iva was in Sugamo, Filipe brought her a letter from her brother, Fred, delivered via the Red Cross, which he had written in the early days of the war. It brought the sad news that her mother died in May 1942 at the age of fifty-four at the assembly center on the way to the Gila River Relocation Center. After her mother's death, the rest of the family—Jun, Fred, June, and Inez—stayed at the concentration camp in the middle of the desolate Arizona desert until 1943, when all the internees were allowed to leave the camps, although they were prohibited from returning to the West Coast. Because of his business experience, her father was hired to buy supplies for the camp and made many business trips to different parts of the country. He came to like Chicago, and when time came to leave, he moved the entire family to the Windy City, where he opened up a small Japanese grocery and dry goods store.

It was during this period in Sugamo that Iva was subjected to lengthy and exhaustive investigations conducted by the army, the Federal Bureau of Investigation, and the Justice Department. She also had to undergo frequent, humiliating visits by curious American dignitaries. The Army Counter Intelligence Corps held an extensive investigation of Iva from October 1945 to April 1946 and found that, although the facts of the case might fall within the definition of treason, there were no offenses against military law, thus no need for the military to hold her. The Legal Section of General MacArthur's General Headquarters (the GHQ) recommended that the findings be submitted to the Justice Department for an opinion and that Iva be released immediately, but instead Iva remained in Sugamo for six more months as a precautionary measure. In July 1946, even a party of American congressmen got into the act of investigating. They conducted "a peeping-tom act" on Iva as she took a shower at Sugamo. Sixteen or seventeen of them, Iva recalled, came to the shower door, "sticking their noses through the door."

At the end of April 1947, Iva was interrogated by FBI Agent Frederick G. Tillman, a second-generation Irish American from Montana. She welcomed the opportunity to talk. Tillman commented that "she wouldn't keep her mouth shut. . . . She was always cracking wise. . . . I got tired of that." As Iva remembered Tillman's interrogation, "Usually we started around 8 or 9 in the morning, and it lasted till 5. . . . The thing that provoked me most was that he kept on insisting I was lying—hiding something . . . I got to where I just didn't give a damn. . . . I was just weary of him and his endless questioning."

At the outset Iva asked Tillman why she had been detained for six months already without being told the reason. She said if she had been accused of something she wanted a speedy trial. The agent replied that the authorities had, in fact, been carrying on an investigation to determine whether or not she should be indicted for treason. Eventually, Tillman produced a twelve-page statement, which Iva read and signed.

This document together with the army materials provided a thorough record of her activities, though it contained no new admissions, denials, or justifications. Some of the important issues discussed during the interrogation were not clearly elaborated in the statement and became heated controversies in the trial. In fact, Iva was tricked by Tillman into making some incriminating statements on such issues as her broadcasting under duress and double meanings of some words she used in her broadcasts.

Iva stated later that Tillman had asked the same things over and over again, "often in a mocking and sarcastic tone of voice." She was eager to explain everything, believing that the questioning might determine whether or not she was to be tried. When Iva found that Tillman seemed to doubt everything she said, she became quite discouraged and dispirited. She thought, according to Duus, she would be willing to sign anything just to get rid of him. At the end of the interview, the agent informed her that she would know the result, whether she was to be indicted for treason, within six weeks, but many more weeks passed without a word.

Tillman's interrogation, no matter how effectively conducted by a seasoned G-man, still came to be challenged as being highly questionable for its validity. Indeed, Iva's statement given to Tillman, as had been claimed, was not admissible in evidence due to her having been in military custody for some time without any charges, military or civil, ever being brought against her. Nor was the questioning done in the presence of a lawyer.

At long last, in late October, over a year after she was arrested, the Justice Department finally decided to release Iva. This action was triggered by James M. Carter, U.S. attorney in Los Angeles and the successor to Charles C. Carr, who had initiated Iva's rearrest. Carter sent a wire to Attorney General Tom Clark on September 13, 1946, stating, "We feel evidence inadequate. . . . Recommend treason prosecution be declined."

In an office memorandum to Theron L. Caudle, assistant attorney general, Criminal Division, Nathan T. Eliff, chief of the Internal Security Section, cited Carter's opinion and added, "We concur in his opinion and suggest that the matter be considered closed at this time, and the War

Department must be advised that we no longer desire that the subject be retained in custody."

Caudle in turn sent the recommendation for Iva's release to Attorney General Tom Clark, emphasizing that "no broadcaster over Radio Tokyo was announced as 'Tokyo Rose,'" and "several women announcers . . . were given that name indiscriminately by the American troops." "It appears," Caudle continued, "that the identification of Toguri as 'Tokyo Rose' is erroneous, or, at least, that her activities consisted of nothing more than the announcing of musical selections." "A few recording cylinders of her broadcasts and a large numbers of her scripts," he went on, "were located," which supported the claim that "she did not do anything more than introduce musical records." Moreover, he pointed out that "'Tokyo Rose' was broadcasting prior to the date of Iva Toguri's employment" and concluded that "Toguri's activities, particularly in view of the innocuous nature of her broadcasts are not sufficient to warrant her prosecution for treason."

It was decided to keep Iva in custody until orders were received from the War Department. On September 23, the Justice Department finally ordered Iva released, and nearly a year after Iva had been imprisoned, the War Department on October 6 cabled Tokyo: "Department of Justice no longer desires Iva Toguri be Detained in Custody. No Prosecution Contemplated at Present."

The finding of the Justice Department, declaring that there was not sufficient evidence for a prima facie case, revealed two significant facts: Iva could not be identified as "Tokyo Rose," and her broadcasts consisted of nothing more than introducing musical records. Almost three weeks later, at eleven o'clock on the morning of October 25, Iva was informed that she was to be released later that day. The arrangements were set for the night to keep the publicity down. When Iva emerged, the prison entrance was brightly lit. A large number of correspondents from the Far East representing Reuters, INS, AP, UP, Domei, and others were there. Through the soldiers forming "double ranks in honor-guard style," as Rex Gunn describes the scene, Iva was "escorted on the arm of the Prison Commander, Colonel Hardy, who presented her with a bouquet of roses." At the end of the walk, she faced "a barrage of press questions." Then, "a small, neatly dressed man" came up to her side and said, "Look, do you want to get away from this?"

"Who are you?" she asked.

"I'm John Rich of INS."

"INS!" she snapped. "Get away from me. I don't want anything to do with INS."

"I don't blame you," said Rich, "but I don't want a story. I want to offer you a cottage that INS maintains for retreats on Enoshima. You can stay there while the story cools off."

Gunn states that John Rich was in fact presenting the sincere offer of the INS correspondents, who had become disturbed by their colleague, Lee, who had treated Iva terribly in the Imperial Hotel interview and his subsequent article that portrayed her as a traitor. The d'Aquinos went to the cottage on Enoshima, and John Rich, true to his word, wrote nothing about her.

A month later, the Associated Press published an article with a formal statement of the U.S. district attorney's office in Los Angeles. "Because Tokyo Rose was a 'composite person' with at least a dozen voices," the article said, "the Federal Government today dropped its plan to prosecute Iva Ikuko Toguri on charges of dispensing subversive propaganda in the South Pacific during the war."

As if to put a nail in the coffin, Tom DeWolfe, who had been with the Justice Department since 1927 and was recently appointed as special prosecutor, seemed to have set forth the department's official stand. In a six-page report to Raymond Whearty, assistant U.S. attorney general, dated May 25, 1948, DeWolfe argued that the three POWs who directed Iva to broadcast, and thus "seem just as much, or more, culpable than she," had been cleared. The scripts of her programs, he further stated, "seem totally innocuous and might be said to have little, if any, propaganda value."

DeWolfe dismissed the "confession" Lee and Brundidge extracted from Iva outright and insisted that "their methods, including the offer of a cash payment for this statement, made the 'confession' of doubtful propriety" and would lead a jury to think it was not given of her own free will. He insisted that "there is insufficient evidence to make out a prima facie case." In order to support a treason conviction, "the accused's overt acts must be accompanied by an intention to betray," DeWolfe asserted, "and the government could not make a case."

During her confinement in Sugamo, government agents lost or destroyed their phonograph records and written transcripts of the alleged "Tokyo Rose" broadcast, and that was apparently the end of any Tokyo Rose treason investigation. The case appeared closed. Iva thought that her troubles were over and that she could return to her normal life. Her troubles weren't over, however. As long as Brundidge was alive and kicking, there were always dark clouds ahead for Iva. Recovering slowly from his earlier setback with *Cosmopolitan*, he was determined to sell his story of how he had trapped America's first woman "traitor" and to somehow bring her to "justice."

CHAPTER 5

The Attorney General's Abrupt Decision

You are directed to arrest, and deliver forthwith to the Sugamo Prison
Ikuko (Iva) Toguri D'Aquino, age 32 years, residing at 396 Ikejiri-machi, Setagaya-ku,
Tokyo, Japan. Upon complaint and sufficient information made to me by the
Department of Justice . . . the person described . . . is suspected of having committed
treasonable conduct against the United States Government during World War II.

Warrant of arrest, issued on August 26, 1948, by W. A. Beiderlinden,
Brigadier General, U.S. Army, Assistant Chief of Staff, G-1, to the Provost Marshal,
General Headquarters, Far East Command

When she was discharged from Sugamo, Iva returned to her former residence at Ikejiri, Setagaya, Tokyo, to live with her husband and became pregnant in the spring of 1947. She received prenatal care from Dr. Amano's wife (a physician) and was treated until her ninth month of pregnancy. Iva decided not to return to the United States immediately but to enjoy her now relatively calm life and wait until things quieted down, hoping that by then she could return with her husband to the United States without attracting anyone's attention.

One year after her release, she renewed her effort to return home. The main reason was that she wanted her child to be born in the United States. On October 20, 1947, when the Passport Division of the State Department asked the Justice Department about the status of Iva, T. Vincent Quinn, assistant attorney general, wrote back and said that "this Department will have no objection to the issue of a passport for Mrs. d'Aquino," because "after a careful analysis of the available evidence, the Department concluded that prosecution of this individual was not warranted."

The approval of the Justice Department to issue an American passport to Iva, however, triggered a renewed hostility toward her. The Los Angeles City Council passed a resolution opposing her return to the city. The American Legion, the Native Sons of the Golden West, and West Coast nativist groups all severely criticized the intention of the State Department to issue a passport and demanded the prosecution of Iva for treason.

The Justice Department, however, instead of convincingly pointing out the insufficiency of evidence and the flimsiness of the charges, tried to respond to public opinion but did so in a haphazard and ineffective manner. Finally on December 3, sensitive to the growing pressure, the department issued a press release, admitting difficulty in securing two witnesses to support a charge of treason. If and when such evidence be obtained, the department promised, the case would be presented to a grand jury.

On the same day, the *New York Times* published an article entitled "SEEK TREASON WITNESSES." It was more than one year after Iva had been discharged from Sugamo as the result of the Justice Department's order that identification of Toguri as "Tokyo Rose" was deemed erroneous. It reads:

Washington, Dec. 3 — Anyone who ever saw Iva Ikuko d'Aquino broadcasting as "Tokyo Rose" or recognized her voice coming over the air waves, should communicate with the FBI, that agency stated today. . . .

Investigation for two years with a view of obtaining . . . two witnesses necessary to prosecute her for treason, had thus far been unsuccessful.

Nevertheless, said the FBI, the inquiry was proceeding and, if possible, the case would be presented to a grand jury. Meanwhile, Mrs. d'Aquino "is not being permitted" to return to the U.S.

This announcement, significantly, rejected two important decisions the Justice Department had made earlier: Iva Toguri was not "Tokyo Rose" and Toguri should be allowed to return to the United States.

The Justice Department was also concerned about Walter Winchell, who had been hosting a very popular radio news show every Sunday evening. In a rich display of journalistic demagoguery, he accused Attorney General Tom Clark and the Truman administration of being "soft on traitors." The Republicans would benefit tremendously in the coming 1948 presidential election, he argued, if something were not done immediately to bring about treason trials of Tokyo Rose and Axis Sally. Winchell was, indeed, angry because the Truman administration was about to clear the way for Iva's return home.

In order to appease the wrath of Winchell, on December 4 Tom Clark sent District Attorney James M. Carter to meet Winchell in Los Angeles. Reporting back to Clark, Carter stated that he had explained to Winchell the department's position on Iva thoroughly and that as a lawyer he would not recommend a prosecution unless there was a solid case against the defendant. Carter also wrote that "I received . . . the impression that somewhere along the line his pride had been injured" and suggested to Clark that "you could go a long way toward smoothing things out, should you have a personal chat with Mr. Winchell."

Carter told Winchell in the end that the government should not seek a prosecution "without having a proper case." It would be bad "if the trial resulted in dismissal or acquittal," to which Winchell agreed readily, saying that "that would be worse than having no prosecution," and they parted "in a very friendly manner." It is strange to see that men like Winchell, who are so sensitive about their own pride and feelings, have no concern about respecting those of others like Iva.

A person who read the *New York Times* "Seek Treason Witnesses" article with great interest was Harry Brundidge, who had manufactured Iva's problem. He had, to borrow Stanley Kutler's phrase, "a long-standing stake in Iva's story" and "a consuming passion for her case," from his initial contact with her in September 1945 to the end of the trial in 1949. He had quit *Cosmopolitan* shortly after suffering the humiliation of having his article rejected by his editor in the fall of 1945 and had joined the *Nashville Tennessean*. Upon reading the FBI's call for witnesses, he immediately wrote to J. Edgar Hoover, offering his service to go to Japan and help find witnesses. "Give me five days in Tokyo," he said to the FBI director, "and I will get the signature" of Iva. Here again, pride was at stake. He hoped that he might be able to recover his damaged fame and restore his pride if he could help bring Iva to trial, even if it required injuring her pride and damaging her individual and political rights.

Brundidge also met Attorney General Clark in Washington and told him that if he were sent to Tokyo he would bring back Iva's signed "confession" thus to bring the Tokyo Rose case to a conclusion. Clark, who had been getting criticism about the case, seemed to be amenable to the offer. On March 12, 1948, Brundige and John B. Hogan of the Justice Department left for Tokyo by a military plane. Brundidge took with him four men's suits made of wool, which was very scarce in Japan, "to bribe potential witnesses." His passport said his trip was on "a special mission for the Justice Department." After spending a week in Hawaii, they arrived in Tokyo on March 22. They scheduled the meeting with Iva for March 26. Brundidge knew by then how to manipulate Iva, who naively thought she could deal with the situation, and he could easily persuade her to do whatever suited his own ends.

On March 26 Iva had two appointments, both at the Dai-ichi Building, the headquarters of General MacArthur. She was not feeling well. Having lost her only child at birth after carrying it full term, Iva was completely devastated, and for some ten weeks she had been in and out of bed. She was invited to meet Earl Carroll, an old friend of MacArthur, who gave him permission to do a documentary film on occupied Japan. He was in Tokyo on his way back to the United States from China, and he was planning to make a musical comedy set in occupied Japan based upon the Tokyo Rose story. The main part of the film was a dramatic treatment of Tokyo Rose, to be played by a leading Japanese actress, Shirley Yoshiko Yamaguchi.

Carroll took pictures of himself and Iva, and he took motion pictures of Iva with Shirley Yamaguchi in the yard of the United Press House. At lunch, he took more pictures of them. Iva told Carroll about her problem, and he was very sympathetic. He assured her that Major General Charles A. Willoughby, who asked Carroll at the GHQ to see her, told him that Iva's trial days were over. Carroll promised that when he got back to the States, he would be meeting with Winchell and would discuss Iva's situation in an effort to set the record straight.

At the Dai-ichi Building, on the same day, she also saw Brundidge and his cohort, John Hogan, without the presence of a lawyer. "I am working with Mr. Hogan on your case," Brundidge said, "acting as an agent of the Attorney General's office. Today may decide whether you will be able to go home, back to the U.S., or have to live in Japan forever." He showed her a photostatic copy of a story written on Tokyo Rose, which looked like what Clark Lee had written from the 1945 interview. After scanning it, she handed it back to Brundidge and said, "That's not the story I gave to Clark Lee. Most of it is made up." Hogan then turned to Brundidge and told him to get the other story. Brundidge then offered her a second document, saying, "You remember the interview. . . . Doesn't that look familiar?"

Iva hesitated, and Hogan told Brundidge to ask her "if those are the notes of the interview." She, finding some errors immediately, continued to hesitate. Brundidge leaned over in his confidential tone again and said, "All it will take to clear your way back to the States is your signature on this document." Iva signed the last page, and under "witness," Brundidge and Hogan signed with the date of March 26, 1948. Hogan then produced copies of some "Zero Hour" scripts and asked her to identify and sign them. She did. They then went to Radio Tokyo, and she pointed out where the scripts were broadcast.

Once again, Iva made a fateful, irreversible mistake, agreeing to have an interview with a man like Brundidge without a lawyer. This was long before the time of the *Gideon* (1963) and *Miranda* (1966) cases, and people often conducted their daily affairs without any advice from lawyers. Nor were American lawyers readily accessible for Americans in postwar Japan, except for lawyers for Japanese war criminal defendants. Few Japanese lawyers were familiar with American law and legal practice. But Iva could at least have gone to the American embassy or consulate in Tokyo for advice, as most Americans traveling abroad would likely have done if they encountered any problems outside the United States, even though her past dealings with the consulate in trying to get a passport had been problematic.

"How incredibly stupid it seems now," Iva recalled, in her interview with Rex Gunn in Chicago in 1957, on the meeting with Brundidge. "I had no lawyer with me," but she still argued that she "really had nothing to hide. I wasn't worried about it." This remark reveals that even at this later time she didn't seem to understand the role of a lawyer.

Earl Carroll, back in California, wrote a letter to Iva in Tokyo, enclosing a brief note he received from Walter Winchell, which stated that "I have confidence in the administration of United States justice, and she will get a fair trial in court." Carroll said he had been mystified by Winchell's phrase "a fair trial in court" for Iva. He repeated that he would have a talk with Winchell when he flew to New York in June and call him off his "howlings" about Tokyo Rose. In June, en route to New York, the DC-6 that was carrying Carroll and forty-seven others crashed into a transformer on a high power line at Mt. Carmel, Pennsylvania, killing all on board. Rex Gunn speculates that Carroll, who had turned "a 1936 bankruptcy in New York into a smash hit in Hollywood," might well have turned "the troubled Tokyo Rose mess into a musical comedy review." Iva now lost another chance to set her record straight. She had to rely on the remote possibility of getting back to the States hinted at by Harry Brundidge.

It was almost three years after he suffered the rejection of his article by the *Cosmopolitan* editor that Brundidge's sensational story on Tokyo Rose was published, not in any magazine but in a newspaper, the *Nashville Tennessean*. The first installment covered the entire front page of the Sunday, May 2 edition (1948), with more on the inside pages, and in it, Brundidge portrays himself as a crime buster and an investigator. Brundidge, Iva, Tom C. Clark, and John B. Hogan were prominently pictured. "Tokyo Rose has now given a full confession," the story informs readers, "and the Attorney General was contemplating her arrest."

In the May 5 continuation, Brundidge was pictured seated with a young Filipino who was identified as Tokyo Rose's disc jockey, now studying at Vanderbilt University. He was the ex–prisoner of war at Radio Tokyo, Norman Reyes. He and his wife, one of the early "Roses" (Katherine Morooka), were living in Nashville on student visas. Reyes, the story said, was expected to be called upon as a witness against Tokyo Rose.

Although public sentiment was mounting against Iva, within the Justice Department a Tokyo Rose treason trial was hard to justify. Both the Los Angeles district attorney, James M. Carter, and San Francisco district attorney, Frank Hennessy, advised against it. For a third opinion, Attorney General Tom Clark appointed as special prosecutor the department's expert on treason, Thomas E. DeWolfe, and obtained his view.

DeWolfe had headed the government's wartime treason cases against Douglas Chandler and Robert Best in Boston, in both of which cases the defendants were convicted. DeWolfe investigated the evidence against Iva thoroughly and came up with a recommendation against trying her for treason. In an office memorandum to Raymond P. Whearty, first assistant attorney general, DeWolfe spelled out the reasons why. The memo was dated May 25, 1948, three weeks after Harry Brundidge had published the emotionally charged story in the *Nashville Tennessean* insisting that a Tokyo Rose treason trial would be held. Since the memo remained confidential and did not become public until 1975, the public had no way of knowing where the Justice Department stood on this matter.

The memorandum consisted of three parts. The "Statement of the Case" succinctly covered the life of Iva, especially her activities in Japan, from 1941 to 1945. Following the Justice Department's position established by DeWolfe's colleagues Nathan Eliff and Theron Caudle for the release of Iva from Sugamo in October 1946, he tried to justify Iva's actions. The POWs selected Iva as an announcer, DeWolfe stated, because she would not betray their efforts to sabotage the Japanese propaganda. Another reason for their selection of Iva was her masculine voice.

In the second part, "There Is Insufficient Evidence to Make Out a Prima Facie Case," DeWolfe went to the crux of the problem, insisting that there had been no intention to betray:

There is no proof available that when subject committed said acts she intended to betray the United States by means of said acts. . . . Federal Judge Ford held . . . that in order for an overt act to be sufficient to warrant submission of the same to the jury the proof thereon must show that the same was actually committed for the purpose of furthering the enemy's war effort. There is no available evidence upon which a reasonable mind might fairly consider guilt beyond a reasonable doubt and consequently a motion for a judgment of acquittal under F. P. Crim. p. 29(a) would probably be granted by the trial court.

·Iva had been pro-American and willing to sabotage the enemy propaganda; her statement for FBI Agent Tillman was not admissible; and the so-called "confession," which Iva gave to Lee and Brundidge, was given only after the offer of a $2,000 payment had been made, not by free will. DeWolfe predicted here the possibility of a directed verdict because the testimony the government offered "will not make out a case."

In the last section, "Recommendation," DeWolfe suggested:

Should the Department disagree with the views herein expressed and desire the case against subject to be presented to a Federal grand jury it is recommended that a no true bill be sought. Should such an indictment be returned against subject under the applicable provisions of Title 18 U.S.C. Sect. 1 (treason) and the cause pushed for trial on its merit before a petit jury, it is recommended that every possible effort be made to secure Federal Communications Commission records of monitorings of subject's broadcasts, which were until recently in the possession of the Federal Bureau of Investigation, together with the Naval sound track film and also the Naval Government recordings made of subject's voice in Guam.

No action was taken on the matter for almost three months. Then, on August 16, 1948, Attorney General Clark suddenly announced that Iva Toguri d'Aquino would be tried for treason before the federal district court in San Francisco. Why did Clark order the trial of Toguri despite virtually uniform recommendations from investigators who found no evidence of crime and from prosecutors who saw no case against her?

The unique relationship between President Harry Truman and Clark, which is vividly portrayed by Henry J. Abraham, explains why the latter acted as he did. Born into a family of lawyers in 1899, Clark attended the University of Texas Law School and joined his father's Dallas firm in 1922. A favorite protégé of the powerful Democratic Texas senator Tom Connally, he spent most of his career in government service, including ten years in the Justice Department. Clark's association with Truman had its genesis in his cooperation, as the head of the War Fraud Unit, with Senator Truman's War Investigation Committee, which found "a powerful working ally" in Clark. In 1942, Clark, the ranking Justice official on the West Coast, helped General DeWitt plan the forced evictions of Japanese Americans, mainly participating in the selection of the camp sites.

Clark helped Truman win the contested vice presidential candidacy in 1944 and was promoted to head the Justice Department as a reward. Throughout the middle and later 1940s, Clark, an assertive, resourceful, and courageous attorney general, became not only a loyal political and personal friend to Truman, but also one of his closest advisers on key domestic issues.

As attorney general from 1945 to 1949, Clark dealt with some of the Japanese rather aggressively. He not only insisted on deporting those who had denounced their American citizenship while interned but supported the deportation to Japan of 200 to 300 Japanese Peruvians brought to the United States during the war for internment, instead of helping them to return to Peru or to remain in the United States. The Justice Department under Clark's direction took an active role in civil rights enforcement and in searching for subversives.

Clark's dedication to civil rights, however, was often compromised by expediency and political considerations. On July 25, 1946, in Monroe, Georgia, when a band of twenty white men dragged two black farmworkers and their wives from a car and fired more than sixty bullets into them, for example, Attorney General Clark ordered "a complete investigation" of the murders. But he failed to see to it that prosecution would result. As a whole, Clark's performance in the Justice Department, as Abraham critically argues, was marginal and authoritative.

With the 1948 presidential election approaching, the Truman administration and the Democrats were facing an uphill battle. The Republicans were charging Truman's administration for being "soft on communism" and "soft on traitors." The Democrats were also facing a tough opponent, the "urbane and experienced" Thomas E. Dewey.

Clark, as attorney general, was willing to make all-out efforts to contribute to the success of Truman's reelection. In July 1948, in order to deflect the "soft on communism" accusation, Clark approved the prosecution of twelve Communist Party leaders, although he had privately doubted that American Communists posed a "clear and present danger" of revolution.

Probably more important, Tom Clark felt the need to take a strong stand against treason and challenge the Republican "soft on traitors" charges. As a result, the Justice Department, before the 1948 election, indicted three individuals for treason. The first was Tomoya Kawakita, whose treason case began in June 1948 in Los Angeles. A Japanese *nisei*, stranded in Japan in 1941, Kawakita became an interpreter at a POW camp. Although he had registered himself as a Japanese, he somehow was able to come back to the United States after the war. A former POW saw him in a department store in Los Angeles and reported him to the FBI. Kawakita was arrested and indicted for treason (beating, kicking, and torturing POWs).

Axis Sally (Mildred Gillars) was arrested in Germany at the end of the war but soon released. In 1948, the Justice Department under Clark changed its mind, rearrested her, and brought her back to Washington, D.C., on August 21 (a month before Iva arrived in San Francisco). Although her trial did not begin until January 1949, she had been indicted for treason long before the 1948 election.

Iva was arrested in October 17, 1945, but released one year later on October 25, 1946. On August 16, 1948, Tom Clark again changed his mind and decided to arrest and indict Iva in spite of the overwhelming recommendations against doing so. Indeed, Clark's decision to indict Iva was clearly an integral part of Truman's reelection campaign. These cases Clark instituted, though no trials ended before the election, succeeded in wiping out the accusation that Truman's administration had been soft on traitors and Communists.

On November 3, 1948, the first Tuesday in November, Truman won the election. In his own way Clark, as attorney general, made a significant contribution to the astounding victory, which was against all odds and predictions. The political goal of the Tokyo Rose trial was achieved. The victory should have convinced the Justice Department to drop Iva's case, but they didn't. What would have happened if the Republicans had won the election? "Most likely," one of the defense attorneys, Theodore Tamba, said, "the trial would have been thrown out to save money." But the Justice Department was determined more than ever to carry on the mission to convict Iva.

In recognition of Clark's crucial role in the reelection campaign, among other things, Abraham argues, Truman decided to reward him with a Supreme Court justiceship as soon as a vacancy occurred. When Justice Frank Murphy died in July 1949, Truman nominated Tom Clark for the position. His nomination, however, was far from a popular one. This was one of Truman's five "crony" appointments to the Supreme Court, "horsemen of mediocrity," but Clark's mediocre opinions were different, to some critics, from those of the other four, being somewhat balanced with "devoted service to judicial reform."

Clark, at forty-nine, became the first man from the Lone Star State to sit on the Court. His role as attorney general, including his indictment of Iva, certainly helped Truman to achieve his victory, and Truman's reelection in turn led to Clark's appointment to the Supreme Court. On August 25, 1949, Tom Clark took the oath of office as a Supreme Court justice, while, ironically, Iva, as a result of Clark's action, was in the middle of her trial in San Francisco, defending herself against the treason charge.

Although as attorney general Clark demonstrated unqualified loyalty to President Truman, he failed to support the president on a few occasions once put on the bench. In the famed *Steel Seizure* case of 1952, for example, Clark cast a crucial vote to disallow Truman's seizure of steel mills that were on strike, forcing the livid president to call Clark "that damn fool from Texas," "my biggest mistake," "such a dumb son of a bitch," and "about the dumbest man I think I've ever run across." Such outbursts on Truman's part, however, didn't seem to have affected their deeper friendship.

In accordance with the attorney general's order, on August 26, 1948, the Eighth Army Counter Intelligence Corps (CIC) arrested Iva at her home. Although this was the first time she was arrested with a formal warrant, the place where Iva lived was not under the direct jurisdiction of American law. The federal arrest warrant was not a trump card; the arrest had to be made only through Japanese authorities. Otherwise, the U.S. attorney general was exceeding his authority in "kidnapping" Iva in Japan and depriving the Japanese court of its jurisdiction over Iva.

She was taken again to Sugamo Prison and kept there for nine days, during which time her husband, Filipe, visited her three times. On September

3, Iva was suddenly taken to Yokohama and put on board the USS *General H. F. Hodges*, which was carrying returning American troops to San Francisco. Her husband was not informed of her departure — he read about it in the newspaper a day after she left!

According to U.S. law, when an alleged act of treason takes place abroad, the trial must be held at the first American territory the accused is returned to. Attorney General Clark publicly admitted that Iva could not receive a fair trial in California. If Iva would travel by plane, she would have to stop first in Alaska or Hawaii for fueling. Alaska was too remote and inconvenient, while Hawaii, with a large Japanese American population, might be too biased in favor of Iva. Clark, therefore, announced that she would be brought directly to the East Coast. It was a "difficult, but not impossible, logistical task," and elaborate plans were made to bring Iva by air through Canada or Mexico. But for an unexplained reason, Clark once again suddenly changed his mind. He ordered her brought to San Francisco, a city regarded as a center of anti-Japanese prejudice.

The troop transport, USS *General Hodges* was not scheduled to take a direct route home. The ship left Yokohama on September 3, 1948, and sailed to Naha, Okinawa. Then it went to Inchon, Republic of Korea, where some of the troops were dropped off, and from there the ship sailed directly to San Francisco, carefully bypassing Hawaii and any islands in the Pacific.

On board, Iva was under the protective custody of Captain John Prosnak of the U.S. Army and two Women's Army Corps officers, Captain Katherine Stull and First Lieutenant Erma D. Keener. It took twenty-two days to cross the Pacific.

The timing was perfect for Clark and Truman. On September 25, less than six weeks before the 1948 presidential election, the *General Hodges*, carrying Iva, a treason suspect, in addition to 2,000 soldiers, sailed under the Golden Gate Bridge and arrived at the beautiful city. "Home at last, but in custody," must have been her reaction. Her seven-year-long quest to return home had at last been achieved, but under deeply troubling circumstances.

While the returning soldiers were warmly greeted by their relatives and friends on the perfect fine day for a homecoming, Iva, escorted by Fred Tillman, an FBI Agent whom she had encountered in Sugamo, and several other federal officials, walked down the gangplank and was escorted through the crowd cheering the returning GIs to a car waiting for her.

After Iva disembarked, her first destination was the office of U.S. Commissioner Francis S. J. Fox, where she was formally arraigned. "I came in without passport, paper, or identification," Iva later remarked. "They asked me where I was born and on what date, and that was it. I was in. Re-entry. I had tried hard enough and I got back, but it wasn't a method I would recommend to anybody else."

Iva sat numbly as the U.S. commissioner read in a stiff voice the formal complaint against her, citing two occasions and charging her with "an undetermined number of acts against the peace and dignity of the United States." She felt isolated, defenseless, and helpless and commented, "Stoic was an appropriate word for me.... I was kind of numb." She had been a pro-American throughout her stay in Japan, and she still believed that "the truth will come out" and sincerely hoped that the trial would finally free her.

In the commissioner's office, Iva found her father, Jun, from Chicago, and her sister, June, who had been married and was living in Los Angeles, waiting for her. They hugged each other. "Girl, I'm proud of you. You didn't change your stripes," her father greeted her. "A tiger can't change his stripes, but a person can so easily." Iva saw "a small, wiry-looking man with short grey hair and bright sharp eyes" standing beside her father, whom Jun had asked for help in defending Iva.

He was Wayne M. Collins, a forty-nine-year-old second-generation Irish American attorney from San Francisco. He was well known for championing the rights of the Japanese Americans, handling such cases as *Korematsu v. United States*. Collins succeeded, as discussed earlier, despite the strong reaction of Attorney General Tom Clark, in forcing the government to restore U.S. citizenship to 5,000 Japanese internees who had renounced their American citizenship (the "renunciants case") and to permit the Japanese Peruvians interned in Texas during the war to remain in the United States.

Collins recruited two other San Francisco lawyers, with whom he had worked before, Theodore Tamba and George Olshausen. The three lawyers agreed to defend Iva without a fee. Local lawyers known mainly within the city, they were dedicated and determined to win, not just for their reputations but, more important, for American justice, which Iva had been denied. Right off the bat, Collins effectively prevented the

FBI special agents' attempt to illegally interrogate Iva, as Tillman did in Sugamo.

The Justice Department assigned Tom DeWolfe as the main prosecutor. Having just successfully prosecuted Chandler and Best, DeWolfe had been appointed to try the *Axis Sally* case, but was reassigned to the "Tokyo Rose" trial, as the department came to recognize it as the most difficult treason case at the time. Despite his earlier assertion that Iva was not indictable, DeWolfe accepted the assignment like "a good soldier who follows orders and does his job," as Masayo Duus puts it. The problem was that he had to destroy his own earlier professional view on the case. Observers could not help but feel that DeWolfe was "under strong pressure" to get "good results." Hennessy, the San Francisco district attorney who had also earlier advised against trying the case, was the nominal head of the prosecution team, which included James Knapp and John Hogan, both of whom were colleagues of DeWolfe in the *Chandler* and *Best* cases.

One nagging problem was venue. When the Justice Department decided that Iva's trial would be held in San Francisco, "a city with a long history of anti-Japanese exclusionist sentiments," it was the result of the careful examination of all possibilities to make the conviction inevitable. Yet many people in the United States doubted the sanity of bringing Iva to trial in California, not so much for Iva's sake as for the sake of the Japanese Americans who had returned to the state from their wartime internment. Jun Toguri, for example, as soon as he got to San Francisco, experienced a cold reception there not only from Caucasians but from the Japanese *issei* and *nisei*.

Even before Iva was arrested in Tokyo on August 26, the presidents of the California Federation for Civic Unity and of its San Francisco Council asked Tom Clark to consider the possible adverse effects upon racial feelings in the area. They argued that the trial would hamper efforts to "weld together" the different, loyal racial elements in the community. Alexander Campbell, assistant attorney general, replied by merely pointing out that the action was "foreclosed by statutory provisions" for venue. Suggestions were also made that the trial be held in the Midwest or in the East, where there were few Japanese Americans and less anti-Japanese hostility. The defense lawyers made a motion to have the trial moved to Northampton County, North Carolina. These requests were flatly rejected. Couldn't the defense ask for a change of venue as a matter of right? Iva was entitled to a jury of her peers, drawn from her own community.

A federal grand jury was convened in San Francisco on September 25, 1948, to determine if there was a "probable cause" for the treason charges. It consisted of twenty-three jurors. They heard testimony of twelve witnesses, eight from Japan (Colonel S. Tsuneishi, Kenkichi Oki, George N. Mitsushio, Hiromu Yagi, Kenichi and Mary Ishii, Emi Matsuda, and Yukio Ikeda), all of whom became prosecution witnesses in the trial, and four from the United States (Norman Reyes, Clark Lee, Harry Brundidge, and Fred Tillman). After their testimony, the Japanese witnesses left for Japan escorted by the CIC agent who had been assigned to conduct further investigations in Japan. They arrived home on October 24 after a two-day vacation in Honolulu. Oki and Mitsushio, both *nisei*, said they were glad to have had a chance to see their families and old friends again.

From the outset the government had problems. According to Francis O'Gara of the *Examiner* (one of the federal court newspaper reporters), the grand jurors on the first day of the hearing threatened to throw the case out. It was revealed, though the hearing was supposedly secret, that jurors were dissatisfied with the way the government was running the case. The FBI witness statements reveal that two Japanese witnesses, interviewed separately, provided identical testimony, over 2,000 words in length! This was the result of the government's desperate attempt to meet the constitutional two-witness standard, by compelling the two witnesses to say the same thing. One witness from Japan was "spirited out of the country" when he insisted on testifying to the truth.

At least one witness committed perjury before the grand jury. An indictment should certainly be defective if it is based solely upon one testimony, which happened to be the perjured testimony of a man from Japan who procured information illegally. Hiromu Yagi claimed in his grand jury testimony that he and his friend witnessed d'Aquino broadcasting. That "friend," Yagi said, did not want to come to San Francisco to testify because he was afraid of getting involved in the case. Yagi's uneasiness and evasiveness naturally provoked the suspicion of the grand jury, and the FBI agents questioned Yagi many times about that "friend," forcing him finally to reveal his identity as Toshikatsu Kodaira.

The truth of the matter as later revealed is that Yagi was bribed by Brundidge in March 1948 in Tokyo into agreeing that he and Tosh Kodaira would testify against Iva in exchange for a free trip to America and some monetary compensations. What Yagi contrived was a purely made-up, incredible story. Neither Yagi nor Kadaira had any contact with NHK; Yagi was an employee of the Japan Travel Bureau and Kodaira an AP reporter. It was Yagi's connection with Brundidge that enabled him to come up with such a fabricated scheme to destroy an innocent person. The story goes:

One day Yagi was walking down a street and met a friend in front of the Radio Tokyo building. Yagi asked the friend, Kodaira, to arrange for him to listen to a "propaganda broadcast." Kodaira agreed, and both entered the building and went to a room where Iva was making broadcasts of musical recordings. Kodaira "opened the door and showed him into the monitor's room," where he saw Mrs. d'Aquino state in substance, "Soldiers and Sailors, your wives and sweethearts are enjoying themselves at home with war workers who are making big wages while you are fighting in the jungles."

When Yagi called Kodaira and said, "Hey, Tosh, how would you like a free trip to the States?" Kodaira became very interested. When Yagi took Kodaira to see Brundidge the next morning, Kodaira found out that he was supposed to testify to a fictitious story that he and Yagi witnessed in a Radio Tokyo broadcasting room, namely Iva broadcasting about unfaithful wives and sweethearts of the fighting GIs. The conversation among them went as follows:

Brundidge: "Mr. Kodaira, Mr. Yagi here tells me that you both heard Tokyo Rose broadcast shortly after the March bombings in 1945 and that you heard her say, 'Soldiers and sailors, your wives and sweethearts are enjoying themselves at home with war workers who are making big wages while you are fighting in the jungles.' Is that true? Did you hear her say that?"

Kodaira: "Wait a minute. That never occurred."

Brundidge: "Well, why don't you talk it over with Yagi, and come back tomorrow morning."

Kodaira refused to go along with the story, and on their way home, he and Yagi stopped at a coffee shop, where Kodaira chewed him up for concocting such a fabricated story: "Damn you, we didn't contact each other during the war, and it was almost impossible for outsiders to get into the Radio Tokyo building, much less the studio where the broadcasting was going on. Do you know how serious it is to perjure oneself in court?"

Yagi listened to him quietly and said finally that he would not go to America to testify either. Despite his promise, Yagi did finally go to the grand jury hearing in San Francisco in the fall of 1948. He had to make up a story to justify Kodaira's not coming to America. Yagi did not tell the name of his "friend" to the grand jury because his friend, Yagi said, was afraid of getting involved.

On the first two days five or six witnesses appeared. After a day's recess, the government attorneys put tremendous pressure on the grand jurors. Special Assistant Attorney General Tom DeWolfe, who five months earlier had insisted that there had been insufficient evidence to make a prima facie case against Iva, completely changed his position and pretended that the decision would be very easy for the jurors. "I believe you have heard enough to convince you that she is guilty," DeWolfe told the jury. "We don't want to waste any more of your time."

One juror flatly stated that the "attempted indictment of the American-born Mrs. d'Aquino was 'unfair' in view of federal failure to seek indictment against 'others just as responsible' for the supposed treasonous wartime broadcasts."

When DeWolfe responded that Wallace Ince was still in the army and outside their jurisdiction, the grand jury adjourned without an indictment, went on "strike," and announced that they would hold no further sessions until prosecutors prepared charges against Ince. The prosecutors then promised that Ince would be charged before an army court-martial.

On November 12, 1948, almost a month later and after Truman had won reelection, DeWolfe wrote a personal memo to his colleague Ray Whearty: "As it was, two of the grand jurors voted against an indictment. It was necessary for me to practically make a Fourth of July speech in order to obtain an indictment." DeWolfe also wrote to Alexander Campbell, assistant attorney general:

I think in retrospect that I personally presented the case against the d'Aquino woman...in a rather forceful manner. I told the grand talesmen that the case as to Colonel Ince, Mrs. d'Aquino's superior at Radio Tokyo, would be presented to a Federal grand jury here in the immediate future, after an exhaustive, factual investigation of the same in the Orient had been undertaken. If the above action had not been taken by me, I believe that the grand jury would have returned a no true bill against Mrs. d'Aquino.

In order to justify the indictment of Iva Toguri in the mind of the grand jurors, DeWolfe had to promise them a treason case against Ince. DeWolfe was indeed willing to risk his integrity promoting a false scheme. Based upon that explicit promise, the grand jury issued an eight-count indictment against Iva. The promise was never kept, and Ince was instead promoted to major shortly thereafter. It was, indeed, a conditional, defective indictment with the promise never kept.

On October 8, 1948, a federal grand jury charged Iva Toguri with committing "each and every one" of the eight overt acts "with treasonable intent and for the purpose of, and with the intent in her to adhere to and give aid and comfort to the Imperial Japanese Government."

All of the eight overt acts used the same form with blanks filled in with particular but imprecise information to fit particular activities for particular overt acts.

Overt Act I: Between March 1, 1944 and May 1, 1944, the exact date being to the Grand Jurors unknown, defendant in the office of the Broadcasting Corporation of Japan discussed with another person the proposed participation of defendant in the radio broadcasting program.

Overt Act II: Between March 1, 1944 and May 1, 1944, the exact date being to the Grand Jurors unknown, defendant in the office of the Broadcasting Corporation of Japan did discuss with employers of the said corporation the nature and quality of a specific proposed radio broadcast.

Overt Act III: Between March 1, 1944 and May 1, 1944, the exact date being to the Grand Jurors unknown, defendant in the office of the Broadcasting Corporation of Japan did speak into a microphone regarding the introduction of a program dealing with a motion picture involving war.

Overt Act IV: Between March 1, 1944 and May 1, 1944, the exact date being to the Grand Jurors unknown, defendant in the office of the Broadcasting Corporation of Japan did speak into a microphone referring to enemies of Japan.

Overt Act V: Between March 1, 1944 and May 1, 1944, the exact date being to the Grand Jurors unknown, defendant in the office of the Broadcasting Corporation of Japan did prepare a script for subsequent radio broadcasts concerning the loss of ships.

Overt Act VI: That on a day during October 1944, the exact date being to the Grand Jurors unknown, the defendant in the offices of the Broadcasting Corporation of Japan did speak into a microphone concerning the loss of ships.

Overt Act VII: That on or about May 23, 1945, the exact date being to the Grand Jurors unknown, the defendant in the offices of the Broadcasting Corporation of Japan did prepare a radio script for subsequent broadcast.

Overt Act VIII: That on a day between May 1, 1945 and July 31, 1945, the exact date being to the Grand Jurors unknown, defendant in the offices of the Broadcasting Corporation of Japan did engage in an entertainment dialogue with an employee of the Broadcasting Corporation of Japan for radio broadcast purposes.

Not only did the grand jury return a conditional true bill, but the indictment against Iva, compared with the indictments handed down in other World War II treason cases involving enemy propaganda broadcasts—such as those of Best, Chandler, Gillars, and Cramer—was so general as to be vague. No specific dates were given, no specific names were mentioned, and no specific broadcasts and scripts were cited. The opening statement of the indictment that "the said defendant . . . with the intent . . . to adhere to and give aid and comfort to the Imperial Japanese Government" is ironic and totally inaccurate because everybody knew that Iva didn't give a damn for "the Imperial Japanese Government"!

Compared also with the landmark cases of treason in American history, the matters set forth in the Tokyo Rose indictment were not only nonspecific but petty. Stanton Delaplane, who covered the grand jury for the *San Francisco Chronicle*, wrote that these charges simply amount to the fact that Iva had worked at NHK, but nothing else.

Upon receiving the indictment, Iva wrote a brief press release, which moved on the wire services:

It was a grave disappointment to learn that the grand jury returned an indictment against me. It is my belief that if the Government attorneys had been interested they could have produced before the grand jury a number of material witnesses who could have cleared me of any suspicion of wrongdoing. The CIC and the FBI conducted a full and complete investigation into my life in Japan, and having found me innocent, they released me after I had been imprisoned for a year. I am innocent of any wrongdoing. I have faith in the court and jury and believe that they will be convinced of my innocence at the trial, and that I shall be acquitted of the charges brought against me.

Following the indictment, defense lawyers made a motion that Iva be permitted bail. Counsel Collins stated that Iva was a person of good moral character, that County Jail No. 3 was too noisy and disruptive to see witnesses and counsel and to obtain restful sleep, and that the defendant was frail and weighed only 110 pounds. Collins emphasized that there was no danger of her fleeing from the area.

The defense motion for bail was challenged by Hennessy, who expressed concern that Iva might leave the country. Treason, he said, though it is the most heinous of crimes and a capital offense, is not an extraditable crime. If she were to flee the country, she could not be forced to return to stand trial.

On October 14, 1948, Federal Judge Louis Goodman upheld Hennessy's argument and ordered her confined without bail. While she could not avail herself of her legal rights to interview witnesses while she was held in County Jail No. 3, Judge Goodman ordered U.S. Marshall George Vice to provide a suitable place of confinement where she would have full opportunity to interview witnesses with her counsel.

It was, however, against the indictment itself that Wayne Collins made a frontal attack. He argued that the indictment failed to state sufficient evidence to constitute an offense against the United States. It simply pleaded, he pointed out, that "the adherence, aid and comfort" consisted of the defendant's work at NHK, without proving them unlawful.

The Rules of Criminal Procedure (Rule 7, c) specifically require that the indictment contain "a plain, concise and definite written statement of the essential facts constituting the offense charged." Collins asserted that the indictment confused the pleader's own conclusions of treason with "ultimate facts of treason." The general allegations would not automatically become treasonous, and since they failed to allege any facts constituting treason, the indictment failed to allege an offense.

Nor was the indictment sufficient because the overt acts were not alleged with particularity as to time, place, and circumstances. Collins further argued that the eight overt acts specifically pleaded as treason were lawful, harmless, and innocent on their face, so the indictment failed to allege an offense unless it is specifically proven.

Treason, Collins insisted, cannot be alleged in general terms. Under the constitutional definition (Article III, Sect. 3, Cl. 1), completed overt acts, in themselves, constitute the offense only when coupled with treasonable intent. Collins, therefore, declared that this indictment had been drawn "as though the *Cramer* case (1945) had not been decided by the Supreme Court" and pleaded in disregard of the principle it established. The actual rule of the case is that a completed overt act constitutes treason only if that overt act is accompanied by or coupled with treasonable intent. It is apparent, Collins insisted, that allegations of overt acts must set forth the particulars wherein and how those overt acts constitute treason, when coupled with allegations of intent.

Collins also asserted that the eight alleged overt acts state nothing except that, corresponding to each act, the defendant (1) discussed, (2) discussed, (3) spoke, (4) spoke, (5) prepared scripts, (6) spoke, (7) prepared scripts, and (8) spoke. "Reduced to their essence," Collins continued, "they allege nothing except that she spoke and wrote words. However, words, so long as they are mere words, will not constitute overt acts of treason."

Collins attacked the indictment in regard to the inherent defects in its content and legal nature. Although his challenge did have some impact on the prosecution, it did not seem to have much effect on the preparation of the trial itself. The indictment not only came under attack from those who questioned certain testimony on which the indictment had stood but also came to be challenged as invalid because the government promise to the grand jury as the condition for them to return a true bill had never been kept.

In the meantime, Yagi's evasive testimony before the grand jury led to several FBI interrogations of him in San Francisco, which eventually forced Yagi to reveal the identity of his "friend" as Kodaira. The information had been conveyed to the Justice Department attorneys, DeWolfe and Hogan, who in turn requested that the CIC agent scheduled to escort the Japanese witnesses back to Japan conduct further investigation in Japan, especially an interrogation of Kodaira.

According to Professor Stanley Kutler, the report the CIC agent prepared was devastating, causing confusion among the Justice Department officials who had been planning Iva's trial. Kodaira flatly denied that he had witnessed any broadcasts with Yagi. Yagi, however, continued to repeat the same story until the CIC agent threatened to confront both Yagi and Kodaira together to solve the problem. On November 5, a month after Iva was formally indicted and Truman had just won his reelection, Yagi confessed everything. The CIC man reported:

Yagi begged . . . not to do so, stating, "I will tell you the truth this time." Yagi then advised, "My friend, Harry T. Brundidge, came to Japan in March or April 1948. He asked me to go to the United States of America as a witness against Toguri. I told him I had never seen Toguri broadcasting." He stated, "If you tell the story to Mr. Hogan, then you will have a nice trip to the United States, and we will have a nice time together." At this point of the interview, Yagi seemed to gain his composure. In response to a question . . . whether he would make a sworn statement to the above, he replied, "Yes, I want to tell the truth now even though it gets me in lots of trouble." Yagi continued, "The statement I signed (that is the statement given to Hogan in Tokyo in March or April, 1948) was not the truth."

Assistant Attorney General Campbell, who received the report from Tokyo, duly sent it to Attorney General Clark on December 2, a month after Truman's reelection. The report called for the dismissal of Iva's case, but the Justice Department instead withheld the statement from the court. Tom Clark could have withdrawn the case, especially because Truman had already won reelection, but Clark's subordinates insisted on damage control and a cover-up. This was gross misconduct by the government officials, including Attorney General Clark, who had been fully familiar with the developments.

The cover-up, which the Justice Department decided to carry out instead of pursuing justice, involved many activities, including a meeting with Brundidge. On Campbell's report to Tom Clark of his interview with Brundidge, Attorney General Clark's assistant, Payton Ford, added his note to his boss, saying that "we can still make the case according to my information from Hogan."

Why did the Justice Department not move to dismiss the case? Since all the information regarding the Yagi-Brundidge episode remained confidential within the Justice Department, the officials were immune from outside criticism and pressure. But that is beside the point. It vividly demonstrates the fact that these Justice Department officials did not have the dedication to carry out American justice.

Despite the overwhelming odds in her favor, Iva seemed to have lost once again, and the trial would now proceed as planned.

CHAPTER 6

Assembling Witnesses and the Jury Selection

Special Prosecutor Thomas DeWolfe was an observer at an earlier treason trial for Tomoya Kawakita in Los Angeles. The three jurors who held out longest against conviction were reported to be minority persons: a Black American, a Jewish American, and a Japanese American.

JAPANESE AMERICAN CITIZENS LEAGUE, *National Committee for Iva Toguri,* Iva Toguri (d'Aquino): Victim of a Legend *(1975), 15*

"Every son of a bitch who ever set foot at Radio Tokyo," Wayne Collins bitterly complained, "was willing to testify against her for a free plane ride and $10.00 per diem." Since the trial could take six to eight weeks to get started and continue for many more weeks, that $10 per diem could become a large sum of money. These economic incentives made many Japanese willingly testify against Iva, whether or not they really believed Iva's guilt, although there were some honest individuals who resisted the temptation.

Hiromu Yagi came to San Francisco, flying Pan American first class and enjoying his $10 per diem at the Whitcomb Hotel, while his friend, Tosh Kodaira, an upright man, who had chastised Yagi for his planned perjury, was struggling in his hard life in Tokyo. None of the witnesses who would testify for Iva would receive a free trip and the per diem. Why was there such a discrepancy between the parties on the witness matter? It was certainly the result of an unfair, discriminatory treatment by the federal district court judge who had been appointed to preside over Iva's trial.

Judge Michael J. Roche, seventy-one years old, was born in Ring, Ireland, immigrated to the United States, and graduated from Valparaiso School of Law. Roche had been a state court judge before his appointment by President Franklin Roosevelt to the federal bench in 1935. His abrupt, crusty, and impatient courtroom manner was notorious and earned him the nickname "Iron Mike." Judge Roche had already made an unpopular, controversial, and delayed decision denying a habeas corpus petition from

Mitsuye Endo, who had been detained despite the government's lack of charges against her.

On January 4, 1949, Iva came before Judge Roche, was arraigned, and pleaded not guilty to all counts. Judge Roche allowed for the prosecution to bring nineteen Japanese witnesses from occupied Japan at the expense of American taxpayers: free air fare and $10 per diem. Iva's attorneys petitioned the court that forty-three persons (including General Douglas MacArthur and General Charles Willoughby) from Tokyo, Hong Kong, and Australia be subpoenaed at government expense to testify on her behalf. The lawyers asserted that these witnesses were absolutely necessary to Iva's defense and to assure her of receiving a fair trial. The Sixth Amendment, they argued, guarantees that "in all criminal prosecutions, the accused shall enjoy the right . . . to have compulsory process for obtaining witnesses in his favor."

The judge, however, denied the petition two weeks later, not only the defense subpoena power but expenses for witnesses needed from Japan. He justified his decision by saying that Japan was a foreign country outside the jurisdiction of American law, contrary to the nineteen such witnesses from Japan he had just permitted for the prosecution! Collins protested that the denial of the petition was "obvious sophistry. Refusal to bring defense witnesses from Japan was because the government did not want to, not because it could not."

Since the government brought witnesses, for defense as well as prosecution, from occupied countries in all the other postwar treason trials, including that of Axis Sally, Iva was entitled to such witnesses as a matter of right under the law (Title 18USC 3005). It provides that in capital cases including treason, the defendant shall be enabled to get witnesses in the same manner as is usually accorded to the government. The government, Collins maintained, had a choice of two courses. If expenses were too great, it could either drop the prosecution or have "a full, regular trial" in the closest possible area relative to the defendant's alleged activities. The government, Collins insisted, could not take the defendant away from the locality of the acts charged (Tokyo) and then try her elsewhere, depriving her of procedural advantages she was entitled to in an ordinary case.

The prosecution made up a list of seventy-one witnesses, nineteen of whom were from Japan (not subpoenaed but "requested" by the GHQ) to testify against Iva, arriving in San Francisco on June 19. Some were those

Japanese *nisei* who registered as Japanese citizens. Oki and Mitsushio, the supervisors of the "Zero Hour," for example, were under strong legal pressure from the FBI, which was suspicious about their loyalty to the United States. They were even forced to try to persuade other Japanese to come to the trial as prosecution witnesses. Others were NHK workers, who were either connected with the Radio Tokyo broadcasts or not connected with them at all but just wanted to take a free trip.

Colonel Shigetsugu Tsuneishi, the military director of the "Zero Hour," supposedly trained to be disciplined, stern, and upright, seemed to have transformed into a sellout in such a short period of time and succumbed to the temptation of a free air trip and per diem to testify against his own former favorite announcer. Or was he thinking about something else?

Financial advantage was obviously the major motive for potential witnesses to attend the trial. The government allowed $10 a day for foreign witnesses and $12 a day for domestic witnesses, in comparison with the Axis Sally witnesses who received only $5 a day. The government seemed so desperate in its attempt to convict Iva that it was willing to spend large sums of money freely.

For many Japanese prosecution witnesses, the trial became a big moneymaking event. They had come from an economically depressed society recovering from war, and they tried to save money. They moved out of the Whitecomb Hotel, which the government had chosen for them, into cheaper boardinghouses. Due to the unfair exchange rate of 360 yen to a dollar, a few dollars saved became a huge amount in Japan. Some bought American goods, especially saccharin, and took them back to Japan to sell on the black market for big profits.

Some witnesses saved enough to go into business after they returned. Kenkichi Oki, for example, used the money he received to start an advertising agency, which later grew to the major Standard Advertising Agency. Kenichi Ishii, a young man who had dreamed of coming to the United States to attend university, took advantage of the trip and, while he was at the trial, visited the University of California, Berkeley; he later enrolled there, eventually graduating with a major in political science. Back in Tokyo, he worked at AP, anchored a television program on foreign affairs, and later wrote a column for the *International Herald Tribune*.

Conspicuously missing from the prosecution list were the war prisoners of "Zero Hour," including Norman Reyes and Wallace Ince. Late in

October 1948, the prosecution announced that Captain Ince would appear as a "star witness against the defendant," but Ince remained steadfast for the defendant and hired his own lawyer. Also missing were other "Roses," female announcers at Radio Tokyo such as Foumy Saisho, Ruth Hayakawa, and Lily Gihevenian. Despite the temptations, they refused to come to San Francisco to testify against Iva.

Not only was the prosecution given numerous advantages over the defense as discussed above, but they were also able to intimidate potential defense deposition witnesses in Japan. When they were provided with a list of potential defense witnesses in Japan, the prosecutors teletyped the names and addresses to the FBI office in Tokyo. Fred Tillman, accompanied by some American soldiers, called on them and, using harassment and threats, warned them not to give testimony in Iva's favor. One of the defense lawyers, Theodore Tamba, who took their depositions in Tokyo, later commented that these potential witnesses who had already been interviewed by Tillman were too frightened to cooperate with him. "I never saw so many scared people in my life," Tamba remarked.

While he provided a generous travel fund for prosecution witnesses from Japan, Judge Roche allowed a budget of only $3,000 for one defense lawyer and one translator to travel to Japan to take written depositions. Tamba went to Japan for the defense on the very tight government budget. On March 25, he left for Tokyo with Tetsujiro Nakamura, a Sacramento-born *nisei*, who had never been to Japan before but whose Japanese was fluent enough for him to serve as Tamba's interpreter. He soon realized that he could have spent more than six months collecting depositions in Japan and petitioned for continuance, but he got a delay of the trial's opening only from May 16 to July 5. He and Noel Storey, a representative of the attorney general who cross-examined the witnesses, took forty-three depositions altogether, including from some of the Radio Tokyo announcers. They were usually sympathetic and were very critical of their colleagues, like Oki and Mitsushio, who went to San Francisco to testify against Iva.

During the Occupation, Japanese travel to the United States was strictly controlled by the American government. Thus the defense could not bring any witnesses, even important ones who could pay their way, without the permission of the American government, which was almost impossible to get. The defense not only lacked a defense fund but, more important, could not offer, as the government did, immunity from prosecution.

Charles Cousens, Iva's former POW boss at Radio Tokyo, was formally accused of treason in his own country, Australia, but the charges against him were dropped in November 1946. When he read in the newspaper that Iva was going to be indicted for treason, Cousens felt a sense of responsibility toward her and agreed to come from Australia to serve as a witness on Iva's behalf. Another Australian, Kenneth Parkyns, a former Bunka Camp POW, also decided to come to testify for Iva. Their expanses were only partially paid by Iva's father, Jun Toguri. When Cousens and Parkyns arrived in San Francisco, they were met by FBI agents, who tried to question them unlawfully.

Filipe d'Aquino also came to appear as a witness in his wife's defense. Since he was a Portuguese national, not a Japanese citizen, the GHQ had no control over his leaving the country. Jun Toguri agreed to pay his passage and expenses. When Filipe arrived in Seattle on June 4, he had been taken into custody for two days. "I arrived in Seattle aboard a ship and immediately I was taken into custody by the FBI and the immigration authorities," Filipe recalled. "When I told them I had come to testify at my wife's trial in San Francisco, they said I wouldn't be allowed to unless I signed a paper saying I would never return to the United States." Filipe was released only on the condition that he was to leave the country within six months and post a bond guaranteeing his return to Japan. On his way back to Japan, Filipe was forced to sign the pledge that he would not come back to the United States, causing the couple's permanent separation and destroying their marriage. The American government simply disregarded the individual and spousal rights of Iva's husband.

Judge Roche's differential treatment regarding witnesses, which was made openly and shamelessly, grossly handicapped the defense; it violated the procedural rules and amounted to judicial misconduct, enough to be a cause to call for dismissal. Moreover, the judge did not allow most of the depositions the defense lawyers had gathered in Tokyo to be admitted into evidence.

———

On Tuesday morning, July 5, 1949, the day after Iva's thirty-third birthday, Federal Judge Michael J. Roche opened the trial by reading the formal indictment. The first order of business was the selection of the trial jury.

Both Article III and the Sixth Amendment of the U.S. Constitution guarantee the right of trial by jury in federal criminal cases. The trial jury (the petit jury) has its origins in medieval England, where King John established in 1215 the right to trial by jury in the Magna Carta. This right was ultimately brought over by the English settlers, transplanted to the American colonies, and has continued to be a vital part of the American criminal justice system. Thus the right of the accused to judgment by his or her peers is as profound today as it was when granted in England nearly eight hundred years ago.

The Constitution says little about the composition of jurors except that they must be "impartial" and drawn from the district where an alleged crime was committed. The function of the federal court jury, consisting of twelve members, is to decide whether defendants in criminal cases are guilty without violating their due process rights.

There are three guiding principles governing methods of jury selection: all citizens have a legal obligation to serve on a jury unless otherwise exempted and excused; the jury pool must be a cross section of the community; and biased jurors who might decide cases subjectively must be precluded from serving. Both defendants and prosecutors have the right to prevent persons called to court from serving on a particular jury if they demonstrate bias. This selection process, called the *voir dire* ("to speak the truth"), is part of the empaneling of any jury; potential jurors are asked a number of questions by lawyers on both sides intended to detect biases and preconceptions.

On the first day of trial, the 109 prospective jurors arrived to be carefully questioned to determine if they had any preconceived notions and if they could be fair and impartial jurors. One of the defense attorneys, Theodore Tamba, set forth the twelve specific questions. The prospective jurors were asked whether they:

(1) had reasonable doubt as to the presumption of innocence,

(2) were free from bias or prejudice regarding persons of Japanese ancestry and nationals of Portugal,

(3) could disassociate themselves from rumors and newspaper reports and try the case upon the evidence produced in Court and the instructions of the Court,

(4) had ever heard a Walter Winchell or Kate Smith broadcast regarding this case,

(5) had lost in the war any members of their family and if so, if such a loss would have any effect on their judging of this case,

(6) were veterans,

(7) had any member of the family who worked for a federal agency,

(8) would believe a government witness in preference to a defense witness,

(9) would be prejudiced against the defendant because she is married to a person of mixed Portuguese and Japanese blood and whether they would be against witnesses of mixed blood or witnesses married to people of mixed blood,

(10) would be prejudiced against black witnesses,

(11) would be disinclined to sit in a trial which may take a long time, and

(12) knew of any reason why they couldn't try the case with a fair and open mind and give the defendant the benefit of any doubt that might arise in the case.

Accordingly, Collins dismissed anyone who had lost a relative in the Pacific War, who had negative attitudes toward Japanese Americans and interracial marriages, and who had heard Winchell's broadcast.

One controversial use of the challenge for cause dealt with capital cases. Since Iva had been accused of treason, a capital crime that carries the penalty of death, this issue must have been crucial, but neither the defense nor the prosecution ever addressed the question to prospective jurors. Jurors who state that they are unequivocally opposed to the death penalty under any circumstances can be removed from the jury, which would have tilted the jury in favor of those who are pro-prosecution because death penalty opponents are usually more liberal in general. On the other hand, those who advocate the death penalty could be removed, tipping the scale the other way, the defense side. Both the defense and the prosecution failed to question jurors on this issue and thus missed the chance of eliminating potential adverse jurors.

The prosecution had made every effort to ensure that they would secure the kind of jury they wanted, an all-white jury. A year earlier, Special Prosecutor Thomas DeWolfe went down to Los Angeles and observed the treason trial for Tomoya Kawakita, who was convicted and sentenced to death. His sentence was later commuted by President Dwight D. Eisenhower, and he was pardoned by President John F. Kennedy. The case was rigorously prosecuted by U.S. Attorney James Carter, who earlier recommended that the case against Iva be dropped due to the lack of evidence. Carter was subsequently appointed to the Ninth Circuit Court of Appeals.

DeWolfe came to recognize in the trial the significant fact that the three jurors who had held out longest against conviction had been minority persons: a Black American, a Jewish American, and a Japanese American. DeWolfe and other government prosecutors in Iva's case were determined to secure an all-white jury and were able to do so without much difficulty.

On the first jury list were seven nonwhites, six African Americans, and a Chinese, an army veteran who had fought in the Chinese-Burma-India campaign. The prosecution used only seven peremptory challenges ("the almost unfettered right to exclude persons without giving reasons"), out of twenty allowed, to remove all seven nonwhites. The prosecution announced their acceptance of the all-white jury, six men and six women, which the defense accepted. The all-white jury with two women alternates was duly impaneled and sworn in at 2:43 p.m. to try Iva's case, relying exclusively on the evidence presented. The court then adjourned until 10:00 a.m. the next day, Wednesday, July 6.

The jurors, equally divided between the sexes, consisted of ordinary middle-class people, professionals, and housewives:

A glass company bookkeeper (Matthew J. Yerbie)
Two paint company employees (Robert Oakes and Robert E. Stevenson, who were employed by two different companies)
A plasterer (Earl M. Duckett)
A certified public accountant (John Mann)
A retiree (Robert L. Stout)
Six housewives (Babette Wurts, Fannie Ibbotson, Adele Grassens, Edith Schlobohm, Flora Covell, and Ival Long)

On the third day of the trial, one of the housewives became ill and was replaced by one of the alternate jurors, another housewife (Aileen McNamara). It seems strange that half of the jurors were housewives, who were not actually Iva's peers. Shouldn't the defense have dismissed some of them by peremptory challenges?

In the selection of the jury, the most serious attack the defense lawyers made was, of course, on the prosecution's use of the peremptory challenges to eliminate all the nonwhite prospective jurors. George Olshausen accused the prosecution of racism. "The prosecution attorney challenged all prospective jurors on a strictly racial basis," Olshausen asserted, and excluded "all the non-whites called to the box and six Negroes and one Chinese American."

In his "It's News to Me" column for the *San Francisco Chronicle*, Herb Caen severely criticized the racial angle in the "Tokyo Rose" treason trial. The prosecution got an all-white jury, he emphasized, after using up only seven of its twenty challenges and disqualified seven, who "just happened to be six Negroes and one Chinese." Caen strongly reproved the government, which was practicing segregation of white and nonwhite witnesses, though it seemed a prevailing fashion, and concluded: "the white witnesses are kept in one room, and the Japanese, Filipinos and Negroes in another."

Tom DeWolfe, a graduate of the University of Virginia School of Law, interjected the typical southern racial attitude into the trial. He not only fully approved the segregation of white and nonwhite witnesses but rarely extended courtesy to Asian witnesses, especially mixed-bloods like Norman Reyes.

Peremptory challenges, which the prosecution had taken full advantage of, are a venerable practice of American courts that grants to both sides in criminal cases a certain number of opportunities to remove jurors without any stated rationale whatsoever. The theory behind giving this "carte blanche" chance to eliminate jurors who have not necessarily evidenced bias is that it allows both the prosecution and the defense to rely on hunches and intuition to eliminate prejudiced people who are able to conceal their convictions.

It has been thought that these exclusions provide for "a cleansing of the jury of people who have made up their minds or who lean in a specific direction even before the trial starts." This process, designed to make the jury more objective by removing anyone who retains preconceptions, was in reality used by both sides to get a sympathetic jury. Especially when it was used by the prosecution to remove all nonwhite prospective jurors, the practice came under attack and was challenged as unfair, aggressive, and arbitrary. Some lawyers, including Iva's prosecutors, were accused of using peremptory challenges to "shape" juries by "purging entire segments" of the community, thus diminishing "jury representativeness." It was in *Batson v. Kentucky* (1986) that the Supreme Court finally accepted this argument, ruling that "race could no longer be used in criminal cases as a basis for striking jurors without cause."

Eight years later, the court in another case held that peremptory challenges could not be used to remove women if "gender alone was the basis for the removal." In practice, it had proved difficult to determine whether the impermissible criteria of race and gender were in fact the bases of peremptory challenges. Such challenges by definition, after all, need not be explained or justified.

At any rate, the Supreme Court decisions limiting the power of prosecutors to exclude jurors on the grounds of race and gender are significant. An all-white jury was no longer acceptable. Prosecutions and defense lawyers must explain their reasons for exclusion if the defendant makes a prima facie case showing that race or gender was a factor. These new legal developments, unfortunately, came too late to help Iva.

As in the striking-down process of eliminating the disqualified, the prosecution succeeded in achieving its own objective, while the defense's attempt to establish a fair jury for Iva had been seriously subverted. The prosecution's effort to make the jury all-white was part of its attempt to prosecute the case as vigorously as possible, applying not just strategy, but pressure, manipulation, and even questionable means at times, in order to get the defendant convicted.

During the fifty-two days of the trial, the jurors were not sequestered. The jury's mission seemed simple enough. All they had to do was to apply the law as explained by the judge to the facts revealed in the evidence presented at trial. In actuality, however, their work was infinitely complex and difficult. They heard a large number of witnesses, presenting conflicting views on the broadcasting activities of Iva.

Despite the judge's instructions, the law seemed vague and self-contradictory, and the facts still remained disputable. Due to the very nature of the American adversary system, the prosecution and the defense presented their own versions of the truth. As a result, the jury's decision making became a "complex judgment process." The essential issue was whether Iva did indeed participate in the propaganda program of Radio Tokyo knowingly, did so only under duress, or fully took part as a "ready accomplice" in the POWs' attempt to undermine the Japanese army propaganda program.

CHAPTER 7

The Prosecution's Case

*You know, I always felt there was something peculiar about that girl's going to
Japan when she did. I always thought she might have been up to something.*

JUDGE MICHAEL J. ROCHE TO CATHERINE RINKHAM AND REX B. GUNN *at the
judge's chambers in the Federal Court Building, San Francisco, December 22, 1958*

In the late 1940s, the United States was in the midst of the Cold War.
Events like the Communist takeover of China and the Russian testing of
atomic bombs alarmed the American people and led to a heightened concern for keeping the country safe from communism, un-American activities, and subversive behavior. The trial of the American Communist Party
leaders for violating the Smith Act and the Alger Hiss trial were among
many criminal trials instituted around the turn of the 1950s. The period
was, as Stanley Kutler pointed out, "the treason season."

It was this America, which demanded loyalty and conformity, that Iva
had to confront in her treason trial from July to September 1949. Press cov-
erage was naturally extensive. On July 6, the courtroom was packed as on
the previous day. Spectators were crammed into 110 seats, and when they
went to lunch, their seats were quickly taken over by others, who would
wait patiently for the afternoon sessions.

The judge who presided over Iva's trial, Michael Roche, was by no
means the best qualified individual to handle a treason case. In fact, some
argued, he was not really a suitable judge for the job. An Irish immigrant,
he became a patriotic American who put himself through college and law
school and was grateful for all kinds of opportunities that this country had
offered him. When he heard the news that President Franklin Roosevelt
had just appointed him to the bench in 1935, he was so grateful that he had
"danced a delighted jig in the marble hallway" of the courthouse. It was
Roche's fourteenth year as a federal district judge.

He was, however, narrow-minded and parochial in his mental outlook
and did not have much understanding and experience with the outside
world. His daily activities and professional career were so limited to local

matters that he seemed utterly unable to understand, for example, the background and circumstances of Iva's trip to Japan and her activities over there. Roche displayed little patience with the defendant, who seemed to him exotic, although she was a *nisei*, a second-generation Japanese American (birthright citizen), compared with the judge, who was a first-generation Irish American (naturalized citizen). He also was impatient with defense witnesses who tried to explain that wartime Tokyo was a different and more frightening place, especially for Americans, than San Francisco, even in wartime.

More serious was Roche's reputation as a federal judge. Even before Iva's trial opened, he had already established himself as an unfair and discriminatory judge, not giving the defense the opportunity to bring witnesses from Japan as he did to the prosecution, among other actions. Judge Roche was also known for giving preferential treatment to prosecution lawyers against the defense, as he frequently overruled defense objections while he almost always sustained the objections of the prosecution. One wonders why such obvious discrimination could occur without serious challenges.

Among the practicing attorneys in San Francisco, Roche had been known for his arbitrary and abrupt moves. His nickname, "Iron Mike," seems to have well reflected his humorless and inflexible nature, as well as his general demeanor. He had the reputation for being "a gruff, crusty courtroom martinet." His lack of patience with lawyers who raised technical legal arguments was notorious. His handling of the Mitsuye Endo case well illustrates his conduct as a federal district judge.

On July 12, 1942, Mitsuye Endo, a twenty-two-year-old clerical worker in the California Department of Motor Vehicles in Sacramento, who had been behind the barbed wire of the Tule Lake internment camp in Northern California, filed a petition with the federal district court in San Francisco, a habeas corpus petition, demanding the court to show cause why she should not be released from internment. Endo's lawyers came to realize that Judge Roche, before whom the petition had to be filed, was going to make succeeding with their case extremely difficult.

On July 20, just a week after filing his petition, James Purcell, Endo's lead attorney, appeared before Judge Roche, expecting that Roche would set a hearing date. Roche shocked both Purcell and his adversary by abruptly demanding that they proceed immediately with constitutional arguments on the detention issue. "Your honor," Purcell demanded, "I understand the hearing this morning was for the purpose of setting a time for argument." Roche declared that right then was the time set for argument. "He tried to catch me unprepared," Purcell recalled later. "Fortunately, I had done my homework."

When Purcell argued, relying on the 1866 opinion of the Supreme Court in *Ex Parte Milligan* as a precedential barrier, that detention was a form of undeclared martial law, Roche was quickly persuaded by the argument. "When this matter was first brought up," Roche openly and inappropriately confided to Purcell, "I was of the opinion that it was a frivolous action. I am no longer of that opinion." The judge then turned to Alfonso Zirpoli, deputy U.S. attorney, and warned him of his task in rebuttal: "Be prepared to answer when court is resumed at 2 o'clock."

The government challenged Purcell's assertion by citing a *Harvard Law Review* article by Stanford Law School professor Charles Fairman that rejected as outmoded and dangerous a distinction between unvarnished martial law and civilian supremacy and insisted on "the reality of the danger" that existed on the Pacific Coast. The article justified the removal of all Japanese persons. It was "the duty of the courts," the article pointed out, to grant "the necessity for the commander's assuming control of the functions of civil government." Zirpoli concluded by urging the court to dismiss the Endo petition. Now Judge Roche seemed to have been swayed to the government position. He then asked both lawyers to submit briefs within ten days, indicating that "he would decide this question five days thereafter."

It was not until July 2, 1943, nearly a year after Purcell filed his petition, that Roche issued an order granting Zirpoli's motion to dismiss the petition without explaining his decision. What the judge had been doing was to stretch the rules while he waited for guidance from the Supreme Court on the Hirabayashi case, which was decided on June 21, 1943.

Finally, on July 2, Roche issued a brief, two-sentence order, which was clearly erroneous. He first dismissed the habeas corpus petition on the ground that it did not present a valid claim of unlawful detention and then ruled that Endo had failed to exhaust her administrative remedies as a precondition to be released from the Tule Lake Internment (Relocation) Center in Northern California. To the contrary, Mitsuye Endo did indeed complete an application for leave clearance on February 19, 1943. Nor had this request any legal bearing on the status of her habeas corpus petition.

After Endo's case was pending in the lower courts for more than two years, the Supreme Court agreed to hear her appeal from a district court ruling that dismissed her petition. Roche's decision was overturned by the Supreme Court in *Ex Parte Endo* on December 18, 1944. The court ruled that a Japanese American whose loyalty to the United States had been clearly established was entitled to a writ of habeas corpus, freeing her from a relocation center.

Nor was the popularity of Judge Roche among the journalists very high. One newspaperman went so far as to accuse Roche of having improperly discussed the case outside of court and "enter[ing] the trial with his mind made up," possibly committing "the gravest dereliction of duty." Judge Roche did indeed preside over Iva's trial, remembered two other reporters, to whom the judge confided later, with the preconceived notion that he "always felt there was something peculiar about that girl's going to Japan when she did," adding that "she might have been up to something."

On the morning of the second day, July 6, the lead prosecutor, Tom DeWolfe, delivered his ninety-minute opening address in "the packed and quiet courtroom." When he was assigned to this case, DeWolfe took on the impossible task of building up a convincing story out of a case he did not personally support, but he resolved, as Russell Howe puts it, to use "courtroom theatrics" and to try to "bully witnesses" to overcome "the burden of a feeble case." DeWolfe, though not happy in his role, was prepared to make an all-out effort. In his room in San Francisco's exclusive Canterbury Apartments, Rex Gunn observes, one could see "his work lights burning into the morning hours." He rarely went out and tended to go alone when he did. In contrast to his emotionally charged appeal to the grand jury nine months earlier, DeWolfe, an effective courtroom speaker, started his statement quietly, "building slowly and deliberately into an oration."

He told the jury it would be their responsibility to decide who was telling the truth. He pointed out that Iva had been "accused of the nefarious and hateful crime of treason, the only crime that the Founding Fathers had felt the need to define in the Constitution." Iva, DeWolfe said, went to Japan but had "voluntarily" stayed in Japan after the Pearl Harbor attack and had participated in Japanese propaganda broadcasts "without duress or compulsion." The government, he said, would show that "she made these nefarious propagandistic broadcasts after it was clearly, fully, and completely explained to her and that she was aware of the purpose of the program and she voluntarily and wholeheartedly participated."

"We will show," DeWolfe told the jurors, "that in one broadcast after the battle of Leyte Gulf, she told American troops: 'Now, you boys really have lost all your ships. You really are orphans now. How do you think you will ever get home?'" DeWolfe continued:

> We will show that she told American troops that their wives and sweethearts were unfaithful, that they were out with shipyard workers with wallets bulging with money; that she told them to lay down their arms, that the Japanese would never give up and had the will to win. And that there was no reason for Americans to stay there and be killed.
>
> We will show that she talked about the mosquitoes and the jungles, and when she heard some troops were short of food, she told them they should go home where they could get steak and french-fried potatoes, that, once, when she heard a certain unit was short of water, she broadcast: "Hello sarge, got any beer down there? Forget about the beer. Wouldn't you like some cold water? Cold water sure tastes good!"

This was an exaggerated story that sounds all made up. "Short of water" seems to have come from the earlier experience in Midway. It was certainly DeWolfe's outright lies designed to impress the jury at the outset, without the defense's immediate rebuttal. Treason was "the only crime that the Founding Fathers had felt a need to define in the Constitution," as discussed earlier, not because it was so serious, as he seemed to imply, but for political reasons.

The picture DeWolfe portrayed seemed a fictional story that did not reflect the condition of fighting accurately in the light of Americans winning the battles in 1944 and 1945. The U.S. troops were not desperate. By mid-1944, the American forces had already won some crucial battles: the Battle of Midway (June 1942), the Battle of Guadalcanal (August 7–9 and November 12–15, 1943), the Battle of Philippine Sea (June 1944), and the Battle of Saipan (June 15–July 10, 1944).

Although they still had to fight fierce battles on Iwo Jima, February 19–March 17, 1945, and Okinawa, April–June 1945, in which the Japanese soldiers resisted the invading forces fanatically to the last man, inflicting a heavy casualty rate on the U.S. forces, the resounding American victories in 1943 and 1944 had made the U.S. troops more offensive, more optimistic, and more hopeful. Indeed, the Battle of Leyte Gulf, fought on October 23–25, 1944, caused the destruction of most of Japan's remaining sea power and gave the United States control of the Philippine waters.

The American fighting men who participated in the campaign knew accurately the situation of the American navy. Few would take seriously and be intimidated by the "Tokyo Rose" taunt of "how will you ever get home now you have lost all your ships?" The United States controlled not only the sea but air with plenty of support, material aid, and rescue efforts. DeWolfe's story is a distorted one, which seems to have been made up possibly after the war and was thus not reflective of the real situation of Iva, POWs, or the Japanese, as he himself depicted in his earlier memo.

DeWolfe's opening statement, was, in fact, contradictory to his May 25, 1948, memorandum. Since this memo was not made public until 1975, only a small circle of his associates and the attorney general knew of the drastic change of his views until then. The comparison between his two statements vividly reveals his drastic change of mind, rejecting his own former view. Could a man, even a prosecutor, be allowed to deceive himself and tell such a serious lie in a court of law?

In his internal memo, "Statement of the Case," which depicted Iva's life in Tokyo, DeWolfe described her many difficulties and fruitless efforts to return to the United States. He continued:

> In November, 1943 . . . Iva was selected . . . to participate as an announcer on Radio Tokyo program called "Zero Hour."
>
> Three prisoners of war, Reyes, Ince, and Cousens, were in charge of the production of Radio Tokyo's "Zero Hour." They had all been cleared by their respective governments of any charge of treasonous activity. . . . They will be the three most important witnesses against her if an indictment should be returned against her by a grand jury. . . . They will testify that she broadcast no information of military or intelligence value and at no time beamed anything to troops in the southwest Pacific of a propagandistic nature. Her sole work . . . consisted of introducing musical recordings . . . to Allied troops in the southwest Pacific. They will testify that they selected her as an announcer because she was the only woman available . . . whom they could trust not to betray to the Japanese their efforts to sabotage any propaganda. . . . The three men . . . will testify that she was likewise selected . . . because she possessed a masculine voice which . . . would not be attractive to Allied soldiers.

"The government's case must fail as a matter of law," DeWolfe emphatically stated, flatly contradicting his opening remark at the trial, "because the testimony will disclose that Iva did not adhere to the enemy or possess the requisite disloyal state of mind.... There is no proof available that when Iva committed said acts she intended to betray the United States by means of said acts."

The question of whether Iva was an American citizen or not was an important issue for the jury. If she was an American citizen, the American court had the right to try her, but if not, the defense would stop the proceedings right away. Collins argued that Iva had been a Portuguese national from the time she married Filipe d'Aquino, but DeWolfe rightly contested that Iva had been an American citizen because she had never formally renounced her American citizenship. Furthermore, DeWolfe insisted that the American government ought to be the judge of her citizenship and argued that Iva had not even been Portuguese by marriage during the time the alleged overt acts of treason were committed.

The first prosecution witness was J. Richard Eisenhart, ex–Eighth Army guard at Yokohama Prison, who came to testify for $12 per diem. He presented a one-yen note with the signature "Tokyo Rose" on it. The government seemed to treat this item as evidentiary dynamite, even though it had absolutely no judicial worth. "Tokyo Rose" had already been discarded. Iva's signing "Tokyo Rose" on the bill occurred before Iva's release from Sugamo upon the Justice Department's decision that Iva was not Tokyo Rose. Even earlier, the Office of War Information just after the war in occupied Tokyo had issued a statement affirming that no such person had ever existed except in the GI imagination.

Thus this witness's testimony was simply immaterial. Collins, in his cross-examination, should have made clear to the jury the fact that the statement "Iva ... was Tokyo Rose" was not only not provable but irrelevant. The real issue was whether Iva had committed treason.

Next came the first important prosecution witness, the tough, arrogant, and straight-backed Colonel Shigetsugu Tsuneishi of the former Japanese Imperial Army. "I was in charge of broadcasting to weaken the morale of the enemy," Tsuneishi said under the direct examination by DeWolfe. "I was in charge of 'Zero Hour,' which was used to make Allied troops homesick and tired or disgusted with the war." He also testified that the POWs were not forced to broadcast, and there was "absolutely no threatening or violent language used in having them do so." DeWolfe's direct examination was brief, and Tsuneishi was already under cross-examination by Collins before noon on Monday, July 12. As questioning continued, this prosecution witness was beginning to sound more and more as if he were testifying for the defense. Tsuneishi couldn't remember any specific quotations by Iva as "Orphan Ann" because he didn't understand English. He said that he had never spoken to Iva individually nor did he assign her to "Zero Hour."

He also testified that there were more than a dozen other English-speaking women who had broadcast from Radio Tokyo to Allied troops in the Pacific and started to name them all by their full names. Responding to Collins, the military boss of the NHK during the war named thirteen other Japanese stations throughout Asia in addition to Radio Tokyo that employed English-speaking women broadcasters. "Zero Hour," he said, never got beyond the point of shortwave entertainment to build up listeners' interest among American troops:

> At that time Japan was suffering rapid defeat and it was satisfactory to me to produce any program appealing to American soldiers. . . . I calculated that we would wait until Japanese troops went over to the offensive, and then the propaganda would be greatly increased. . . . It was unfortunate, but the opportunity did not present itself to do the real, true propaganda program that I wanted.

Tsuneishi's testimony thus far was very significant. The defense must clearly have impressed the jury in Iva's favor. The prosecution had been saying that it was prosecuting "Tokyo Rose," but Tsuneishi said there had been more than a dozen such announcers at the Tokyo station. Moreover, the colonel testified that Radio Tokyo's overseas broadcast was nothing but entertainment because they had not had the chance to implement the propaganda program in their broadcast before the end of the war.

More crucial, why didn't the trial end right then? Tsuneishi's testimony, which shocked the very foundation of the prosecution's case, was sufficient enough for Collins to enter a motion for a mistrial, to dismiss, or for a direct verdict of acquittal. The testimony under the cross-examination had clearly demonstrated not only that Iva could not have broadcast the propaganda program, because it had not yet been instituted at Radio Japan, but also that there was a burden of proof to show that Iva—among numerous NHK women announcers throughout East and Southeast Asia—was indeed Tokyo Rose. The testimony effectively challenged the two key points on which the prosecution had been basing its accusation of Iva for treason. Or, could the prosecution, against all these odds, hope to prove Iva's culpability beyond a reasonable doubt through the testimony of subsequent witnesses?

Collins's questioning got tougher when it shifted to the topic of duress, specifically on the conditions under which the defendant and the POWs had broadcast at Radio Tokyo. "You told Lt. Reyes and Capt. Ince," Collins demanded, "to obey orders the same way that Major Cousens was compelled to obey your orders." "I don't believe I told them to obey my orders," Tsuneishi answered, adding that "these were not orders but instructions or directives." All the POWs knew that they had to obey Tsuneishi's orders. "No one," as Ince put it, reflecting the general feeling of the POWs, "was going to say no to a mad Jap." DeWolfe, sensing that Collins's cross-examination was leading to a duress argument, repeatedly objected, most of which were sustained. Collins protested and read Tsuneishi's order to the assembled POWs at Bunka Camp on one fall day in 1943 in "an offer of proof," in order to get it into the trial records over the prosecution's objections: "If you will cooperate with my wishes and ideas, you will broadcast to the American people that the unfortunate war be terminated as soon as possible. If there is anyone present who does not wish to do this, please step forward."

"Who stepped forward?" Collins asked.

"A Britisher, George Williams," answered Tsuneishi, "a splendid type of Britisher."

Judge Roche, for some unexplained reason, allowed no further questions to Tsuneishi about the Bunka Camp incident. "We desire to show," Collins protested, "that there was continuing duress stretching from the day Major Charles Cousens was assigned to perform duties on the 'Zero Hour' to the date that it was concluded; that it was not hearsay but part and parcel of the *res gestae* [facts of the case, admissible in evidence]."

As Collins's questioning became tougher, DeWolfe raised more frequent objections (which were sustained) to prevent Tsuneishi from answering as to the meaning of the order and the presence of an unsheathed sword during the incident. Collins finally turned to the bench. Judge Roche recessed court, providing both sides, in the absence of the jury, the opportunity to argue whether or not the alleged duress used to force the Bunka Camp POWs to do their wartime broadcasts might also have relevance for the defendant in this trial.

DeWolfe argued that "alleged duress of others" had nothing to do with "the defendant's intent in any manner whatsoever." "The government,"

George Olshausen quickly responded, "can prove matters not pleaded in the indictment in order to show guilty intent, and we say for the same reason, we can prove matters not pleaded in the indictment to prove innocent intent." "Duress on others," he continued, "so far as communicated to the defendant and so far as it is part of the duress on the defendant, is relevant to the question."

Judge Roche ruled "There is nothing before the court," thereby preventing Tsuneishi from either acknowledging or denying "his threat of Cousens or the presence of his bared sword when he ordered Cousens to broadcast or else." This arbitrary ruling, which profoundly affected the trial, once again vividly reveals misconduct on the part of Judge Roche, who did not even try to understand Japanese society during the war, which had been under strict military rule and was oppressive both among the military and toward civilians. The ruling drew the line between oppressive conditions that had applied to the war prisoners at Radio Tokyo and those that might have applied to the defendant. Since the ruling would not permit testimony on depositions by the war prisoners in the court records, the jury would never hear the vivid, detailed descriptions about Tsuneishi's "persuasion" methods used on the POWs and the terrible food situation at Bunka Camp.

It was difficult for the majority of the American people in the late 1940s, especially Judge Roche, to understand the oppressive nature of the military-controlled wartime Japanese society. Nor did the judge allow the opportunity for the jury to see the hint of such society by allowing some witnesses or depositions. Iva's broadcast, simply stated, took place in wartime Tokyo, not in San Francisco in a time of peace, where a strong anti-Japanese sentiment still existed.

The close familial relations that developed between the POWs and the defendant were exactly what Collins wanted to establish and could have established if the defense had been given the opportunity to examine the context in which the defendant had given sustained aid to the war prisoners. The broadcasts made by the POWs and the defendant were the result of the close, strong anti-Japanese and pro-Allied feelings among them. The objective of the prosecution, especially DeWolfe, was to draw a distinct line between the prisoners of war and the defendant.

Clark Lee, the forty-two-year-old, well-known war correspondent, was the "first celebrity of a sort" among the witnesses. Lee was the author of Iva's story, mislabeled "confession" by Brundidge, which did not in fact contain anything that was not known when the attorney general had thrown out the case two years before. It was not an admission of guilt. Nor had there been any new information that would support suspicion of her guilt since then.

DeWolfe a year earlier had expressed considerable doubt on its usefulness as evidence. The so-called "confession" or "admission against interest" given by Iva to Lee and Brundidge, DeWolfe stated in his memo to one of his colleagues on May 25, 1948, "was given only after they offered her $2,000 for exclusive right for her story," money that had never even been paid. The method by which these newspapermen obtained the "confession" from Iva, DeWolfe reasoned, appeared "at least questionable and of doubtful propriety." Now, however, DeWolfe, who believed that his memo had been sealed and that no one, except he and a few of his colleagues, would ever realize he had done a complete turnabout, was presenting the "confession" as an important piece of evidence.

Lee testified, in response to DeWolfe's questions about the interview, that Iva had told him about the content of one propaganda broadcast: "She said that in the fall of '44 at the time that Japan claimed they had sunk a number of American ships off Formosa, a major came to her from Imperial headquarters and bluntly suggested that she broadcast as follows: 'Orphans of the Pacific, you really are orphans now. How are you going to get home now that all of your ships are sunk?'"

This testimony had apparently been a false story, considerably altered from the original notes of Lee's interview, which had been more terse and ambiguous, to fit in the situation in Overt Act 6. The "major," who came from the Imperial headquarters, for example, could have been no one but Tsuneishi, but he had just said, in his testimony in court, that he had never spoken directly to a subordinate staff person such as Iva. Moreover, Lee, who could only testify as to what she allegedly told him at that interview, had no direct knowledge of what went on at Radio Tokyo.

When it was time for him to interrogate Lee under cross-examination, Wayne Collins, instead of pursuing the altered part of the "confession," asked Lee about the identity of "Tokyo Rose." Lee said that he had heard "Tokyo Rose" was a Canadian *nisei* girl and that he had first heard of "Rose" in 1942, which Roche ruled inadmissible hearsay evidence.

Collins had brought to court a copy of Lee's *One Last Look Around* (1947), an account of his postwar experience in Asia, especially Japan, a chapter of which, "Her Neck in a Noose," dealt with the Tokyo Rose matter. His story in the book was an exaggerated account, and he was careful not to present such distorted reports in open court. When Lee came to realize that his book and articles about Iva partly led to her trial, he regretted that he hadn't written them differently, to avoid the anti–Tokyo Rose furor he might possibly have caused.

Collins suddenly changed topic and asked if Lee knew Hiromu Yagi, who had testified at the grand jury proceedings. "Now, Mr. Lee," Collins asked, "isn't it a fact that you and Mr. Brundidge requested me to go to the St. Francis Hotel on October 25, 1948, because you wished to ascertain from me . . . whether or not I knew that Harry Brundidge had gone to Japan in 1948 and . . . advised Yagi to come before the grand jury and testify falsely in this case?" "You know that's nonsense!" DeWolfe shouted, even though he already knew all the facts of the Yagi-Kodair matter.

"We'll demonstrate it in this court!" Collins declared.

"No, you won't!" DeWolfe responded.

"I will," Collins insisted.

"You're talking through your hat!" bluffed DeWolfe, who knew he was lying himself.

Judge Roche once again sustained DeWolfe's objection and directed the jury to ignore the exchange. The jury, however, had already heard the remarks to Iva's advantage, helping to establish the unreliability of both Lee and Brundidge.

DeWolfe changed his mind and decided not to call Brundidge as a witness, although the jury might not have realized the significance of the change. The defense could not call Brundidge to the stand, and the government chose to not call him, Stanley Kutler asserted, because "the common law rule then in effect required one to vouch for the veracity and truthfulness of one's own witness."

The reason for the prosecution's change of plan was openly revealed when the next prosecution witness, Frederick Tillman, was cross-examined. On July 27, Collins asked if the FBI agent had not told Collins's colleague Ted Tamba that Yagi had confessed that he had been bribed to lie to the grand jury. DeWolfe immediately objected, but Collins insisted that the court should know if there had been an obstruction of justice, to which Roche responded this time positively. Tillman, to whom all eyes in the courtroom turned, said, "Yes." An observer reported, "There was a ripple through the audience." Roche, however, prevented Collins from elaborating the point further.

As already described, Brundidge in April 1948 had called on Yagi and asked him whether he and his friend wanted a free trip to the United States. The next day, Yagi had taken Kodaira to see Brundidge at the Dai-ichi Hotel. Brundidge asked them to testify that they had jointly witnessed Iva making certain broadcasts, but Kodaira refused to comply. Yagi had perjured himself at the grand jury hearing, although Kodaira refused to come to San Francisco to commit perjury. Yagi had finally confessed to the FBI that he had lied at the instigation of Brundidge. When he was questioned by Assistant Attorney General Alexander Campbell, Brundidge denied everything.

Campbell had then sent Tillman back to Tokyo in December 1948, and Tillman had reported that both Yagi and Kodaira had agreed that Brundidge had tried to bribe them to lie. Tamba questioned Tillman at that time, who had conceded that this was the case. Why did DeWolfe not indict Brundidge? Campbell told Attorney General Tom Clark that arresting Brundidge for "subornation of perjury" would "completely destroy any chance of a conviction in her case." Why didn't they drop Iva's case? Could the Justice Department still indict Iva based upon the perjury that they, the attorney general, assistant attorney general, and special prosecutor, all came to know to have been clearly proven? Campbell thought, he even added, that no California court would convict a white man on the testimony of two Japanese.

When Lee quit the witness stand, the prosecution feared the credibility of their witness had been damaged. According to an observer, the jury had been very sympathetic to Lee, even when he was rigorously pursued by Collins under cross-examination. As he finished his testimony and left, Lee was "followed by the admiring glances of just about everyone in the courtroom" and gave "a favorable impact" for the prosecution case "far in excess of any factual basis that he had in his testimony."

Next came the prosecution's star witnesses, Kenkichi Oki and George Hideo Mitsushio, the two supervisors of "Zero Hour." They had been well coached and carefully rehearsed on what they might say in the courtroom. These two men were in a vulnerable position. They were both California *nisei* who had gone to Japan before the war started and later took on Japanese citizenship by signing their names in the Japanese family registry. According to the *jus sanguinis* (the right of blood) laws of Japan, in contrast with *jus soli* (the law of the place of one's birth), this action made them Japanese citizens, but they did not legally renounce their American citizenship before the U.S. consul. They were technically citizens of both countries and were, therefore, subject to treason charges by the United States.

Well aware of the situation, the prosecution took advantage of the precarious position they were in and threatened them with possible treason trials if they did not cooperate and if they did not confirm each other's rehearsed testimony. The prosecution had indeed been able to get the kind of testimony it wanted.

DeWolfe, on direct examination, questioned Oki and Mitsushio quickly and tried to get them off the witness stand fast. They testified to the eight overt acts of alleged treason. Their testimonies were identical, with words right out of the indictment. They recited a word-for-word quotation about what Iva was supposed to have said into a microphone at Radio Tokyo several years earlier, "Now you fellows have lost all your ships. You really are orphans of the Pacific. How do you think you will ever get home?"

Judge Roche, who began to develop a distaste for Oki and Mitsushio, even asked Hennessey, one of the prosecutors, "where in the world he got witnesses like those two." Roche accordingly allowed Collins more opportunities for questioning. "Can you repeat the oath of allegiance to the flag?" Collins asked Mitsushio, fully aware of the fact that he had been a Boy Scout and an ROTC student at UC Berkeley. DeWolfe objected, but Judge Roche overruled the objection, forcing Mitsushio to answer. When he went so far as "One nation . . . invincible. . . ," he stopped, then murmured, "I don't remember." Roche completed the oath from the bench, "with liberty and justice for all."

Collins then turned to Oki. He testified that he was not appearing voluntarily but had been brought forcibly to San Francisco by order of the U.S. Occupation forces. Collins drilled him for not being able to recall anything about the happenings of the day at Radio Tokyo in October 1944, except the exact words broadcast by Iva. What did he have for breakfast and dinner? What time did he go to work and what did he wear? What kind of day was it? Mitsushio and Oki had not only remembered the same things in the same words, but they had remembered them in great detail, including the wrong dates. Collins said to Oki in court, "Are you a man or a parrot?"

At the end of the cross-examination, Collins was able to extract from Mitsushio that, immediately after his arrival in San Francisco, he had been given a copy of the indictment by the prosecutors and that he had met with DeWolfe and other prosecutors and FBI agent Frederick Tillman almost every day. The *San Francisco Chronicle* reporter Stanton Delaplane commented, "On the face of his letter-perfect, unchanging word structure," it was "a damaging admission."

The reporters were certainly not much impressed by these two key witnesses. They were American-born traitors who had served Japan, but no one would be willing to say in public that this made them vulnerable to pressure by the prosecution, amounting to contempt of court.

The jury's crucial verdict would depend entirely on how much credence it attached to these two men's testimony. Iva emphatically denied the testimony of these men, the constitutionally required two witnesses. They had not met the burden of proof, clearly proving that Iva had committed treason beyond a reasonable doubt. At any rate, it was up to the defense to discredit them and convince the jury of their unreliability. It had been demonstrated to the jury that Oki had simply countersigned Mitsushio's responses and that their very testimony was suspect.

Mitsushio and Oki, who had been two supervisors directly in charge of the program "Zero Hour" and directing Iva's role in it, were the ones who turned Iva in, without assuming any liability themselves for the alleged treasonous acts. They were more responsible than Iva for the content of the broadcasts. She was just doing what they had formulated and ordered her to do.

Iva's broadcast was not a solo undertaking, like the discovery of the New World by Christopher Columbus. Rather, it was part of an integrated group effort, like the landing on the moon in 1969, an accomplishment of not just those three young heroes who had actually landed on the moon but of some 400,000 individuals and billions of dollars. The broadcasting similarly involved many people, script writers, administrators, planners, technicians, and other announcers, all contributing to the integral whole. It is unconscionable to single out a part-time announcer and place upon her responsibility for the entire work.

If Iva's broadcasts were a treasonable act, so were the actions of all the members of Radio Tokyo who were American citizens, and some were even more liable than Iva. Newspaper commentary focused on the irony of Iva being charged with treason because she insisted on holding on to her American citizenship, while the key witnesses against her were "turncoats."

What does the constitutional requirement of the testimony of "two witnesses to the same overt act" really mean? Treating Mitsushio and Oki as the required two witnesses is highly questionable. These "two witnesses" could be either two independent individuals who witnessed the same act at the same time or witnessed the same act at two different times or witnessed different parts of the same act. In any of these situations, the two witnesses should produce two different reports.

On the other hand, when these two persons would, as a pair, witness one identical incident, they should be able to produce two independent, different reports, two different versions of the same incident. If they produce two identical accounts and give identical testimony, they should not be treated as two *separate* witnesses.

Oki and Mitsushio, who presented identical testimonies, should be treated as one witness, not two. Such a situation does not clearly meet the constitutional requirement for treason. The court, therefore, needed one more witness to the same overt act. The testimony of these two witnesses, instead of proving Iva's guilt beyond a reasonable doubt, should have served to implant doubt in the minds of the jurors.

Before the trial began, Lieutenant Norman Reyes had been subpoenaed by both the defense and the prosecution. One of the three POWs who had been in charge of Radio Tokyo's overseas broadcasts, in November 1944 Reyes married Katherine Morooka, a typist who later became an announcer. He came to the United States in 1947 to study at Vanderbilt University, majoring in English. He also worked at a local radio station as an announcer. He had been a witness at the grand jury, and he had also given three lengthy statements to the FBI, one in Nashville in April 1948 and two in San Francisco at the time of the grand jury hearings. The prosecution had been certain that he would testify for them. But several days before the trial, on June 30, he met with the prosecutors and told them he would testify first as a defense witness.

Besides Oki and Mitsushio, six other witnesses had been brought from Japan to testify that they had seen Iva in the NHK studios broadcasting as "Orphan Ann." These witnesses, who came to San Francisco to take advantage of free trips and per diems, did not help the government's case very much. "I was surprised at these witnesses I'd never seen before," Iva commented later, "who came out and said they knew me." Kenichi Ishii, a young man in his early twenties, testified against Iva on Overt Act 7. He testified that he had seen Iva broadcast, that she had not been coerced, and that Major Cousens had selected her because she had the voice he wanted. Ishii said that "she could have stayed in the typing pool, but she wanted to help Cousens and the other prisoners." To Ishii, who was only nineteen then, Iva had a voice that "sounded very sexy over the air." The jury, however, did not seem to have been much impressed by him.

The other prosecution witnesses were even less effective. One conceded that his English was so poor that he could not understand what Iva said on her broadcasts.

A prosecution witness waiting to be called to testify, David Seizo Hyuga, had told Collins and Tamba during the lunch recess that he could prove that what Mitsushio and Oki had recited from the witness stand was "pure nonsense, that the events narrated had never happened, and that their testimony was downright perjury." He then requested that "certain questions be asked of him on cross-examination" and said that "he was sure the ill-founded case against Tokyo Rose would collapse." If he was allowed to testify, Hyuga might surely have influenced the outcome of the trial. The prosecution, however, found out that Hyuga had been talking to the defense attorneys and suddenly sent him back to Japan.

In response to the FBI's request for witnesses in December 1947, several hundred ex-GIs replied. Some said that "Orphan Ann" reported troop movements, others testified "Orphan Ann" made remarks about the unfaithfulness of their wives and sweethearts at home, and still others reported "Orphan Ann" tried to make the GIs homesick by talking about ice cream and beefsteaks.

Under cross-examination, Collins didn't have much difficulty in demonstrating that the "Orphan Ann program" the former GIs allegedly heard was in fact the fictitious "Tokyo Rose" broadcasts. Collins exposed their fallacies that they heard "Zero Hour." In most cases, due to the different time zones, the time they claimed to have heard "Orphan Ann" did not match the time at which the broadcasts were actually made. If the American fighting men heard the Japanese broadcasts that didn't include the identifier "This is Ann of Radio Tokyo," they were not listening to the ones announced by Iva, period.

A total of thirty-three statements the ex-GI witnesses alleged to have heard on "Orphan Ann" broadcasts were all firmly denied not only by Iva but also by Cousens, Ince, and Reyes, who had written Iva's scripts for her. Although some GI witnesses displayed rather positive memories, none of those who had been directly connected with "Zero Hour" and had actually seen and heard Iva in the studio, including those who testified for the government, ever remembered any of those alleged broadcasts having taken place.

While most of the GI witnesses had turned out to be unreliable, a small number of witnesses did make strong impressions on the judge and the jury. Marshall Hoot, chief boatswain's mate on a PT (motor torpedo) boat patrolling between the Gilbert Islands and Saipan, was one of them. On June 3, 1944, Hoot had heard Orphan Ann's broadcast. "Wake up, you boneheads. Go and see your commanding officer and demand to be sent home," he remembered Orphan Ann announcing. "Don't stay in that mosquito-infested jungle and let someone else run off with your girlfriends." Hoot said that he heard "Zero Hour" between six and seven o'clock in the evening just after dinner. "Zero Hour" had, in fact, been broadcast between these hours, but in Tokyo time. There was a three-hour time difference between Tokyo and the Gilbert Islands, where the program should have been heard from three to four o'clock in the afternoon. Apparently, the time zone problem had been overlooked by DeWolfe and his prosecution gang, who had been coaching their witnesses. How could Hoot claim he had heard Iva's announcement if he did not hear the real "Orphan Ann" and "Zero Hour"? His "Tokyo Rose" seemed to have been a totally different announcer from Iva. The defense lawyers had many options available to pursue, such as confronting Hoot not only on the words he said he specifically heard but on the quality of voice he had heard.

When Collins asked the witness how he was able to remember the date of the broadcast, he seemed to have been readily prepared. He pulled out a thin green paper, a letter he wrote to his wife between June 2 and 6, 1944. Hoot started reading:

We have a radio now, and we get Tokyo best. They have an American-Japanese girl who has turned down the United States for Japan. They call her Tokyo Rose and does she razz us fellows out here in the Pacific; telling how well Japan is getting along and to hear her start out you would think she was broadcasting from the United States and sorry we were losing so many men and ships. It sure makes the fellows sore.

The letter said nothing about frequencies, "Orphan Ann," or "Zero Hour." The witness testified, however, that he had heard the "Orphan

Ann" broadcast and "Zero Hour" but failed to recall any of the details about them, quite in contrast with his specific and vivid description of Tokyo Rose and her announcement! He definitely seemed to have confused Orphan Ann's "Zero Hour" with other broadcasts. At the end of his testimony, he again stated that he had listened to "Zero Hour" without specifying it. Hoot also contradicted himself by first saying that he listened to the program "not for entertainment but for another purpose" but later stated that the main reason was "to hear the recordings of popular music . . . not available to us at the time from other sources."

The letter told about a bombing attack by Japanese planes, which killed two of Hoot's shipmates. "Honey babies," the letter concluded, "I hope I dream of you tonight as I think of you all day." This letter, though it had nothing to do with Iva and her treason trial, made a very strong impression on both the judge and the jury. It sent "the six women jurors fumbling in their handbags for handkerchiefs" and "hardened the jaws of men." At the press tables, said Delaplane, the odds for acquittal "broke like the 1929 stock market."

In reality, the letter did not prove beyond a reasonable doubt that it was Iva who broadcast what Hoot was supposed to have heard. It was, moreover, the war itself that made the separation of Hoot and his wife intolerable, not Iva's alleged announcement.

The letter was indeed suspect. It obviously was part of a well-planned drama, made up after the war and well coached by the prosecution. The contents of the letter didn't seem to reflect the general view of the fighting GIs in the central Pacific. The PT boat operation was by no means a picnic, but most of the American fighting men were in a more upbeat mood than the letter had depicted. The overwhelming victories at Midway and Guadalcanal and the death of Admiral Isoroku Yamamoto all contributed to the optimistic outlook.

The shortwave radio broadcast was usually listened to by a group, not individually, and the propaganda announcements were not taken seriously by American fighting men but instead were joked about, especially since the beginning of 1944, when the tide of the war had definitely turned in favor of the United States. Only the losing side was likely to be subject to "rapid psychological demoralization by the propaganda," and the winning Americans essentially became impervious to propaganda. The group listening to the shortwave radio did not usually allow for any listener to be sentimental. There must, of course, have been some emotional and fainthearted men who on rare occasions were nostalgically longing for their homes, especially their wives, girlfriends, and sweethearts.

The statement in the Hoot letter, "They have an American-Japanese girl who has turned down the United States for Japan," is a kind of remark that could have been made only after the war, probably by the coaching of the prosecution. No one at Radio Tokyo had announced such things as who and what the broadcasters were, and American GIs in the central Pacific in 1944 had no way of knowing about Tokyo Rose or Iva. "They call her Tokyo Rose" is another made-up remark, specifically intended to identify the person as Iva. No one at Radio Tokyo had ever used "Tokyo Rose," and it was American GIs who called all announcers at Radio Tokyo and other Japanese stations in Asia "Tokyo Rose." The defense could have also called expert witnesses, though doing so sometimes requires considerable recruitment, preparation, and expense, to testify on the genuineness of the letter, regarding the quality of such things as the ink, envelope, and paper available at the time in the South Pacific.

In addition, the letter allowed into testimony information (whether true or not) regarding the effectiveness of the supposed propaganda broadcasts in damaging the morale of the U.S. servicemen. In a treason trial, it was the conduct itself that matters. The effectiveness of the propaganda broadcast, therefore, would not in any way aggravate or mitigate the offense. It follows that the judge should not have allowed Hoot to read his letter. But since he had done it, the judge should have instructed the jury to disregard the letter.

The judge didn't seem to fully understand the law of treason. Quite contrary to the general rule that treason should be adjudged solely by the conduct of the offender, Judge Roche not only allowed the prosecution to present the witness to testify to the effect of the act but also denied comparable opportunities to the defense.

The greatest damage of Hoot's letter, however, did not become apparent until about a decade later. Three days before Christmas 1958, two newspaper reporters, Katherine Pinkham and Rex Gunn, called on Judge Roche in his office at the Federal Court Building. He was eighty-one, one month away from his retirement. Roche confided to the reporters:

I think if it wasn't for the witness from Los Angeles, the reluctant witness, I might have considered her innocent. They pressed him to tell and he produced that letter. I think . . . that was the turning point.

Up to the time that fellow pulled the letter out of his pocket ... with all my experience ... I was up in the air as to what might or might not ... have happened.

Here it is. The culpability for treason should not be adjudged by the effect of the act, but Roche's remark clearly showed that he had had no understanding of the law of treason. The judge, who had presided over a treason trial, was exhibiting not only his ignorance but his unawareness of the inherent problem of the crime. His instructions would have been clearly defective. He should have told the jury that the effect of the broadcast was to be disregarded, and he himself should have stuck to the same instruction. He, instead, shamelessly allowed the effect of the act to influence the jury as well as allow himself to be deeply swayed by it. This was a treason trial. Judge Roche's instruction to the jury would, unfortunately, have already been crippled by his inadequate understanding of the law of treason.

The Defense Rebuttal

If I got on the witness stand and told only the truth, then the truth would win,
I thought. My family was very worried when I took the witness stand.
But I wasn't all that worried. I did not feel the least bit as though
I had betrayed America. If I had felt that way, I wouldn't have stood up
in court. I would have run away to Lisbon. I had the chance to do so.

IVA TOGURI D'AQUINO'S INTERVIEW WITH MASAYO DUUS,
May 20, 1976, quoted in Duus, Tokyo Rose *(1979), 203*

The defense's opening statement was delivered by Theodore Tamba on August 13. In his forty-minute speech, Tamba pointed out that the prosecution had tried to prove that the defendant not only had the will to commit the act but committed the act with the intent to betray her country. He then insisted that the defense was going to show that Iva did not have any treasonous intent and that she had broadcast "under threat and duress."

As a matter of fact, the prosecution had failed to prove beyond a reasonable doubt that Iva had committed treasonable acts in her broadcasting. They did not prove in the witnesses' testimony that Iva broadcast with the intention to betray her country despite their pledge at the outset in their opening, nor were they successful in identifying her, beyond a reasonable doubt, as the announcer of the statement set forth in the indictment and the voice the GIs were supposed to have heard in the Pacific. Since the defendant had a presumption of innocence, the defense did not have to prove anything. The only thing they had to do was to destroy as effectively as possible the credibility of the prosecution's arguments and evidence presented in court.

The main defense witnesses were the three former POWs who worked on the "Zero Hour" program. The first witness called to the stand was Charles H. Cousens, who had been previously cleared by an Australian court and voluntarily came from Australia to testify, paying most of his own expenses. Cousens, who had been a war prisoner of the Japanese for almost four years, tried to establish the groundwork for a defense plea of duress by describing the scene on the deck at Singapore in March 1942 and what had befallen a fellow soldier:

> The word got around amongst the boys that he was starving and had rushed in and had tried to snatch a can of food from a Japanese soldier.... They threw him to the ground and put his head under a tap so that as he drew breath and screamed, he drew water into his lungs. And then they drew him away, and he got up and they proceeded to beat him again, and then they put him under the tap again.... Eventually, they put him under the tap, and I suppose he clenched his teeth because they broke his face open on the tap, turned the water on, drowned him, and threw the body away.

"What did you see with reference to the other man?" Wayne Collins asked. "He was an Australian and they beat him to death," Cousens's voice broke as he spoke. He lowered his head and started to cry. It was painful to watch, one reporter commented, and people looked away. In quite a contrast to the reaction to Marshall Hoot's letter, no handkerchiefs appeared in the jury box. Something unusual, the reporter continued, must have happened; "men trained at Sandhurst don't break down like that, not in public, among strangers." To Collins's question, "Was he a soldier?" Cousens answered:

> Yes, sir. He had stolen a can of onion [*rakkyo*]. Two Japanese held him while a third beat him.... They had stripped his shirt off and beat him across the back, and then when he was on the ground, on the ankle bones and on the kneecaps in order to bring him to his feet again. Each time he got to his feet, they would beat him down again. He kept on getting up.

"Did the man die?" Collins continued. "Later, when he didn't get up again," Cousens responded, "the man grunted at us to take him away. We did, and he died before they could get him on board ship."

DeWolfe asked Judge Roche to excuse the jury so that counsel could argue the issue of duress. The judge so ordered. James Knapp argued for the prosecution, while George Olshausen joined Collins to assert the defense's position. Eventually, Judge Roche ruled, prohibiting Cousens from relating any force or threat of force used against him by the Japanese. When Cousens testified that he was knocked about by a Japanese in civilian dress at *kempei-tai* headquarters and that he was forced to stand before

Tsuneishi and face an unsheathed sword as Tsuneishi read his order, the prosecution objected, which was sustained by the judge.

On the morning of the second day of direct examination, Collins continued his questioning of Cousens in order to establish the close relationship of the defendant's broadcasting to the starved condition of the POWs, but the judge advised, "We have had this witness on the stand for a day and a half." "I know, your honor," responded Collins, "but I think he is our most important material witness, because he was at Radio Tokyo with the defendant," and proceeded to ask Cousens to spell out in detail the valuable aid Iva had given to him and other POWs.

Shortage of food was a serious problem for all Japanese during the war, but Cousens testified that "the prisoners at Bunka Camp . . . were in very poor condition; we badly needed medicine . . . citrus fruit, I recall, because men had pellagra." Besides food, Cousens said, Iva purchased for them "vitamin pills, tobacco, and a blanket on one occasion." Knapp objected, saying that "the defendant's aid doesn't go to the intent to commit an act of treason at all . . . it only shows she might be a kindly, kind-hearted person." The objection was sustained.

When Cousens went on to testify that he had informed the defendant of the condition of the war prisoners, Knapp again spoke up, "Objection, your honor. The question of the reason for which she gave food and medicine is immaterial. The fact is she gave it. The reason for which she gave it is of no concern." Once again, Knapp's objection was sustained. The action of the judge was crucial, changing the course of the trial. From this point on, the defendant's aid to the POWs was not considered related to Iva's intentions in broadcasting as Orphan Ann. It is incredible that the significance of Iva's action in aiding the POWs, to her especially, "had been tossed aside as if it were of no consequence."

"I guess I should have jumped up and shouted, 'No. I'm not a kind-hearted person!' I should have done something," acknowledged Iva later. "But I was so dumbfounded, I just sat there, I couldn't believe it." Another point on the issue of intent was Cousens's reason for selecting Iva as his confrere on "Zero Hour" and his instructions to her. Responding to Collins's question, Cousens explained his position in detail:

As near as I can remember, I said to her, "Here is tonight's script, Ann. Now, I want you to read this in this way. You will notice we have got a satirical bit here about "Strike up the Band." Take that sergeant's part tough, like this. . . . in that next part, take it very light, rather sissy, and I would have done that for her because it was a specific reference to a comic record . . . then, to come in very fast on what I explained to her was what were called a wipe in radio terms.

If you have a commercial program and the commercial has just been read, if the next unit on the program jumps in fast, you get entirely the wrong effect from what the sponsor wants, because the listener's mind is jerked away from what has just gone on, and you get, in effect, a wipe (erasure). . . . I explained to her many times to pick this up as soon as the "Home Front News" was over, not just "Thank you," and into the program, but "Thank you, thank you, thank you, thank you," and it was written in here a multiplicity of times, to jump in and take that fast.

Cousens then read the script as he had instructed the defendant to read it:

Hello, there, enemies. How are tricks? This is Ann of Radio Tokyo, and we're just going to begin our regular program of music, news and the "Zero Hour" for our friends—I *mean* our enemies in Australia and the South Pacific. So, be on your guard and mind the children don't hear! All set? Okay. Here is the first blow at your morale, the Boston Pops playing "Strike up the Band."

There was no doubt about "the skills of the performance or of his ability to weave double meaning into the script he was reading," but Judge Roche, who didn't appreciate the show, or more accurately refused to understand the importance of it, finally interrupted, "Is that all from this witness?" "No, no, your honor," reacted Collins, "I want to get to some further explanations because these require explanations."

"I recall this phrase which occurs here," Cousens took up the Orphan Ann script of March 9, 1944. Referring to the island-hopping campaign that was then going on under General MacArthur, Cousens coached Iva to say, "that's not bad atoll, atoll; all right boys, one more left and then you can have your beer." The meaning behind his instructions to the defendant, Cousens concluded on direct examination, was "to sabotage" the Japanese purposes "in every way possible."

Cousens stated that he had chosen Iva as Orphan Ann because she had a "gin-fog voice—I hope I can say this without offense," which was what Cousens needed to make "a complete burlesque" of the propaganda content on the "Zero Hour." He testified that he had talked her into broadcasting by assuring her the program was "straight out entertainment," and that he had said if she would "place herself under my orders, I would see to it that she did nothing harmful." Cousens said only bright, pleasant music was played, and community sing-alongs were used as morale-building devices. He said also that he wrote in British idiom so Iva could not have spoken with the alleged American slang. Thus, not only Iva but the entire POWs' broadcasts sabotaged Radio Tokyo's program.

Evidence indicates that, in her broadcasting, Iva did not have any intention to betray her country. When she decided to take the job as an announcer, not only did Cousens guarantee that she would not betray her people and the United States but also she herself was entirely certain that she was not betraying her country.

The prosecution's cross- and recross-examinations were very brief. They did nothing to shake the credibility of the witness. DeWolfe must have thought that he encountered a witness who was as quick "to grasp a rhetorical opening as DeWolfe."

To DeWolfe's question, "Any other Japanese bring you goods besides the defendant?" Cousens quickly responded, "The defendant was not Japanese. She was an American." Except for the one breakdown at the beginning, Cousens left the witness stand without any difficulty, but it was hard to assess the impact on the jury.

The next witness, Wallace Ince, who had been earlier cleared by the U.S. Army and promoted to major, corroborated Cousens's testimony. Ince was a cautious witness because of the grand jury's demand for his prosecution. He came to court with his attorney, Alfonso J. Zirpoli, a former deputy U.S. attorney, who had earlier argued against Mitsuye Endo's habeas corpus petition.

Both Ince and Reyes had testified at the grand jury. But shortly before the trial began they agreed to testify as defense witnesses, due probably to Cousens's persuasion. Since they were still under the threat of indictment themselves, it took courage for them to change sides and testify for the defense. It is indeed an irony that Iva, a civilian, had been indicted for treason for the wartime broadcasts, created by the POWs, and that one of whom, Ince, a military man, had not only escaped prosecution but been promoted.

The tall, red-haired major, who had fully recovered his normal weight since his days in Tokyo, was very composed at first, but when Collins started to ask about the treatment of the POWs at Bunka Camp, Ince became very emotional. "We were beaten, starved, subjected to indignities," said Ince, and then stopped and buried his head in his hands. "Sobs racked him. His shoulders heaved as he tried to control himself," an observer noted. Again the jurors and spectators stared and then looked away. Finally Ince spoke again: "It is not so easy . . . to talk so matter of factly of brutality. It is quite a different thing." To the prosecution's objection that the witness was not relating what happened, Ince sharply retorted, "I am telling what happened. . . . Men you knew well, lived with, worked with, fought with, died horribly."

Like Cousens, Ince had broadcast, he said, under threat of death. His life was threatened frequently by Lieutenant Hamamoto, by George Uno, and by Tsuneishi. Ince also testified that Iva's aid to him and his fellow prisoners had included eggs, noodles, rice, vegetables, fruit, vitamin pills, tobacco, the woolen blanket that Cousens had mentioned, and almost daily news of Allied victories. "The POWs were all hungry — always," Ince concluded.

On cross-examination Ince told of an initial reaction of distrust when Cousens first wanted to include Iva as confrere on "Zero Hour." "I told him [Cousens] I didn't like it. We had a working agreement between three of us [Cousens, Ince, and Reyes], and I didn't want to take chances on Toguri."

> KNAPP: You didn't trust her.
>
> INCE: Certainly not.
>
> KNAPP: Then, you don't know whether she was ever part of that agreement?
>
> INCE: I believe she was.

Norman I. Reyes was the third and last of the three war prisoners from "Zero Hour." He had been widely publicized as a star prosecution witness since March 1948, but decided to testify for the defense. Reyes, who likewise had been cleared by the Philippine government, also confirmed Cousens's testimony and testified on Iva's loyalty to the United States: "I would put my life in her hands." He added that she was part of the POW plot to sabotage the "Zero Hour" and that he was the recipient of food, medicine, tobacco, and news items from her. Reyes further testified that Iva had broadcast under duress and that she had often expressed a desire to stop working at the station.

It was DeWolfe's turn to cross-examine Reyes, and the lead prosecutor led with his main weapon: FBI statements Reyes had earlier signed, in order to discredit his truthfulness as a witness. The statements, about which Reyes had never told Collins, contradicted almost everything Reyes had just testified in court as a defense witness: Reyes was never under duress to broadcast at Radio Tokyo; Cousens wanted a benevolent Japan to dominate the Pacific; Ince had broadcast because of "inducements of better living quarters and more freedom"; there had been "no threats, duress or coercion that was exercised or directed to influence Iva Toguri" in her broadcasting; and no plot had existed among the POWs to sabotage Japanese purposes on "Zero Hour."

After two days of questioning, on August 23, DeWolfe tried to get Reyes to admit he had been lying in his statements to the FBI. "Norman," DeWolfe asked, addressing him without his title and family name as he usually did to other witnesses, "you were never threatened with death or torture if you stopped working at Radio Tokyo, were you?" "I was," Reyes answered. DeWolfe responded by pointing out one of Reyes's earlier statements: "at Radio Tokyo I was never conscious of threats of death or torture if my radio activities stopped" and asked Reyes whether the statement was false. Reyes answered, "Yes, sir." "Then since you testified here this morning that everything you told was true, consequently everything you told the FBI was a false statement, wasn't it?" "Yes," Reyes responded, "without reading the statement." "How many other lies have you told here, Reyes?" demanded DeWolfe, whose own contradiction about his views on Iva's culpability had been obvious but never revealed publicly.

If Collins had known that the government had Reyes's statements that contradicted his testimony, he would never have put Reyes on the witness stand. In response to Collins's redirect-examination, Reyes testified about the FBI tactics:

The agents told me Ince and Cousens and the defendant aren't going to worry about you—you are in a highly questionable position. If you want to go over to the other side, all right. I want you to know we had got a lot of stuff on you. I'll pass this on to my CIC friends in the Philippines and you won't like it a bit. . . . I could see them building up overt acts, and I thought if overt acts were all that was needed for a case of treason, I might be held as guilty as the defendant.

Without doubt, the FBI used Reyes's vulnerability to frighten him into giving unfavorable statements against Iva. The same tactic had been used by the FBI on other prosecution witnesses from Japan such as Oki and Mitsushio, who were equally prosecutable.

Reyes did not break down but devastated the defense position. Reyes at least had the courage to stand up and recant his statement publicly in court. Even though he might face charges of perjury, Masayo Duus remarked, it was "a brave act for a young man with his future ahead of him." Judge Roche ruled Reyes to be an unreliable witness and disqualified all of his testimony. Instead of ruling so arbitrarily, why didn't the judge let the jury decide on Reyes's reliability?

The next witness for the defense was Captain Edwin Kalbfleish, Jr., a former POW at Bunka Camp, who had been starved, beaten, and nearly executed for refusing to do radio work for the Japanese. He testified on direct examination that "Cousens is the type of man who would have been followed through hell," but he wasn't allowed to testify about the aid that he had received from the defendant because he had not received it directly from her hands. Kalbfleish had to sit on the witness stand for fifteen minutes without saying a word, because of the prosecution's repeated, sustained objections. The judge eventually ruled his testimony was not related to the case, but how would Roche know that had been the case without actually hearing the testimony?

After Kalbfleish was disqualified and removed from the witness stand, three other Bunka Camp POWs appeared on the witness stand for the defense. But they were all silenced due to their lack of direct contact with the defendant.

There were several GIs for the defense who claimed to have heard the "Orphan Ann" broadcasts in the Pacific. "Orphan Ann" called them "boneheads," but they all said they did not feel any viciousness in the broadcasts. They had, instead, enjoyed listening to them. Sam Stanley, a former baker in the Seabees who listened to her broadcasts nearly every day in the Admiralty Islands, said that the "Orphan Ann" program was so popular that the radio tent could not hold all the GIs who came to listen. "Often there was a large crowd standing outside to hear the show, even when it was pouring rain," Stanley remarked. "I was hoping . . . like a lot of other people who hadn't heard her," he went on, "that we would hear a Tokyo Rose who was witty and smutty and entertaining and telling dirty stories, but we never heard anyone of them."

Robert Speed, an ex–marine lieutenant who had served on Saipan and Okinawa as an intelligence interpreter, stated that he "listened to 'Zero Hour' originally with this specific purpose in mind [to learn about Japanese propaganda techniques] and did not find propaganda." His chief purpose thereafter "in listening to 'Zero Hour' was just entertainment." He also testified that he had never heard of the naval intelligence circular, regarding the movement of Japanese ships and planes, which Marshall Hoot had mentioned in his testimony for the prosecution.

Probably the most crucial former GI defense witness was Kamini Kant Gupta, an American citizen of Indian descent. Gupta, who had been a warrant officer in the judge advocate's office stationed in Alaska, testified that the staff officers were informed by the Alaskan Command that the Orphan Ann broadcasts were a strong factor in building up troop morale in Alaska. This clearly demonstrated the fact that the U.S. Army had recognized that the Orphan Ann broadcasts were bolstering morale, instead of demoralizing the Allied troops. Gupta's testimony was not very effective because he had been interrupted by "repeated and heated objections" by DeWolfe.

Under cross-examination, these ex-GI defense witnesses were rigorously questioned by DeWolfe about their attitudes toward the U.S. government. He blamed them for supporting the Japanese American woman indicted for treason against the United States. All of these witnesses, it was reported, had been visited by the FBI and, as with all the other defense witnesses, encountered prosecutorial harassment.

The two witnesses who undermined the contention that Iva had been the only Tokyo Rose beaming toward the South Pacific were Ruth Yoneko Kanzaki and an Australian woman named Kramer. Kanzaki testified that as a student she had to work at a war plant in the morning and in the afternoon was assigned to work as an English-language announcer on the "German Hour," under the control of the German embassy. As a disc jockey she played almost the same records as those on "Zero Hour," although her scripts were written by the famous German propagandist Reginald Hollingsworth, making her announcements not innocuous but filled with propaganda. Another announcer, Kramer, who later married Hollingsworth, testified that she broadcast her program at 5:30 p.m., just before "Zero Hour." Quite naturally, Kanzaki and Kramer were more likely Tokyo Rose candidates than Iva.

In addition, two Americans, Mark Streeter, a construction worker captured on Wake Island, and John D. Provoo, an army sergeant captured in Corregidor, testified they were forced to do broadcast work at Radio Tokyo like the defendant. Though they were both American citizens engaging in radio broadcast work for the Japanese, Streeter had never been charged with treason, while Provoo had been indicted and convicted, as will be discussed in Chapter 10, but his conviction was overturned on appeal.

The nineteen depositions Theodore Tamba had taken in Tokyo were read in court. They were the only available substitute for testimony by the Japanese witnesses, because the court refused to pay their expenses to come to San Francisco to testify. As Duus notes, DeWolfe used constant objections to disrupt the flow of defense question-answer, preventing much of the deposition content from reaching the jurors. The depositions that the defense considered most important were those by two of Iva's former co-workers. Ruth Hayakawa stated that she "has not heard her [Iva] broadcast anything detrimental to America." Lily Gihevenian stated that she had never typed anything in Iva's scripts about unfaithful wives and sweethearts, the loss of American ships, or the movement of Allied troops.

According to Duus, the deposition by Ken Murayama, a New York *nisei*, seemed more crucial. A Domei News Agency reporter in Manila, Murayama had written scripts for Myrtle Lipton, known as "Manila Rose." Murayama, in his deposition, testified that the scripts he wrote for her "were designed to create a sense of homesickness among troops in the Southwest Pacific. Their tone was one of trying to make the soldiers recall certain good times they might have had when they were back in the United States. . . . We had stories of girls having dates with men at home, while possibly their sweethearts and husbands might be fighting in the Southwest Pacific area."

Murayama also testified that Myrtle Lipton had a very sexy voice, like "a torch singer . . . quite low-pitched, husky . . . the sort of voice that would carry well and was in keeping with the general tenor of the program itself."

The objective of the defense in the trial was to distinguish the "Orphan Ann" broadcasts from those of Tokyo Rose, which were originating either from Radio Tokyo or from one of the other Japanese stations in Asia, like the "German Hour" and Myrtle Lipton's broadcasts. The latter two certainly more closely resembled "Tokyo Rose" broadcasts of rumor. More specifically, Myrtle Lipton, whose broadcasts were confused with Iva's, was the strongest candidate for "Tokyo Rose." The government had thus failed to prove that Iva had been Tokyo Rose and had made those announcements that Myrtle Lipton was supposed to have announced.

Next came the deposition of Toshikatsu Kodaira. It told the full story from the time when his friend Hiromu Yagi had phoned him, saying, "Tosh, don't you want a trip to the United States?" to Kodaira's refusal of the free trip and his lecture to Yagi about the seriousness of perjury. When the prosecution objected, the judge dismissed the jury to hear the arguments from both sides.

DeWolfe insisted that the deposition was based upon hearsay and should not be allowed into evidence because it focused upon two people (Yagi and Brundidge) who had not appeared as witnesses in the trial. Olshausen responded that the prosecution was accountable for Brundidge's actions with Yagi and Kodaira in Japan in March 1948. "Mr. Brundidge," Olshausen continued, "said he made the trip at the request of Attorney General Tom Clark, telling him. 'Give me five days in Japan, and I can find all of the witnesses you need.'"

When Roche ruled Kodaira's deposition hearsay, Collins asserted the ruling incorrect, pointing out that the testimony as to Brundidge's attempted subornation was given by the person to whom Brundidge spoke. "Brundidge's utterances in attempting to suborn perjury," Collins declared, "are themselves part of the issue, so not subject to the hearsay rule."

Collins then insisted upon reading the depositions aloud, question by question, in the presence of the jury so that the court might rule whether each was admissible or not. DeWolfe objected to every question. After forty-six sustained objections Judge Roche stopped the reading of the deposition. "It is my frank opinion," Collins asserted, "that it is clearly admissible testimony." "It is hearsay," the judge responded. "I don't want to deny you any legal position . . . but it is obvious to me, and I think should be to you, that there is clearly hearsay testimony. I say that advisably to you."

"Well," responded Collins grudgingly, "I have no alternative . . . except to read the deposition, to have your Honor make what rulings your Honor sees fit to make." As Collins read the deposition, DeWolfe objected 160 times, all of which were sustained. A total of 39 answers were allowed because none were related to Brundidge's or Yagi's propositions and gifts to Tosh Kodaira.

Although the deposition did not gain the court's favor, the impact on the jury was uncertain. Collins's assertion was correct. Kodaira's deposition might have contained some hearsay portion, inadmissible as evidence, but that shouldn't have meant the entire deposition was hearsay.

The fact remained that the serious bribery had been ruled irrelevant by Judge Roche.

Filipe d'Aquino presented the husband's view of Orphan Ann. He testified that he had heard the "Zero Hour" broadcasts between November 1942 and May 1944 four times a week, between May and October 1944 most of the programs but only Iva's part of the program, and between October 1944 and August 1945 only once a week or less. Collins asked, "What did you hear?" "I never heard one damaging remark against the Allies," was the answer.

Unfortunately, October 1944, when Filipe heard Iva's broadcast only once a week or less, was the very period during which time the prosecution accused Iva for making treasonous remarks on the radio. It was the time when Cousens was hospitalized and Ince had been transferred to another program. Most of the recordings of Orphan Ann during this time, moreover, had been discarded by the U.S. government.

Concerning Iva's exclusive interview with Lee and Brundidge at the Imperial Hotel in 1945, her husband's testimony was drastically different from Lee's. "One [Lee or Brundidge] asked, 'Are you Tokyo Rose?' ... and my wife said she was not. And then she told them there were many women, approximately a half dozen women who had broadcast on the 'Zero Hour.'" Filipe also testified that none of the "quotes" regarding 4Fs dating the wives of GIs, sunken ships, and the joys of working at Radio Tokyo were true.

DeWolfe, for some reason, never questioned d'Aquino about the Lee-Brundidge interview. During Collins's redirect-examination, Roche, at seventy-one, started to doze off and was suddenly awakened by a prosecutor's objection. The judge had to ask the court reporter to reread the question, but he had to ask the reporter to reread one earlier than that, which he also missed. One of the reporters recorded the following exchanges:

> COUNSEL: Have you any children?
> WITNESS: I have no children. I had one, but it died at birth.
> COUNSEL: When did that occur?
> DEWOLFE: Objection to that as incompetent, irrelevant, and immaterial.
> (After a silence in the courtroom, the judge woke up.)
> COURT: Read the question, Mr. Reporter.
> COURT REPORTER: When did that occur?

COURT: When did what occur?
COLLINS: The death of her child?
COURT: Objection sustained.

After his testimony for his wife, Filipe had to go back to Japan, as if the American law did not recognize the spousal right. Though he might have been able to come to the United States as an immigrant from Portugal, Filipe, as mentioned earlier, had been required to sign a statement that he would not try to come back to the United States except as a trial witness. Although it was not a legal statement, he was forced to sign it.

Exactly two weeks after Tom Clark took an oath of office as an associate justice of the Supreme Court as the reward for his work as Truman's attorney general, which, conspicuously enough, included his indictment of Iva for treason, Iva Toguri was desperately defending her case, unjustly and unfairly instigated by Tom Clark. In the early afternoon of September 7 (the forty-sixth day of the trial), Wayne Collins said, "Iva, take the stand, please." Iva stood up, walked to the witness stand, and took an oath.

During the nine months since her arrival in San Francisco, she had kept herself busy in the prison, helping at breakfast, waiting on tables, and cleaning up afterward. She came to be known as "the little nurse," as she took care of anybody who was sick or needed help. Iva Toguri decided to take the witness stand because she hoped that "if she told only the truth, the truth would win." So Iva as the final defense witness told her own story to the court. She emphasized she had no intent to betray the United States and believed she was only entertaining American troops. She said she retained her American citizenship and loyalty throughout the war years, despite threats and pressure. Iva turned out to be a sympathetic and convincing figure for the courtroom audience.

As Iva answered Collins's questions under direct examination, the audience came to realize that her voice was opposite from the one described in the press as "syrupy," "sexy," "velvety," and "seductive." Collins asked her, one by one, if she made any of the forty-one inflammatory "quotations" put into the trial record by prosecution witnesses.

"Welcome to the First Marine Division, the bloody butchers of Guadalcanal?"

"No."

"Your wives and sweethearts are leaving you servicemen because you are overseas too long?"

"No, never could say that."

"Why don't you stop fighting and listen to good music?"

"Never."

"This program is dedicated to the Jolly Rogers, the 90th Bomb Group. I know you are moving from Dobodura to Nadzab, New Guinea, on January 17, and I will have a reception committee there waiting for you?"

"No, never any mention of any island, any place."

In this way, answers to Collins's questions were "no" or "never." When Collins read off the broadcasts alleged in the eight overt acts in the indictment, she answered with the same strong voice, "Never." Her answers were especially emphatic, denying Overt Acts 5 and 6. Not only did Iva deny having ever made any of the broadcasts but also the testimony did not describe accurately whether they were Iva's.

On the third day, when Collins, who had been unsuccessful in pursuing the question of duress, asked her about Seizo David Hyuga, Iva became very emotional. Questioned by Collins, Iva was able to tell how in the fall of 1944, Hyuga, a liaison man between Radio Tokyo employees and the Imperial Japanese Army, told her that Major Tsuneishi wanted a verbal assurance from her that she would cooperate with the army; otherwise she would be conscripted. Hyuga told Iva she had been the only one yet to give her signature for the verbal assurance.

"I told him," Iva said, "he would never get an agreement out of me. I told him, 'I'll quit today; I'll take the consequences.'" "I told him I was only on the Zero Hour for one purpose." She told the court, "I told him I was going to stick by the POWs until the house collapsed." Then she had the same reaction as Cousens and Ince. She cried and collapsed into tears. "Slowly, painfully, the dark eyes brimmed with tears." She bit her lip to stop crying and, in a low voice, told how Hyuga had urged her to say something accommodating, but had finally made up something himself, in her place. The tears of Iva, as the observers noted, induced little sympathy or show of emotion from the jurors, as had been the case with Cousens and Ince.

She told the court how she had refused to buy war bonds, despite repeated demands, or contribute to the Japanese Red Cross. When old clothes were called for, she again refused to give but sold some to buy food for the prisoners. She had refused to take part in air drills, using the excuse of her poor knowledge of Japanese. These activities clearly demonstrate the fact that Iva held a strongly patriotic, anti-Japanese attitude during the war.

Iva's American patriotism, which had never faltered throughout the war in the enemy country and had been demonstrated on every possible occasion, clearly revealed the fact that she would not do anything to betray the United States. Glimpses of her patriotism, vividly demonstrated in Master Sergeant Okada's remarkably detailed story of Iva's daily life in wartime Tokyo, which had never been presented in court, could be clearly detected in the testimony of Cousens, Ince, Reyes, and others in the depositions. Judge Roche did not allow them to fully testify on Iva's behalf.

The defendant throughout direct examination denied all the allegations made by the prosecution in the trial. She said she had not ever broadcast "any smut," "obscenity," "predictions concerning troop movements," "any statement relating to casualties suffered by the United States or its allies," or "any casualties of Japan or its allies." On the fourth day of direct examination, Collins finally turned to prosecutor Tom DeWolfe and said, "Your witness."

On cross-examination, which was to last four days, DeWolfe treated Iva "as if she were dirt" and used all the rhetorical tricks he could muster to confuse and intimidate the defendant.

"Did you ever broadcast about the loss of ships?" demanded DeWolfe. "I did not broadcast anything about the loss of ships, Mr. DeWolfe," she answered.

> DEWOLFE: Never did.
> WITNESS: Never.
> DEWOLFE: Never in July, 1944, did you broadcast about the loss of ships?
> WITNESS: July?
> DEWOLFE: Yes.
> WITNESS: Not that I recall.
> DEWOLFE: What is that?
> WITNESS: No, Mr. DeWolfe.
> DEWOLFE: Are you sure?
> WITNESS: Yes.
> DEWOLFE (picking up a note): This note on p. 14 of Exhibit 15 is correct, is it, about the loss of ships?
> WITNESS: May I see it? [The note simply said that she had not broadcast about the loss of ships.]

WITNESS: Yes, this is correct.

DEWOLFE: That is correct?

WITNESS: Yes.

What was the point of DeWolfe asking about Exhibit 15, except to attempt to trick the defendant and confuse the jury? DeWolfe continued:

DEWOLFE: Somebody told you or suggested that you should broadcast about loss of ships, is that right?

WITNESS: Oh, no, not to me.

DEWOLFE: Not to you. Well, you heard Mr. Nakamura testify that you broadcast about the loss of ships, didn't you?

WITNESS: Yes, I did.

DEWOLFE: His testimony is false, wasn't it?

WITNESS: I don't know whether I am in the position of saying that anybody's testimony is false.

DEWOLFE: I see. Well, you never did broadcast to any American troops at any time that their ships were gone, did you?

WITNESS: No.

DEWOLFE: And "how are you going to get home now?"

WITNESS: No. I can't—

DEWOLFE: You didn't tell Clark Lee that you broadcast in 1944, "You boys are all without ships now, you are really orphans of the Pacific. How are you going to get home now?" You didn't tell Mr. Lee you broadcast that, did you?

WITNESS: That's right, I didn't tell him I broadcast that.

DEWOLFE: You didn't tell him that?

WITNESS: No, I didn't tell him I broadcast that.

DEWOLFE: You heard him testify that you did tell him that.

WITNESS: Yes.

DEWOLFE: Did you hear Mr. Reyes testify something about a broadcast about a loss of ships made by you in July of 1944?

WITNESS: I don't remember.

DEWOLFE: Did you hear anybody make such a broadcast as the broadcasting I am referring to?

WITNESS: No.

DEWOLFE: No such broadcast was ever made, according to your personal knowledge?

WITNESS: To my personal knowledge, no. No.

DEWOLFE: Well, somebody suggested that you broadcast to the American troops, "You fellows are all without ships. What are you going to do about getting home? You are orphans of the Pacific now?"

WITNESS: That is what I heard two or three other people talking about. You see, Mr. DeWolfe, a lot of phrases that were used in Major Cousens's scripts were borrowed for other purposes. There were six or seven copies made, and I heard that suggestion one day when I came late to the studios.

There had been no accurate information on the loss of ships as to who had said what to whom over Radio Tokyo. No scripts were extant for the month of October 1944 of the alleged broadcast about "loss of ships." Thus, Orphan Ann's explicit broadcasts for October 1944 remained conjectural. This broadcast, if it were indeed made, was so out of touch with the reality of sea battles in the Pacific that it is difficult to imagine who would have made up such a story. No one on the Japanese side, including the POWs, would make up such naive, rudimentary accounts. Every American GI fighting in the Pacific should have known that if he lost his ship and survived, there were plenty of ways to get home, if he were allowed to do so.

The prosecution's questioning continued.

DEWOLFE: You did not think the Japanese, Mrs. d'Aquino, were paying you to get up and entertain American troops, did you?

WITNESS: That is what they were doing.

DEWOLFE: That is what they were doing. You honestly, Mrs. d'Aquino, and sincerely thought the Japanese were paying you money to entertain American troops, is that right?

WITNESS: No, that is not right.

One wonders why DeWolfe, after Tsuneishi's testimony earlier, which had clearly stated Radio Tokyo's objective in the propaganda broadcasting, had to ask Iva this question. DeWolfe did not seem to have paid attention to Collins's cross-examination of Tsuneishi. Most important, had he been able to demonstrate that Iva broadcast with the clear intention to betray her country?

Wayne Collins tried to put into evidence the "Navy 'Citation' for Tokyo Rose of Radio Tokyo," which had been issued on August 7, 1945, praising her for "meritorious service contributing greatly to the morale of United States armed services in the Pacific." Judge Roche, however, ruled it out of the trial record.

On the seventh day on the witness stand, when Collins on redirect asked her his last question, whether she "still wants to be an American citizen," Iva "burst into tears" and then answered, "Yes . . . that's why I made all these applications." She stepped down from the witness stand and stumbled back to her seat at the defense's table. She "sat with her head in her hands" and "closed her eyes and pressed her fingers into her temples."

The testimony finally ended, and both sides rested on September 19. The prosecution had called fifty witnesses to the stand and the defense, forty-five, nineteen of whom were deposition witnesses. The cost of the trial to the government had gone up beyond the estimated $500,000. Did the defense successfully challenge the prosecution, asserting that the prosecution had been unable to prove the guilt—the alleged traitorous intent—beyond a reasonable doubt?

The defense in its rebuttal seemed to have been able to create as required by law a reasonable doubt in the minds of the jury. The defense lawyer, Collins, therefore, could have requested a directed verdict of acquittal on three possible grounds: First, the two witnesses to the same overt act, Oki and Mitsushio, were highly questionable to meet the constitutional requirement; second, none of the broadcasts that Iva had allegedly made were ever proven to have been made by Iva; and third, it had not been proven that Iva had made her broadcasts with a clear intention to betray the United States. At the end of testimony, the evidence seemed to be abundantly clear about her innocence. Iva accepted Cousens's request to be an announcer only when he guaranteed that she wouldn't be doing anything against her country, and she and the POWs all sabotaged the Japanese broadcasts in every possible way.

The defense, however, must have felt that Judge Michael Roche had always been on the side of the prosecution; the judge seemed to handle the case with bias and prejudice throughout the trial and sustained almost all the objections to the testimony crucially important to Iva's case. He especially denied her telling about her experiences with the *kempei-tai* that would vividly illustrate duress and about her work with the POWs that could clearly reveal her strong anti-Japanese and pro-American attitude, the essential ingredient for evaluating the intention in her activities.

For the reason that the defendant had to defend herself and prove the accusation false, the defense should be given ample opportunity to challenge the prosecution's allegations. The judge proved to have been very stingy about giving such opportunity. Moreover, courtroom observers, especially newspaper reporters, and the defense lawyers noticed that Roche started to doze off more frequently during the defense phase of the trial than in the earlier prosecution session. Was it because the judge had already made up his mind during the earlier phase of the trial?

On September 20, 1949, the closing arguments started. The chief prosecutor, U.S. Attorney Frank J. Hennessey, who, like DeWolfe, had earlier doubted Iva's culpability for treason, made his two-hour presentation. He outlined three points as the basis of the government's case:

> First, there is no validity to defendant's claim that she should be exempt from trial by the basis of her Portuguese citizenship acquired through marriage. Six of the eight overt acts of treason charged against her occurred before her marriage on April 19, 1945.
>
> Second, she was neither ordered, threatened, or coerced to broadcast over Radio Tokyo on the "Zero Hour" program beamed at American troops fighting in the South Pacific.
>
> And third, she did not conspire with other prisoners of war to sabotage the defeatist propaganda aims of the broadcasts.

Hennessey was simply bluffing in his speech in order to impress or at least confuse the jury. The problem of duress, for example, was a point of controversy between the prosecution and the defense as the result of Roche's ruling rejecting some defense depositions. The crucial point that could never have been brought out in the trial was the fact that she could not back down or get out of broadcasting once she had gone in. On the third point, Iva did indeed participate in the sabotage of the Japanese propaganda broadcasts, and Hennessey was apparently ignoring the indispensable testimony of Cousens just after he himself had been heard in open court.

Olshausen delivered a forceful summation on Iva's behalf, charging that the government had been interested not in developing the facts but in only obtaining a conviction. "This case isn't a case of treason at all," he continued. "It's a story of intrigue, the kind you see in the movies but seldom in real life."

Olshausen concluded his summary with an appeal for acquittal and a charge of attempted bribery. He told the jury that Harry T. Brundidge was the man who was responsible for the case being reopened, and he argued that the eight alleged overt acts were "clearly pieces of an entertainment program." As for the two key prosecution witnesses, Mitsushio and Oki, Olshausen charged: "They knew the story they were telling was not true. . . . The witnesses were perjuring themselves to bring a conviction in against this defendant, which they knew would be unjustified. . . . They were in the position of falling over themselves to please occupation authorities. . . . They were just going out of their way like a lot of dogs to please their masters."

Olshausen also challenged the testimony of prosecution witnesses from the defendant's audience in the Pacific. He noted that none of the "Zero Hour" program scripts produced by the prosecution, including several recorded by the Federal Communications Commission monitoring stations, contained any treasonous material.

Olshausen argued further that time differentials in the Pacific and the Far East demonstrate that the prosecution's witnesses were all mistaken, confusing the "Zero Hour" program with some other programs emanating from Radio Tokyo. The witnesses, Olshausen insisted, "don't remember clearly in their own minds what they heard by radio and what they heard by rumor."

In American criminal law, the prosecution, which has the burden of proof beyond a reasonable doubt, has the right to make the final remarks. It was Tom DeWolfe who made the government's final statement. He attacked the defense position that Iva went on the air under duress. In quite a contrast to his earlier, sympathetic portrayal of Iva's life in Tokyo, DeWolfe viciously assaulted the conduct of Iva, calling her,

> a smart plumber and cleaver . . . a woman quite ambitious to better herself, even though it be by working for the land of the enemy . . . a betrayer of her native land and a betrayer of her government in time of need, . . . a female Nipponese turncoat and a female Benedict Arnold. The defendant says she was one of our little soldiers—our little Nell—working behind the enemy lines. . . . This is, to the government, a very odious comparison, when you think of our young men and women who were risking their lives fighting the government which paid her, the woman they knew as Tokyo Rose. . . . [The trial] should serve as a warning to others that they cannot in an hour of great peril . . . adhere to the enemy with impunity.

Once again, like his colleague before him, Hennessey, DeWolfe openly rejected or ignored all the evidence presented in the trial, which the jury also heard.

Now, the case was finally to go to the jury.

When it opened on July 5, in San Francisco, where a long history of anti-Japanese sentiment prevailed, the trial started out in the strong anti-Japanese mode. An all-white jury was selected, and Caucasian and non-white witnesses were segregated into separate waiting rooms. But by the time the trial was ending, newspaper reporters noted that courtroom spectators were nearly unanimously sympathetic to the defendant. The straw vote of the press corps, for example, was 9 to 1 for acquittal on all counts. It was the persuasiveness of the defendant's case that brought about this significant transformation.

The Verdict and the Sentence

*This is an important case. The trial has been long and expensive to both the
prosecution and the defense. If you should fail to agree on a verdict, the case is
left open and undecided. Like all cases it must be disposed of some time. . . .
Any further jury must be selected in the same manner and from the same source as
you have been chosen; so, there appears no reason to believe that the case would ever be
submitted to twelve men and women more intelligent, more impartial, or more competent to
decide it, or that more or clearer evidence could be produced on behalf of either side.*

JUDGE MICHAEL J. ROCHE *to the deadlocked jury in the evening of the second day of
deliberation, Tuesday, September 27, 1949*

On September 26, 1949, Judge Roche instructed the jurors regarding the
overt acts of treason by Iva Toguri. He read fifty pages of instructions for
the crime of treason, which had been stated in the Constitution in only
four lines. His instructions proved to have been very misleading to everybody in the courtroom, especially to the jury.

When he was a little over halfway through, on the topic of food, the
judge injected a little story. In his effort to distinguish intent from motive,
however, he gave a puzzling example, confusing the jurors:

The element of intent is an essential element of every crime . . . intent
and motive should never be confused. . . . Good motive is never a defense where the act done is a crime. If a person does intentionally an
act which the law denounces as a crime, motive is immaterial.

Let me illustrate. I belong to a benevolent society — one that feeds
the poor. The organization is badly in need of an automobile to make
deliveries of food. This circumstance induces, moves me to steal an
automobile from my neighbor. My motive is a laudable one, but the
intent is an entirely different matter. I intend to steal, commit larceny,
and it is no defense at all to a charge of larceny that my motive was
praiseworthy.

The defense objected, insisting that "the theoretical crime in the story did not fit the case on trial" and that "the use of food in the story made it seem as if it applied directly to the situation in which the defendant had aided prisoners at Radio Tokyo and Bunka Camp." The objection was, however, overruled. To elaborate the defense protest a little further, it must be pointed out that "to feed the poor" and "to steal an automobile," though they may be the cause and effect in Roche's example, are not inherently related to each other. Iva's broadcasts, directed by the POWs on one hand, and her aiding the POWs, on the other, had the basic common denominator, Iva's pro-American and anti-Japanese sentiment, which was not a motive of one for another but the essential ingredient for both of her actions. This strong position of hers was the essential element that would clearly have challenged the notion of intent to betray her country. She helped the POWs as much as she could and fully participated in the broadcasts because she knew they had been directed and sabotaged by her trusted prisoners. Simply stated, Iva was too anti-Japanese an American to have intent to commit a treasonous act. The judge's erroneous distinction between motive and intent in an irrelevant and hypothetical situation was unfortunate because it seems to have misinformed and frustrated the jury. This instruction and his refusal to permit the defense to elaborate on the relationship between the POWs and Iva would surely constitute clear judicial misconduct, based upon his ignorance, lack of proper legal reasoning, prejudice, and intentional bias.

The next point the judge explained in his instructions was rather obvious. "Adherence to the enemy," Roche said, "may consist in nothing more than a disloyal state of mind and heart—an intent to betray one's country." "But," he continued, "adherence to the enemy in thought, in intellectual or emotional sympathy, without more, does not constitute the crime of treason. The crime is not complete unless one or more acts—overt acts of treason—be committed."

Then Roche urged the jury to give full consideration to the testimony of the ex-GI witnesses, the statements given to the FBI, and other evidence, especially to the testimony of Oki and Mitsushio, who alleged to have seen Iva commit the overt acts. This section of the instructions is highly questionable. The judge asked the jury to consider fully the testimony of ex-GI witnesses, who testified to the effect of the broadcasts, not fully identifying whether Iva actually made them. Moreover, the effect of the broadcasts should not be a factor in assessing culpability for treason. Roche also urged the jury to pay special attention to the testimony of Oki and Mitsushio, whom Roche himself, ironically, had once thought unreliable and asked Hennessey "where in the world he got witnesses like these two."

The reliability of Oki and Mitsushio had already been challenged in court, and the attentive jurors must have noted it then. One of the defense attorneys, Olshausen, too, clearly pointed out the flimsy value of their testimony in his summation. Despite all this, Judge Roche urged the jurors to pay attention "especially to the testimony of Oki and Mitsushio." This intentional misleading of the jury on the part of the judge would definitely constitute another instance of judicial misconduct.

Roche's other contradiction soon became obvious. Just after he had stated that the jury should give full consideration to the testimony of the ex-GI witnesses, he contradicted himself, stating that actions of giving aid and comfort to the enemy were distinct from the effects of these actions. "It is not necessary that one single soldier, sailor, or marine be affected in any manner whatsoever by enemy propaganda or by anything said or done by the defendant to establish treason. . . . It is immaterial that the enemy mission as a whole, which the defendant assisted, if she did assist, did not achieve its purpose."

What Roche was saying here, just after he had urged the jury to pay attention to the GI testimony, is that it made no difference whether the GIs had enjoyed Iva's broadcasts or whether they had been made homesick by them. The effect of the broadcasts was not at issue. Why, then, did the judge all along permit ex-GIs, especially Marshall Hoot, to give testimony in court for the prosecution regarding the effect of the broadcasts and also allow himself to be deeply affected by it? This conduct constituted not only the misguiding of the jury but the subornation of the office and duty.

A little later in the instruction, Roche went on to explain the problem of duress or coercion. Without even trying to understand the oppressive Japanese society under military rule and Iva's working conditions at NHK under Tsuneishi and without allowing testimony and depositions that would surely have proven the oppressive circumstances and conditions surrounding the POWs and Iva, which could have been at least considered as extenuating circumstances, Judge Roche instructed the jury with the textbook account and stated simply what was not sufficient to justify the excuse of coercion or duress:

In order to excuse a criminal act on the ground of coercion, compulsion, or necessity, one must have acted under the apprehension of immediate bodily harm. Fear of injury to one's property or of remote bodily harm do not excuse an offense. . . . The fact that the defendant may have been required to report to the Japanese police concerning her activities is not sufficient. Nor is it sufficient that she was under surveillance of the *kempei-tai*. If you find that she, in fact, was under such surveillance, it is not sufficient that the defendant thought that she might be sent to a concentration or interment camp or that she might be deprived of her food-ration card. Neither is it sufficient that threats were made to other persons and that she knew of such threats if you find, in fact, such threats were made to her knowledge.

Judge Roche had no capacity nor even tried to understand duress during the wartime Japan controlled by the military. How could the judge boldly state that threats made to others were not sufficient to constitute duress to Iva without fully examining in court the specific relations between the POWs and Iva, which he had refused to do?

At the press table on the afternoon of September 26, as the jury began its deliberation, the reporters voted, 9 to 1, for acquittal. "My overriding conviction," said Francis O'Gara of the *Examiner*, the sole exception in the straw vote, "is that, legalistically, she committed the crime of treason, but actually was not a traitor in the true sense. What she really was doing was playing both sides — trying to work for Japan and the United States at the same time."

Iva was sitting "slumped in her chair," Masayo Duus notes, "looking as shocked as if she had been struck in the face" when Judge Roche finished reading his instructions. The judge rejected all the major arguments of the defense, including the nature of Iva's relations with the POWs in sabotaging the Japanese broadcasts and the coercion and threat under which Iva claimed to have acted. "She sat motionless, her back hunched, her lips closed tightly, her fingers clinched," and as the court bailiff, Herbert Cole, came to tell her that reporters were waiting outside to take some pictures, Duus's observation was moving, "Iva started to rise from her chair, sat back, tried again, and shook her head at Cole." It was only five minutes later that she finally "set her jaw and stood up" and walked out of the courtroom supported by Cole into the reporters' flashlights. Iva then went downstairs to the bailiff's office to wait for the verdict.

In the meantime, just before noon on September 26, 1949, the sixtieth day of the trial, the jury, six men and six women, retired to the jury room to deliberate. Their job was to reduce the massive amount of testimony (a million words in 125 documents and the fifty-page court's instruction) into a simple verdict of "guilty" or "not guilty." The deliberation was private, and they were allowed to speak only among themselves. When they went to their hotel rooms, where telephones had been disconnected, radios removed, and newspapers not allowed, they were totally incommunicado; they could contact their families only in the marshal's office.

John Mann, "the small, neat, soft-spoken" certified public accountant, was elected as foreman. At the first voting, the jurors split, 6 for conviction, 6 for acquittal. As for the overt acts, there had been "a general opinion that they had been committed," Mann recalled, "but the question boiled down to the sixth essential element of treason—that she must have had intent to betray the United States." In the jury room, two jurors strong for conviction, a man and a woman, who refused to let their emotions sway them, insisted that all jurors "rule their emotion out," based upon the judge's instruction that "the law does not permit jurors to be governed by sympathy, prejudice, or pubic opinion." What they were doing was, in a sense, forcing the rest of the jury to take a hard line against Iva. Accordingly, they were all forced to agree formally to rule "their emotion" out, leading, significantly, to "the scant margin" by which Iva eventually lost acquittal on treason charges.

The jurors then eliminated from their consideration all overt acts except five and six, which alleged that the defendant wrote a script and broadcast about "loss of ships." As the deliberation dragged on, and the chance of acquittal became less likely, Iva "wept intermittently . . . stared silently at the floor or moved restlessly to the powder room." The jury finally gave up for the night at 11:40 p.m.

The next morning, Tuesday, September 27, at 9:30, John Mann again polled the jury. The vote was 9 to 3 for conviction. The argument was concentrated on those statements about "loss of ships." Mann sent a note to Judge Roche, asking for the transcripts of the testimony of Lee, Oki, and Mitsushio regarding Overt Acts 5 and 6. The requested materials were sent, but the jury was back in the courtroom, requesting the entire testimony of the defendant. The jury soon afterward asked for another document, Exhibit 15 (Lee's news notes). The defendant, who had to be present in the courtroom whenever the jury was in, came to realize where

{ *Chapter 9* }

the deliberations were centered, on Overt Act 6, "That on a day during October, 1944 ... said defendant ... did speak into a microphone concerning the loss of ships."

That evening there was a heated debate in the jury room. The two jurors who had demanded to leave emotion out were "hotter than pistols for conviction" and pressured the three holdouts (John Mann, Earl Duckett, a San Francisco plasterer, and Flora Covell, a dentist's wife) to give in. A majority leader said, "We've got to get the thing over with." After thoroughly examining the testimony of Lee and others, the minority came to the conclusion that there was a "reasonable doubt" of guilt. "How would you like to be sitting out there," a majority spokesman responded emotionally, "ten thousand miles away from home, with her telling you all your ships are sunk?" (The jurors had just decided to leave the "emotion" out, and, moreover, the jurors had not only been told not to consider the effect of the announcement but witnessed the highly questionable testimony of Oki and Mitsushio.)

By late evening on Tuesday, with the same 9 to 3 deadlock, John Mann sent another note to the court, informing it that the jury could not reach unanimity. Defense hopes suddenly rose; a hung jury would be a victory for the defense, and the government would not pay for another Tokyo Rose trial. "The jurors have reported," Judge Roche announced, "that they are unable to reach a unanimous verdict." He then started to pressure the jury:

> This is an important case. The trial has been long and expensive for both the prosecution and the defense. If you should fail to agree on a verdict, the case is left open and undecided. Like all cases it must be disposed of sometime.

As the jurors grasped that they were not going to be allowed to quit with a hung jury, the judge continued:

> There appears no reason to believe that another trial would not be equally long and expensive to both sides, nor does there appear any reason to believe that the case could be again tried better or more exhaustively than it has been tried on each side. Any further jury must be selected in the same manner and from the same source as you have been chosen; so, there appears no reason to believe that a case could ever be submitted to twelve men and women more intelligent, more

impartial, or more competent to decide it, or that more or clearer evidence be produced on behalf of either side.

Though Roche did not realize it, the defense by then should have been convinced that a new trial presided over by a judge, "more intelligent, more impartial, and more competent," to borrow Roche's own words, would have made a big difference. On a consoling note, Judge Roche then suggested:

You may conduct your deliberations as you choose, but I suggest to you now, retire for the night and reconvene tomorrow morning and carefully reexamine and reconsider all of the evidence bearing upon the questions before you. You may be as leisurely in your deliberations as the occasion shall require, and you shall take all the time which you may feel is necessary.

Roche told the jurors that the bailiff had been instructed to take them to their meals at any time they wished and at their pleasure, and to take them to their hotel at their own request at any time they wished and whenever they were prepared and ready to go. The judge then urged the jurors to retire for the night and continue their deliberations in the morning "in any manner that you determine by your own good and conscientious judgment as reasonable men and women." Why did the judge have to tell the jury such obvious things? To show the jury that he was a considerate, kind, understanding, and benevolent person? It seems clear that the judge had been determined to push the jury to return a verdict; the judge, who might have been fairly certain by then that most of the jurors favored conviction, did not have a hung jury.

On the morning of Wednesday, September 28, the third day of deliberations, John Mann began to feel the pressure from the majority's attack on the three holdouts. He was holding his ground, mainly upon two points. One is "the presumption of innocence," which is "sufficient to acquit a defendant, unless the presumption is outweighed by evidence . . . beyond a reasonable doubt of the defendant's guilt," based not only upon "the evidence produced" but upon "a lack of evidence." The other is intent to "betray the United States," to "adhere to the enemy for the purpose of giving aid and comfort to the enemy," and to "give aid and comfort to the enemy." John Mann came to be convinced that the prosecution's case failed on both these counts.

{ *Chapter 9* }

A majority spokesman, basing his argument on the quotation from the judge's instructions that "intent may be inferred . . . and there need only be proved by the testimony of one witness," insisted that there were "five of them." (All of them, however, had already been proven in court either as defective or questionable.)

The jury sent for another thousand pages of testimony by Cousens and Ince and the depositions of Ruth Hayakawa, George Ozasa, and Lily Gihevenian. At 5:20 p.m., the jury came back to the courtroom for another question. Although the judge suggested they go to the hotel to retire until the morning, the jurors went back to the jury room to deliberate, without progress, until 8:00 p.m., when they decided to quit.

On the fourth day, September 29, the jury still maintained the 9 for conviction (4 were vocal) and 3 for acquittal (none were vocal). The arguments still boiled down to the defendant's intention and to how many witnesses heard the defendant broadcast about a loss of ships, but nothing could change the 9 to 3 lineup. In the early evening, John Mann sent a note to the judge, which dealt with his erroneous instruction on intent:

> The jury is at a temporary impasse relative to the full interpretation of intent and motive. On page 41 of your instruction, it reads " . . . the crime of treason consists of two elements: adherence to the enemy; and rendering him aid and comfort . . ."
>
> On pages 45 and 46 [third paragraph], "good motive is never a defense where the act done is a crime. If a person does intentionally an act which the law denounces as a crime, motive is immaterial."
>
> Overt acts of an apparent incriminating nature, when judged in the light of related events, may turn out to be acts which were not of aid and comfort to the enemy.

"What," asked John Mann, "is meant by related events?"

The judge addressed the jury and gave his answer, which was, however, not really an answer:

> In relation to your request for instructions, the Court desires to instruct you further in this regard; you are cautioned not to select a single instruction or portion of an instruction alone, but to consider all of the instructions in determining any issue in this case. It is the duty of the jury to give uniform consideration to all of the instructions herein given, to consider the whole and every part of them together, and to accept such instructions as a correct statement of the law involved.

The judge obviously avoided giving a specific answer. How can one understand "the whole and every part of them" without fully understanding each individually? John Mann certainly felt rebuffed and discouraged. He sought clarification of the instruction, and Roche could not or refused to answer! "It is time to go to dinner," the judge said, telling the jurors that they afterward "may come back here or retire to the hotel for the evening."

As the jury filed out and retired to the jury room, the jurors did not want to eat or talk together anymore. John Mann felt that the judge's refusal to clarify instructions was a reprimand to him and a denial of the case for acquittal. Reluctantly, the three holdouts were "cajoled to capitulate to the majority decision," based upon Overt Act 6, that on a day in October 1944, Iva Toguri had broadcast something about "the loss of ships."

The jury returned to the courtroom with the verdict, only 33 minutes after they had left. It was 78 hours and 20 minutes after they received the case. Jury foreman Mann, who couldn't look at the defendant but "saw her in his mind," recalled later, "She was such an inoffensive little thing, sitting there—working against herself with her impassive expression."

As the court clerk pronounced the word, "Guilty," a disappointed "oh" was heard among the audience. The jury convicted Iva upon Overt Act 6 alone, to the effect: "That on a day during October, 1944, the exact date being to the Grand Jurors unknown, said defendant, at Tokyo, Japan in the office of the Broadcasting Corporation of Japan, did speak into a microphone concerning the loss of ships."

How could anyone be convicted of a serious crime like treason for such a vague, imprecise charge, based upon the perjured testimony of Hiromu Yagi before the grand jury? Although Iva broadcast for little more than a year, supplying a twenty-minute entertainment segment on an hour-long program, from November 13, 1943, to August 13, 1945, her brief, alleged broadcast shortly after the Battle of Leyte Gulf for the American fighting men, who were upbeat because of their overwhelming victories, even though she did actually announce it, was a very trivial matter, indeed. She was convicted for reading over the air, "Orphans of the Pacific. You really are orphans now. How will you get home, now that all your ships are sunk?" How could American troops have been demoralized by such words just after their resounding victory? It must, surely, have sounded "like hilarious comedy." She was declared guilty without being proven "beyond a reasonable doubt" of announcing a single sentence of which there is no script or recorded evidence that she ever spoke, which Iva herself vehemently denied, and which may not have been broadcast from Radio Tokyo at all. It was a "forced" verdict of a jury that could not reach unanimity, under pressure from the judge.

Slumping into her seat, Iva was just staring at her hands. Alternate juror Aileen McNamara kept repeating, "How could they possibly do it?" Wayne Collins said in disbelief that the verdict was "guilty without proof." Tom DeWolfe, who had been forced to take on the case against his own convictions, nevertheless expressed his satisfaction, stating that "the United Sates feels that the verdict was a just one and one which was rendered after patient and persevering deliberation."

When Stan Delaplane asked him, "Did you at anytime consider her not guilty?" John Mann answered, "If it had been possible under the judge's instructions, we would have done it." "It is an interesting point that most of the regular spectators who sat through 13 long weeks," Delaplane remarked, "had concluded the girl was not guilty." The reaction of the newspapers was very critical. Katherine Pinkham of AP was appalled and said, "Americans believe strongly in fair play, and that sense has been violated here." Another said, "they have convicted her on a legend," and still another said, "she did just about what you could expect of a loyal and reasonable person." "The judge's instructions (or rather his lack of clarification at the end)," Delaplane rightly accessed the situation, "swung them over. The acquittal forces had banked on a clarification that would enable them to hold out—and make it a hung jury." Twenty-seven years later, Mann said to the *San Francisco Chronicle* interviewer, "I should have had a little more guts and stuck with my acquittal vote."

The sentencing took place a week later on October 6, 1949. Judge Roche, who had given the terribly biased instructions to the jury that made acquittal difficult, imposed a rather stiff penalty. The punishment for treason could range from death to a minimum of five years imprisonment and a fine of no less than $10,000 at the option of the court. What Iva got was not the minimal sentence for the crime; the judge sentenced Iva to ten years' imprisonment in the Federal Reformatory for Women, Alderson, West Virginia, and a $10,000 fine. Loss of American citizenship was automatic according to law. At thirty-three, Iva thus lost the citizenship she had held onto so firmly throughout the past eight years.

All the members of the jury were shocked by Roche's "savage sentence," the foreman John Mann later stated, and the "three holdouts," including himself, "instantly regretted our compromise." Although they had the power of returning the verdict of "guilty" or "not guilty" but had nothing to say about the punishment, the foreman and the rest of the jurors were expecting a much lighter penalty. Since Iva had already served in Japan and in San Francisco for about two years altogether, the jurors were tacitly speculating that even if she were found guilty and sentenced to the minimum five years, she would just serve her remaining three years in prison, together with a possible minimum $5,000 fine. Out of all their expectations, the severity of the sentence surprised most of the jurors, who deplored their decision for a long time.

The jail matrons, the bailiff, the court reporters, and other federal workers connected with Iva's case one way or another expressed their sympathy toward Iva and were disappointed about the verdict and punishment. Iva's father, Jun, attended his daughter with perfect faith. He met the ship that brought her to San Francisco to face treason charges, brought food, sat through the trial, was to frequently visit her at the Alderson prison, and even paid her fine by a provision in his will. He was a proud American citizen whose sickly wife died at an assembly center on the way to an American concentration camp in 1942.

In the meantime, the defense made motions for a mistrial, for arrest of judgment, for clemency, and for bail pending appeal, but they were all denied by Judge Roche. After the judge denied bail for Iva, his decision was appealed to the U.S. Court of Appeals for the Ninth Circuit, which affirmed the decision below and held Iva nonbailable. The Supreme Court justice William Douglas, sitting in the U.S. Court of Appeals for the Ninth Circuit, reversed the decision and granted Iva bail for $50,000 pending appeal. "The question of the guilt or innocence of an appellant is not an issue on application for bail," Justice Douglas asserted. "It has long been a principle of Federal law that bail after conviction and pending appeal is a remedy normally available to a prisoner." "The existence of power to grant bail," he further insisted, "is, indeed, essential for the protection of the right to appeal. Otherwise a short sentence might be served before the appellate court could set aside the judgment of conviction for infirmities in the trial. An effective right to appeal would then be lost." Douglas then cited the precedent:

The matter has best been summarized by Mr. Justice Butler sitting as Circuit Justice for the Seventh Circuit in *United States v. Motlow*, 10 F.

(2d) 657, 662. He wrote, "Abhorrence, however great, of persistent and menacing crime will not excuse transgression in the courts of the legal rights of the worst offenders. The granting or withholding of bail is not a matter of mere grace or favor. If these writs of error were taken merely for delay, bail should be refused; but, if taken in good faith, on grounds not frivolous but fairly debatable, in view of the decisions of the Supreme Court, then petitioners should be admitted to bail." That test has been incorporated in Rule 46 (a) (2) of the Federal Rules of Criminal Procedure.

Iva, however, was not able to raise $50,000 for bail.

Upon Roche's sentencing, Wayne Collins, speaking for his client, said that "her own conscience is clear. She is sorry because she wishes she could say the Government's witnesses' consciences were also clear." Neither Collins nor Iva had the ability to question the consciences of the prosecutors, the judge, and others who had determined Iva's fate.

Iva took the long train ride to Alderson, West Virginia, high up in the heart of the Appalachian Mountains, where she had never been before. "I took her off the boat, and my wife and I took her to Alderson Prison," said Bailiff Herbert Cole, who had escorted Iva, as he recalled the trip in an interview with Rex Gunn in December 1958. The Federal Reformatory for Women at Alderson was where Iva's German "counterpart," Mildred (Axis Sally) Gillars, had already been serving her time for some seven months. Gillars was convicted and sentenced to ten to thirty years' imprisonment and a $10,000 fine for broadcasting Nazi propaganda over Radio Berlin and with "intent to adhere to the enemy," which had been clearly proven in court. In stark contrast, Iva's broadcast and intent had never been decisively proven.

"I will do the ten years," she said to Bailiff Cole on the way to Alderson, "and I will sleep every night of it, but I don't think the same will be true for Mitsushio and Oki." The arrival of Tokyo Rose brought out new excitement. The matrons, according to Rex Gunn, had expected Iva to appear "all decked out in mink and pearls," as Axis Sally had been several months earlier, but they were surprised to see her in her old plaid two-piece suit. Alderson was a pleasant surprise for Iva. It was a "small and homey" place situated in the wilderness, way up in the mountains, with an inmate population between 300 and 500 but very few "hardened" criminals. Most of the inmates were moonshiners from the Carolinas and the Smokey Mountains of Tennessee, incarcerated for violating federal liquor tax laws. "There was no criminal element about her—nothing at all.... It really hurt when we had to leave her back there," Bailiff Cole later remembered of the time when he and his wife said good-bye to Iva at the Alderson prison: "It was like leaving one of our own."

CHAPTER 10

Appeals, Threat of Deportation, and Pardon

Great cases, like hard cases, make bad law. For great cases are called great, not by reason of their real importance in shaping the law of the future, but because of some accident of immediate overwhelming interest which appeals to the feelings and distorts the judgment. These immediate interests exercise a kind of hydraulic pressure which makes what previously was clear seem doubtful and before which even well settled principles of law will bend.

JUSTICE OLIVER WENDELL HOLMES, JR., *dissenting opinion in* Northern Securities Co. v. U.S., *193 U.S. 197, 420–421, quoted in George G. Olshausen, "D'Aquino v. United States, the So-Called 'Tokyo Rose' Case," 15* Lawyers Guild Review, *6–10 (Spring 1955)*

As soon as the trial ended, the "fiery" defense attorney, Wayne M. Collins, started to appeal the district court decision. He continued his tireless fight to reverse the conviction of Iva until his death in 1974, on an airplane on his way home from a trip to Hong Kong.

All the appeals Collins and his cocounsels instituted repeatedly during 1951, 1952, and 1953 to the U.S. Court of Appeals, Ninth Circuit, and to the Supreme Court of the United States had been turned down. The district court's judgment of conviction and sentence were appealed for the first time in 1950. The appeal was based upon more than twenty major contentions that largely fall into two categories: calls for a dismissal of the judgment of the district court, and charges of alleged errors, which would require a new trial.

They included, to name some of the most important issues, unlawful detention; denial of speedy trial; destruction of evidence, scripts, and records; the "posse comitatus" act; questions relating to the sufficiency of the evidence; questions relating to duress; denial of legal counsel; misconduct of prosecutors; refusal to permit defense offers of proof, especially to produce defendant's witnesses from Japan; perjured testimony before the grand jury; the Geneva Convention; and prejudicial instructions by the judge.

On October 10, 1951, the U.S. Court of Appeals for the Ninth Circuit, to which the case had been appealed, turned down the appeal and affirmed the judgment below. The Circuit judges, William Healy, Homer T. Bone, and Walter L. Pope, are the panel that previously held Iva nonbailable and had been reversed by Supreme Court Justice William Douglas sitting on the Court of Appeals for the Ninth Circuit.

Upon receiving the ruling that the Circuit judges had found no prejudicial error in the record and had affirmed the original judgment, Iva's attorneys on November 8, 1951, filed with the same court a petition for rehearing, but it was denied on December 17. Responding to the extensive opinion written by Circuit Judge Pope, rejecting Iva's appeal, the defense lawyers prepared detailed statements and petitioned the Supreme Court that a writ of certiorari be issued to review a judgment entered against her on October 10, 1951, and a denial of rehearing on December 17.

The attorneys for Iva as the petitioner contended that the Court of Appeals admitted at least twelve errors in the trial court, but excused them as simply nonprejudicial. The cumulative effect was not even considered. This isolated treatment, Iva's lawyers continued, particularly obscured the concentration of errors on Overt Act 6, upon which Iva was convicted. Collins and his colleagues followed the court's subject order examining the prosecutor's misconduct on Overt Act 6, the categorical instruction, and the failure to instruct the jury on the cumulative effect of duress. (The government witnesses, especially Mitsushio, said Overt Act 6 was broadcast in response to their direct order.) Failure under such circumstances to consider the cumulative effect of admitted errors on the pivotal issues, her attorneys insisted in their petition for certiorari, "so far departs from the accepted and usual course of judicial proceedings as to call for an exercise of this court's power of supervision."

The attorneys for Iva also argued that the conviction of Iva violated the constitutionally guaranteed equal protection. They pointed out that Mitsushio, Oki, and others who had been naturalized from American to Japanese citizenship after the outbreak of the war worked at Radio Tokyo in executive positions and supervised Iva. Those who gave aid and comfort to Japan "after publicly announcing that they spurned the United States for good" are exonerated, while those accused of doing the same thing without formal and permanent renunciation are punished for treason. The petitioner's attorneys contended that "this reverses all concepts of justice; it is an irrational classification. As such it denied equal protection which is guaranteed by the due process clause of the Fifth Amendment."

John J. Hada, who extensively studied Iva's appeals, analyzed over a dozen major contentions in the petition for certiorari. An examination of just a few of the most serious contentions of the petitioner will suffice to see some fundamental problems inherent in this trial.

On the issue of duress, Iva testified in court that she had been ordered to broadcast under threat, after she had been told "You know what the consequences [of disobedience] are. I don't have to tell you that." Most of the evidence introduced to show what these "consequences" were, however, was rejected.

The Court of Appeals tried to define the standard of duress, which would operate as a defense to a criminal charge in an ordinary, peaceful, and orderly society, where the defendant claims that some private criminal coerced him to do the act charged. In such cases, the defendant could have invoked the protection of the police or other authorities. In times of war or rebellion, where a person, caught in hostile territory, is ordered to act against the country to which he owes allegiance (like Iva in wartime Japan), the defendant cannot get the protection of the government of his own country.

The Court of Appeals refused to distinguish these two classes of cases and doggedly applied the rule of private lawlessness that duress can be a defense only where there is a threat of immediate death or serious bodily injury. The law regarding individuals stranded in an area of rebellion or war had a long tradition in the English common law originating in the Stuart Rebellion of 1745. Duress will constitute a defense, the common law principle concluded, if "upon the whole he may fairly be presumed to have continued amongst them [the rebels] against his will, though not constantly under an actual force or fear of immediate death." The Court of Appeals rejected this argument for Iva, due to the fact that: "However appropriate such quoted language might be in the case of a person impressed into military or naval service of the enemy, we think that under the circumstances here there was no occasion for departing from the ordinary rules applicable to the defense of duress or coercion."

The Court of Appeals did not even attempt to clearly distinguish the difference in treatment, if any, between soldiers and civilians under the strict Japanese militarism. Was the court advocating the rule that treated civilians more severely than soldiers?

The Geneva Convention, which had been ratified by the United States and became part of the Statutes at Large, was another of the defense's issues of contention. The convention accorded "a detaining power"—the right to utilize "the services of prisoners of war"(Article 27) except that "labor furnished by prisoners of war shall have no direct relations with war operations"(Article 31). All other work may thus legally be demanded even though it may indirectly aid the war effort of the detaining power. Although the Japanese diplomats signed the convention, Japan did not ratify it. The United States and Japan, however, exchanged notes, making the convention applicable to prisoners of war and interned civilians, but the legal effect of the notes was later contested, as Yuma Totani argues, at the war crimes trials in Tokyo.

The Court of Appeals maintained that none of these provisions of the convention covered Iva, who had been an uninterned civilian. "The Geneva Convention," the court went on, "did not change the law of treason, and, therefore, if a prisoner performs the acts authorized by the Convention with the intent of adhering to the enemy, he is guilty of treason," and the court cited *Haupt v. U.S.* and *Cramer v. U.S.* as authorities. The petitioner's lawyers, however, challenged the court for misconstruing both *Haupt* and *Cramer* in holding that the Geneva Convention was not to be read in *pari material* (on the same subject) with the treason statute.

In *Haupt*, it was held that the overt acts were ambiguous, and the jury had to decide whether they were a help to the accused's son, Herbert Haupt, a Nazi saboteur, or to the enemy. In *Cramer*, on the other hand, it was held, as the petitioner's attorneys had precisely argued, that if the overt act is indisputably legal, intent cannot turn it into treason. The same result follows in the case of an overt act legalized by the Geneva Convention. Iva's attorneys contended that she, wholly in the power of the Japanese and subject to internment at any time, must have the benefit of the Geneva Convention to the same extent as citizens whom the Japanese saw fit to intern. This was, indeed, a crucial issue, but the Supreme Court, in retrospect, denied certiorari and decided not to examine the question of the extent to which Iva's case follows *Haupt* and *Cramer*.

There were several issues surrounding Iva as a suspect for treason committed abroad. She was charged with violation of a domestic statute of the United States, not with the breach of any law or ordinance for the government of occupied Japan. Iva's yearlong incarceration in Japan that denied her a speedy trial; her travel from Japan to San Francisco under army guard for the purpose of laying venue, not jurisdiction; illegal use of the army as *posse comitatus*, and the statement taken from Iva during her unreasonably long detention all caused confusion in the administration of extraterritorial laws and statutes.

Iva's lawyers pointed out that she was imprisoned on suspicion of treason for a year and was held incommunicado for the first two months. Afterward, her husband could see her once a month for twenty minutes at a time. The first six months of her confinement were done by the military, and the next six by the military on behalf of the Department of Justice. This imprisonment resulted in two legal issues: whether the defendant had been given a speedy trial and whether the statement (Exhibit 24), taken at the end of six months of army confinement, was admissible into evidence.

The defense contended that this yearlong incarceration amounted to denial of a speedy trial and blocked subsequent prosecution on the same facts, citing *U.S. v. Fox* (1880), which expressed the general principle, "The government of U.S. cannot cast a man into prison and then fold its arms and refuse to prosecute."

The Court of Appeals held that the year's imprisonment in Japan had no legal effect whatsoever. Specifically it ruled that the Sixth Amendment did not protect a defendant in Japan and that in any event it applies only after the filing of a formal complaint. Responding to Iva's petition for rehearing, the court, in a supplemental opinion denying the rehearing, drastically changed its mind and said that this was not what it had meant, but, "Counsel assumed that our decision is based upon a determination that, when appellant was in detention in Japan, she had no rights under the Constitution. We did not and do not so hold. On the contrary, we assumed that she was at all times entitled to such rights."

The court tried to justify its position by stating that what it had "attempted to say is that the facts here do not disclose a denial of the rights to a speedy trial granted by the Sixth Amendment" and continued:

What appellant argues is that she must be immune to this prosecution because at some former time she was detained for a period, when no prosecution was proceeding. First, the detention was by the military. Second, whatever may be her situation, where the decision so immediately precedes the attempted prosecution as fairly to be deemed a part thereof, here the detention had long since terminated.

We think that the detention by the military authorities, which so long preceded the initiation of the present prosecution, is simply not relevant to the question of a speedy trial.

Reacting to the farfetched, inexcusable, and unconstitutional reasoning, the appellant's lawyers brushed aside this comment as superfluous, insisting that the court could not justify the government's revival of its right to proceed after doing nothing for two years. Indeed, what the court did was to simply avoid a frontal confrontation of the problem of dismissal of the case as the remedy for a violation of the speedy-trial right.

Another effect of a lengthy detention is the legality of a statement taken under such circumstances. The defense objected, under *Upshaw v. U.S.* (1945), to the admissibility of Exhibit 24, a statement taken from Iva after she had been in jail for six months in Japan. The U.S. Supreme Court in the *Upshaw* case holds that a statement taken from the defendant after an unreasonably long preliminary detention is inadmissible in the federal courts. Confinement originally lawful would become unlawful if continued unjustifiably without the defendant brought before a magistrate. Even lead prosecutor Tom DeWolfe earlier conformed to this argument before he took on the case against Iva.

In its original opinion, the Court of Appeals came up with a strenuous excuse without the least understanding of postwar Japan as well as the personal character of Iva as a person. It held that the arrest had been necessary for a prophylactic purpose: "That she might be capable of fomenting disorder among the Japanese population then being subjected to the Yoke of military occupation, and of inciting discontent among the troops of the occupying powers was a sufficient basis for the military to take the precautionary measure of interning appellant."

And the court held that this "was legal and authorized under the laws of war." The Constitution and laws of the United States seemed to have had no bearing at all. Where had Judge Pope gotten such erroneous notions of postwar Japan to justify his assertion? For those Japanese who lived through the war and postwar years and those American soldiers who came to occupy Japan after the war, Japanese society was, despite the physical devastation and serious shortages of food and other daily necessities, not crumbling but was functioning smoothly, in an orderly and respectable manner.

On denial of rehearing, the Court of Appeals conceded that Iva had been arrested for past acts. It went on to say: "We think the quoted phraseology of the order does not negate the military character of the detention. The order, taken as a whole, appears to direct the exercise of one of the powers incident to military occupation. It would be presumed to be for that purpose. We think the detention cannot be characterized as an unlawful one."

Was the Court of Appeals justifying the position that if an arrest by the military is originally legal, detention without trial continues to be legal indefinitely? The fact remains that the arrest and detention of Iva were made by the American occupying forces in Japan on the assumption that she was an American citizen. At any rate, it was the length of the detention that the court should have been concerned with, not whether the detention had been lawful or unlawful.

Title 18 U.S.C. 3238 stipulates that a crime alleged to have been committed outside the United States shall be tried in the district to which the defendant was first brought. This law, therefore, deals with the matter of jurisdiction, not the matter of venue because it was not a question between districts. There had been confusion over venue and jurisdiction, but in the case of Iva, the question was simply one of jurisdiction.

Iva was brought from Japan to San Francisco by the U.S. Army as an agent for the Justice Department on the army transport under army guard, with the Justice Department reimbursing the army. The petitioner's attorneys challenged that this violated Title 10 U.S.C. 15 forbidding the army to be used as a *posse comitatus* except in Alaska and that the court below was without such jurisdiction because Iva was brought to San Francisco in an illegal and unlawful manner by the military authorities in violation of the Posse Comitatus Act of 1878. The Court of Appeals insisted that the same arguments were made unsuccessfully in *Chandler v. U.S.* and in *Gillars v. U.S.,* but Iva's attorneys insisted that the analogy was erroneous.

The destruction of evidence had been one of the serious concerns of the defense. When the Pacific War ended, the government destroyed all the recordings taken by the Hawaiian monitoring station "in the process of the routine closing of such stations." Iva's lawyers contended that all extant written and other records of her broadcasts contain not a single treasonable word by her and that it is a denial of due process to prosecute her when such scripts and records were unavailable. They argued that "it was unthinkable that U.S. officials would have destroyed the records . . . if they had contained treasonable matter." So, they reasoned, it may reasonably be inferred that there were "no treasonable materials," thus favoring Iva's position.

Although the records were destroyed by way of routine rather than from evil motives, Iva's attorneys insisted that prosecuting with knowledge that the government had made relevant evidence unavailable to Iva's attorneys was "on par with prosecuting on known perjured evidence." The Court of Appeals ruled that there was no basis for the appellant's contention and for the missing scripts and records favorable to the defendant.

On the subject of reasonable doubt, Iva's counsels maintained that under Rule of Criminal Procedure 29 (a), a defendant is entitled to a judgment of acquittal if, under any view of the record, there is a reasonable doubt upon an essential issue. The Court of Appeals said that the petitioner's contention could be sustained if it were psychologically impossible for the defendant to harbor a treasonable intent while aiding Allied prisoners. "If it were impossible," Iva's lawyers sharply contended, "there would be much more than a reasonable doubt." What the Court of Appeals was demanding would be "a demonstration of innocence," they aptly pointed out, but the defendant need only raise "a reasonable doubt." The attorneys for Iva further asserted that her helping Allied prisoners, established by both sides as a fact, raised a reasonable doubt as to whether she had an intent to betray the United States, an intent which is a necessary element of treason.

The appellant's lawyers asserted that on numerous occasions during the trial, prosecutors were guilty of such serious misconduct that the record in respect to it would require a new trial. These claims of misconduct related to alleged misstatements of the record during the argument to the jury of other witnesses. Iva's attorneys contended that Prosecutor Tom DeWolfe repeated his misstatement that Clark Lee was a witness to Overt Act 6, not Overt Act 5. They further contended that the record affirmatively showed that the jury accepted the prosecutor's misstatement that Clark Lee was a witness to Overt Act 6, which, they insisted, "goes to the core of the conviction."

They also pointed out that the Court of Appeals omitted to mention another misconduct involving Exhibit 52 (the one used as the source of affirmative facts to impeach defense witness Charles Cousens). Iva's attorneys argued that the government, moreover, mislabeled twenty-five subpoenas, directing the subjects to appear before the trial started at 9:00 a.m, instead of 10:00 am. The court held that these time mix-ups, though occurring rather systematically, were insufficient to take the issue of intentional mislabeling to the jury. Iva's lawyers also claimed that the question of Kodaira's testimony showed it was not hearsay and argued that Brundidge's attempts at subornation and bribery were the very facts in the issue and, therefore, not hearsay.

The petitioner's attorneys contended that a writ of certiorari should be granted accordingly and the judgment of conviction reversed. The Supreme Court, however, rejected appeals for review three times. On April 28, 1952, the court denied both the motion for leave to file the briefs of Milton J. Javis and others as amici curiae and the petition for certiorari (Justice Clark took no part in its consideration and decision). A month later, on May 26, 1952, Iva's petition for rehearing was also rejected (Clark did not participate in it either). Finally, a year later, on April 6, 1953, the Supreme Court (without Clark participating) denied another petition for rehearing.

In comparison, another treason trial discussed earlier needs to be mentioned here, that of John David Provoo, a former POW at Bunka Camp. In fact, most of the prosecution witnesses from Japan in Iva's trial went to New York as soon as the trial was over to be witnesses in the Provoo trial. Due to his mental illness, the trial had been delayed, and finally in February 1953, he was found guilty of four overt acts of treason and sentenced to life imprisonment and a $10,000 fine. On appeal, in contrast to Iva's case, the Court of Appeals for the Second Circuit in August 1954 overturned his conviction and sentence on two grounds: (1) the government had illegally tried him in New York instead of Maryland and (2) it had made "wrongful insinuations about his sexual preferences" before the jury.

Although the government was attempting to try him a second time, a federal judge ruled in February 1955 that Provoo could not have a fair trial so late in time and that he had been "denied the right of a speedy trial under the meaning of the Sixth Amendment." Iva, whose rights under the Sixth Amendment had been similarly violated, on the other hand, had then still been serving her term in prison. All the appeals she had filed had been denied, with the ruling that her original conviction, including denial of her right of speedy trial under the Sixth Amendment, had been proper.

One wonders why all the appeals of Iva were so persistently denied by the appellate courts, including the Supreme Court's three rejections within two years. "Great cases are called great, not by reason of their real importance in shaping the law of the future but because of some accident of immediate overwhelming interest which appeals to the feelings and distorts the judgment," Justice Oliver W. Holmes, Jr., emphatically remarked in 1903 in his dissenting opinion in one of the important Supreme Court cases. "These immediate interests," Justice Holmes went on, "exercise a kind of hydraulic pressure which makes what previously was clear seem doubtful and before which even well settled principles of law will bend." Iva's trial was, indeed, one of these cases.

George G. Olshausen, one of Iva's defense lawyers, went further and declared that public interest and opinion had determined the outcome of Iva's case. Criminal cases, Olshausen argued, could be divided into three classes. First, "the run of the mill," in which there is no public interest; second, those cases in which there is public opinion supporting each side; and third, those in which all public opinion supports the prosecution. Where public opinion is overwhelmingly in favor of the defense, on the other hand, "the prosecution usually is either not brought at all, or is handled very perfunctorily." Olshausen continued as if putting Iva's case fittingly in the third category:

> In the last class the accused has no chance. Punishment is not demanded by hysteria, but is assumed as axiomatic. A defendant is not rushed to conviction; the government can afford the luxury of slow motion and profits from the resulting illusion of fairness. Complicated process passes for due process. When, after a procedure which would bring a mistrial in any ordinary case, the victim is found guilty and sentenced for something which he may never have done, no one sees anything wrong; the "sense of injustice" is quiescent.

This analysis convincingly explains why Iva did not, or more precisely could not, have fair treatment in court. Treason was one such crime in which the entire public opinion supports the prosecution. Whether those charged with this crime are real traitors, just suspects for treason, or falsely accused persons, they will be treated the same by public opinion. The hostile public view would clearly reflect on the minds of the jury and the judges on both the trial and appellate levels.

Such an attitude seemed clearly to have been reflected in Justice

Holmes's opinion cited above. Great cases are great, to highlight Holmes's point once again, not because of "their real importance" but because of "some accident of immediate overwhelming interest." Such an interest, Holmes ventures, will very often exert immense force to make even clearly established principles and concepts of law dubious. Iva was thus convicted for treason, Holmes might have reasoned, not because she was really guilty but because the existing law of treason was ignored or not adequately interpreted and applied for the benefit of the compelling public opinion and interest.

The lead counsel for Iva, Wayne Collins, reflected a similar sentiment at the end of the trial. "There was no way that Iva could escape the guilty verdict for treason," he asserted, "as long as she was paid for the work for the Japanese government in some capacity," regardless of what kind of work she had done.

———

Iva's life at Alderson Prison was, unexpectedly, quiet, pleasant for the most part, and passed quickly. Her family visited frequently, but her husband, Filipe, could not. He was forced to go back to Japan before he could see her off at Oakland for Alderson and was compelled to sign a statement at Hawaii that he would not ever come back to the United States. It was not "a full time, by no means a complete life," Iva commented later, but it was a time away from crowds and publicity. She really hoped that by the time of her release, the public could have completely forgotten Tokyo Rose, enabling her to live her normal life again.

In prison Iva found some good bridge players, including Mildred (Axis Sally) Gillars, whom Iva found to be "a brainy person." She said, "We never talk about what had happened." The inmates, according to Iva, "ranged from women who have never before worn shoes to brilliant and sophisticated women." "In a way, I appreciated the time to myself," she recalled. "I always had thought that prison time would be wasted and go very slowly." She became a model prisoner, holding a series of jobs. She became a supply clerk first, then became assistant to the medical aide, then X-ray operator, and then medical purchaser. Finally, she was a laboratory assistant and ran the X-ray lab, tested basic metabolism rates (the highest one she tested was her own), and took electrocardiograms.

Iva served over two-thirds of her ten-year sentence. At the time of the sentencing, the newspaper reporters predicted that Iva would be freed on parole within three and a half years. Iva, however, had to wait for six years and two months, even though it was reduced time for good behavior. Mildred Gillars, on the other hand, stayed in the prison for another five years after Iva left. Gillars's sentence, ten to thirty years in prison, was much lighter than those accorded to Robert H. Best and Douglas Chandler, two other Americans who made broadcasts for the Nazis. She became eligible for parole in 1959, but she didn't pursue it until two years later, and on June 10, 1961, she was finally paroled after serving for eleven years.

In late 1955, when Iva's early release had been under consideration, her brother, Fred, made a public statement in Chicago, where the Toguri family had moved thirteen years previously, and he helped his father build a $5,000 investment into "a prosperous, three-store business" (a grocery, a bookstore, and an import store). "She hopes to settle down here, quietly and inconspicuously," Fred said. "She has been working as an assistant to prison doctors and dentists, and she hopes to get a job like that here."

Despite her hopeful expectations, anti–Tokyo Rose sentiment remained strong, and the newspapers and magazines only helped to fan the flames. A 1955 *Newsweek* article, "Once Again, Tokyo Rose," viciously denounced Iva: "You stuck a knife into the USA," it charged, and as Abe Burrows's song goes, "you forgot what they learned you at UCLA."

On January 5, 1956, when the prison authorities formally announced that Iva was to be released later that month, the press once again got excited. As the time of Iva's release neared, reporters started to congregate around the prison preparing for the occasion. It so happened that there was only one farmhouse close to the prison and one telephone in it. Every room in the house, Duus reported, came to be rented by the newspaper reporters. The latest arrival, an International News Service reporter, had to settle for the kitchen but gladly found that the telephone was in it, which he refused to share with other reporters.

In order to avoid the crowd, the prison officials chose the release time of 6:15 a.m., but their discretion was useless because the release attracted a large crowd like the one at Sugamo Prison almost ten years earlier. Among the crowd who were standing outside the gate, Iva first found her family. Back in 1949, when Iva had boarded the train at Oakland for this prison, her father and her sister June had come to see her off. Now a little over six years later she saw her father standing at the prison gate, flanked by brother Fred and sister Inez, ready to take her to Chicago.

Iva now became the first person in American history convicted of treason to regain freedom. To the group of reporters, who were waiting at the entrance to hear Iva's first comments, Iva said tersely, "I am going into darkness. All I ask is a 50-50 chance to get back on my feet." She then quickly got into a waiting car with her family. Before Iva climbed into the automobile, however, an agent of the U.S. Immigration and Naturalization Service was waiting for her, as if he didn't want to think Iva had suffered enough, and served her a warrant for her deportation. But to where? Surely, the treason conviction carried a loss of citizenship rights, but Iva could not be deported because she was a native-born American. The irony was that the conviction of treason was the result of her stubborn claim of American citizenship, which was in turn taken away from her because of her conviction.

If she were deported as an alien, she would not be allowed to return. She was right back where she had started from at the time the trial had begun. Was she brought back to the United States just to be tried, convicted, and punished? And as soon as she completed the punishment, as if to add insult to injury, was she to be pushed out of the country? She understandably became adamant, enraged, and angry. "This is my country!" she shouted. "I was born here. I belong here. I'm going to stay."

As the door closed, the car sped off for the long ride to Chicago. The *Chicago Tribune* seemed to reflect the general, diehard public sentiment against Iva when it published an article about her release with the headlines "Tokyo Rose Quits Jail, Shows No Repentance." The Tokyo Rose hunt seemed to have started up again.

The deportation order was the result of the government's calculated move. On January 27, one day before Iva's release, the U.S. Immigration and Naturalization Service in Washington announced that the government intended to deport Iva as "a stateless person" as a result of her treason conviction. On the following day, Iva was freed only to receive the deportation notice that forced her once again to confront her citizenship.

The government ignored the United Nations Universal Declaration of Human Rights—a declaration that the United States, Iva's own country, sponsored—which among other things pledged never to remove the citizenship from anyone who had no other nationality (Article 5[2]). This notice simply claimed that Iva was an "undesirable alien" and deportable under the provisions of the McCarran-Walter Immigration and Naturalization Act of 1952. She had served her sentence and in so doing paid her debt to society. Exile, it should be emphasized, was not part of her sentence. The 1952 law, moreover, was passed after she had been sentenced and was thus as the JACL's National Committee for Iva Toguri, in its support for her pardon, decidedly claimed in 1975, ex post facto. The government, nevertheless, gave her only thirty days to leave the United States, or she would be forcefully deported.

After she arrived and settled down at her father's house in Chicago the following day, Iva released a statement that she was determined to fight deportation "every step of the way" in order to remain in the United States as an American.

On March 13, 1956, the Chicago office of the Immigration and Naturalization Service issued a formal order for Iva to leave the country within thirty days or face deportation proceedings. In San Francisco, Wayne Collins called this action "cruel and needless." "They know she is not legally subject to deportation," he said, "but they still insist in persecuting this harmless little typist." He declared that he would use every possible means to fight the order.

The deportation order prohibited Iva to move beyond fifty miles from Chicago, but she was finally allowed to move to Collins's home in San Francisco in April 1956, to defend herself in the deportation hearings, and spent most of the next two years with the Collins family. It was here at the breakfast table that Iva first met Collins's eleven-year-old son, Wayne Merritt Collins, who later took over his father's practice when he died suddenly in 1974 and became her lawyer. As soon as Iva moved back to San Francisco, Collins arranged a press conference for her in his Presidio home. She stated, basically reiterating the statement she had made in Chicago in late January:

> This is my country! I was born here. I belong here. I'm going to stay. . . . When I was caught in Japan at the time of the war, I asserted my American citizenship three times. I asked the American Government to help get me home. Nothing happened. I asked to be interned by the Japanese as an enemy alien. They didn't do it. I was an alien all the time I stayed in Japan. Now, they say I am an alien here. But I was born in L.A., and I have always been an American citizen. I want to stay that way.

Why was Iva threatened with deportation, while Axis Sally was not? Why was the Immigration office so fierce about deporting Iva? They had already succeeded in eliminating her husband completely from the

United States by barring him from coming back either from Japan or from Portugal. Were the Justice Department and the Immigration and Naturalization Service as its agent trying to expel Iva as soon as she was released from prison? If she would be deported, Iva had no way to come back to the United States, since she had already lost her citizenship and had not regained it yet. Perhaps this was the intention of the government.

The prosecutors seem to have been trying to get rid of her permanently, by deporting her and thus putting her in a position in which she could not come back to the United States, so that they could eliminate the possibility of her challenging their judicial misconduct, of which they were all fully aware. What the government was attempting was doing away with any potential future challenges to the prosecution.

Even after all the appeals to the U.S. Court of Appeals and the U.S. Supreme Court were denied, Iva and her attorneys still presented some kind of potential threat to the prosecution. The prosecutors must have well recognized all kinds of misconduct they had carried out during the entire process of the trial. It was thus very natural that upon Iva's early release from prison, an effort had to be made to put her out of reach of the prosecution. The deportation order against Iva seems thus to have been initiated by the Justice Department merely to be carried out by the Immigration and Naturalization Service.

Who was actually doing all this? Were the Justice Department officials, DeWolfe, Hennessey, Hogan, and others, including former attorney general Tom Clark, who had been fully familiar with and personally responsible for various acts of misconduct, trying to eliminate all the potential problems by permanently expelling Iva from the United States?

The main villain in Iva's affair, DeWolfe, retired early at fifty-three, just a few months after Iva's release from prison, after working for the Justice Department for twenty-nine years. He had been a special assistant to U.S. Attorney General Tom Clark for six years, during which he had prosecuted Iva, against his own deep-seated conviction of her innocence. Was it just a coincidence that Iva's release from prison and DeWolfe's early retirement occurred in the same year? It was only three years later, on June 18, 1959, almost a year after the deportation order against Iva was revoked, that DeWolfe shot and killed himself in a hotel room in downtown Seattle.

For Iva, who had been living at the home of her attorney, Wayne Collins, since 1956 to protect herself, the matter was finally settled on July 10, 1958, when the Immigration and Naturalization Service canceled the deportation order against her "for a rather tame reason"; they had nowhere to deport her to since she held neither Japanese nor Portuguese citizenship, which they should have known from the very beginning in January 1956. More significantly, according to the holding of a recent Supreme Court decision, Iva could not have lost her citizenship before conviction, and, therefore, she was not deportable.

She was finally able to return to Chicago to live with her father and work in the family store. Reunion with her husband was not possible. Contrary to the UN charter on human rights, she was declared a stateless person, and with no passport, she could not visit her husband in Japan. Nor could her husband come to visit her in Chicago because he had been forced to sign a statement that he would never return to the United States even for a visit. The forced separation by the American government eventually ruined their marriage. Because they were Catholics, they still did not divorce, but they had ceased to correspond shortly after Iva's release from prison. Before long, he had found "a companion to look after him."

The government, however, hadn't given Iva up so easily. In 1968 the Justice Department demanded payment of the $10,000 fine, which Iva had not paid because she was without assets and worked only for subsistence in the family store. The federal district court in Chicago ordered her to surrender the cash value of two life insurance policies on her life, which had been taken out by her father at the Chicago Japanese Civic Association Credit Union. The CJCACU granted a loan equal to the cash value for $4,745, to pay the fine partially.

Three years later, the Justice Department, under Attorney General John Mitchell, again summoned her into court and demanded payment of the balance of $5,255. Attorney Jiro Yamaguchi represented Iva in the Chicago proceedings, but Wayne Collins, who continued as associate counsel for Iva, denounced the government "for capricious harassment." "The Government," Collins severely charged, "must have billions of dollars in fines which they never try to collect." On November 14, 1972, the Seventh U.S. Court of Appeals denied her a hearing to show why she should not be made to pay the remaining fine.

Iva had been urging her father, who had no legal obligation whatsoever to pay any of her fine, as Article III, Section 3 of the U.S. Constitution clearly states, not to go into debt any more to pay the rest of her fine, but when her father died in 1972 at the age of ninety, he stipulated in his will that the remaining fine be paid from his estate. The government thus mercilessly collected the last bit of her fine and finally closed her case, when she was fifty-nine years of age. By then, Iva must have, as Russell Howe insists, "overpaid her dues to the United States." Still, she remained without American citizenship and a stateless person. She managed the family store for a living and tried to remain as inconspicuous as possible. She had to stay away from publicity and to live with fear. Every time articles appeared in the newspaper about "Tokyo Rose," she said, she received threatening mail and telephone calls.

On June 7, 1954, almost five years since she arrived at Alderson, one of Iva's attorneys, Theodore Tamba, filed a petition for executive clemency (pardon) on Iva's behalf with the president of the United States, Dwight Eisenhower. This petition accompanied a letter to the president. Its excerpts read:

> The most shocking experience I had was the alleged conduct of a man named Harry Brundidge, a newspaperman ... [who] accompanied to Japan a man named Hogan, an attorney for the Justice Department.... Mr. Brundidge is alleged to have deliberately bribed witnesses by promises of trips to the United States and other gifts. While Brundidge was in Japan with Hogan, he made contact with [Hiromi] Yagi who was induced to come to the United States as a witness for the United States Government, and who testified before the United States Grand Jury....
>
> My investigation developed that Yagi was then an employee of the Japanese Travel Bureau ... and I went to the Japanese Travel Bureau and there met Yagi.... I then asked [Yagi] what he knew about the case of alleged treason against [Iva Toguri]. [Yagi] then gave me a narrative of one of the most obviously fictitious stories I have ever heard in my professional career. Finally, under questioning by me, Yagi stated that this was a story he and Brundidge had concocted....

Theodore Tamba, who had had the occasion to meet a man named Toshikatsu Kodaira, a Japanese newspaperman working for the United Press in Tokyo, further explained:

> Mr. Kodaira then proceeded to narrate the events truthfully and his statements are supported by his deposition on file in the United States

District Court in Northern California, much of which was not allowed in evidence. [Kodaira stated he accompanied Yagi to a meeting with Brundidge, and that Brundidge attempted to bribe both of them with whisky, clothing, and a trip to the United States.] Kodaira was summoned by the [United States] Occupation to the Office of Occupation Intelligence Service and there he confronted Yagi who admitted that the testimony he [Yagi] gave before the United States Grand Jury was pure fiction. Kodaira produced the suit of clothes given him by Brundidge. The trouser and coat bore the name of Harry Brundidge.

Convincing though this letter was, Tamba's petition was not even answered. Who were the attorneys in the Eisenhower administration reviewing the petition? If any of the Justice Department officials, who had been somehow connected and related with Iva's case, were involved in the review, Iva's pardon had no chance of approval. At any rate, Tamba's letter has the appearance more of an appeal, pointing out the prosecution's misconduct, rather than a petition for pardon.

The presidential power to pardon, vested in Article 2 of the Constitution, was exercised for a variety of reasons and a variety of offenses. The pardons have also been used in the "justice neutral" situation and the "justice enhancing" situation (to rectify miscarriages of justice, remedy disproportionate punishment, ascertain actual innocence or uncertain guilt). If a pardon were to be issued, in the second situation, to remedy procedural unfairness or to correct misconduct of the prosecution or the judge, it should be granted before the punishment starts or in the early part of the punishment to have the full effect of the pardon.

Wayne Merritt Collins, the son of Wayne Mortimer Collins, filed a second petition for presidential pardon on November 4, 1968. In his letter to the president, Collins pointed out the prosecution's mishandling and mistreatment of the defense witnesses from Australia before the trial, the refusal to accept defense witnesses from Japan, not allowing defense depositions, and abuse and coercion of defense witnesses by FBI agents, including Fred Tillman.

Lyndon Johnson was president, and Richard Nixon was elected one day later, but again no response to Collins's petition was forthcoming from the White House. Then Attorney General Ramsey Clark, son of Tom Clark, who indicted Iva for treason as attorney general and was eventually promoted to the Supreme Court as a reward, had tried to bypass the embarrassment, simply saying that he had no recollection of hearing about the petition. Since a petition for presidential pardon can be filed only once during a six-year period, the next petition had to wait until 1975.

In the middle of the seventies there was a gradual change in public feeling and sentiment. In March 1976, the *Chicago Tribune* published a two-part article by its Tokyo correspondent, Richard Yates, vividly depicting all kinds of irregularities, abuses, and misconduct on the part of the prosecution. "We had no choice," Oki was reported to have said. "U.S. Occupation police came and told me I had no choice but to testify against Iva, or else. Then, after I was flown to San Francisco for trial, along with the other government witnesses . . . we were told what to say and what not to say two hours every morning for a month before the trial started." Oki also told Yates, "She got a raw deal. She was railroaded into jail."

"We were told that if we didn't cooperate," former witness Mitsushio told Yates, "Uncle Sam might arrange a trial for us too. All of us could see how easy it was for a mammoth country like the United States to crucify a Japanese-American—all we had to do was look at Iva." These and other statements by Ruth Hayakawa, Teruo Ozasa, Tsuneishi, and others had considerable impact, abundantly demonstrating that "Iva never made a treasonable broadcast in her life." All these allegations and misconduct revealed by Yates were really pointed toward acquittal rather than pardon.

Resolutions for Iva's pardon were passed in the California Assembly and the Senate and in the city governments of San Francisco, Honolulu, Los Angeles, and San Jose. The Los Angeles City Council rescinded its resolution of 1948 opposing her return to the United States. Veterans' associations added their support for Iva. Also crucial was the change in the attitude of the Japanese American community, which had been very hostile toward Iva earlier. The Japanese American Citizens League (JACL) started to take an interest in Iva's trial beginning in the early seventies and published an important pamphlet to promote her cause.

In 1975, Dr. Clifford I. Uyeda, a retired pediatrician in San Francisco, organized a JACL committee to campaign for a presidential pardon for Iva. The new campaign was extremely effective because it was supported by the entire JACL national organization and backed by a number of prominent Japanese American politicians as well as Americans not of Japanese descent.

Wayne Merritt Collins, who had lived with the Iva case since childhood, announced, as he had long planned to do, the filing of a petition for a presidential pardon on November 17, 1976, calling a press conference symbolically at the site where the old courthouse had once stood. Iva optimistically said at the conference, "Times have changed. If the trial was held today there is no way I would be convicted." The petition, backed by many famous individuals including educator and politician Samuel I. Hayakawa, was sent to President Gerald R. Ford, who was fortunately "notoriously open-handed with pardons."

On January 20, 1977, the elaborately sealed pardon arrived at Iva's Chicago home. It said that President Ford "had this day [January 19] granted unto Iva Ikuko Toguri d'Aquino a full and unconditional pardon" and that he had instructed Attorney General Edward H. Levi to "sign this grant of executive clemency." It was the first-ever pardon in a case of treason.

"After all these years," Iva said, "it's hard for me to believe that the pardon is really true." She wrote to President Ford thanking him for his "compassion and sense of fair play." In a press conference held by the Chicago chapter of the JACL, Iva repeated, "After all these years, it's hard for me to believe it's all over." There was talk of Iva going to revisit Japan for a "joyful reunion" with Filipe in Yokohama and with many old friends. Iva soon denied this as just a rumor. The treason trial instigated by the Justice Department had ruined Iva's marriage.

The presidential pardon, however decent and proper it had been, was "too little, too late." It not only was a belated gesture but did not go far enough; it did not erase the guilt that unjustly stained Iva nor reverse the conviction as the appellate court would do. "I am all for a pardon," former FBI agent Fred Tillman commented upon hearing about Iva's pardon. "She took her punishment. It's O.K. to pardon her now." Is that all that could be said by a person who had railroaded her? He must have well known that Iva had been innocent and that her trial was all made up, based upon false evidence, which he himself contributed to illegally. "The pardon," Russell Howe commented, "was the belated work of people who had let Iva Toguri down the most in the past . . . the Japanese American community."

A presidential pardon for Iva, to be sure, was the fastest way to regain her citizenship rights, but there is a vast difference between pardon and innocence. Could she just accept the pardon resignedly? It was not pardon but the proclamation of innocence that Iva was entitled to. She was declared guilty of treason because of the perjured testimony of the two witnesses even though she thought she was innocent. Pardon, as Howe aptly points out, is only forgiveness of guilt, not an acknowledgment of innocence. It presupposes the fact that the person is culpable and guilty but has suffered enough and does not proceed on the belief in the innocence of the person pardoned. Repeated petitions for pardon insisting that there had been prosecutorial misconduct and coerced, perjured testimony should have been used to void the decision, not to support a pardon. Why, Iva must have thought, had she to be pardoned for a crime she did not commit?

Prosecutorial Misconduct and the Coram Nobis Relief

Normally, criminal defendants cannot ask judges to reopen their cases after appeals have been exhausted and sentences completed. The only exception to the "finality" rule stems from one of the "ancient writs" of English law, called the writ of error coram nobis. This term is legal Latin for "error before us," referring to the trial judges. This application for judicial relief is related to the better-known writ of habeas corpus.... In coram nobis cases, the former defendant must show that "prosecutorial misconduct" during the original trial deprived him or her of a fair trial.

PETER IRONS, A People's History of the Supreme Court *(1999), 361–362*

Iva's life was a sad, painful, but courageous story of a Japanese American *nisei*. As demonstrated throughout the book, she believed in the American system, upholding and adhering to it, even when it worked against her beliefs and ideas. Iva had dutifully accepted her conviction and sentence and had courageously endured the punishment, even though she was certain of her innocence, as if it were her duty to comply as a patriotic American.

Such American patriotism has been abundantly exhibited throughout American history, especially during the American Revolution. A large number of American POWs, for example, were kept on British prison ships and harshly treated, but only 8 out of 100 chose to defect. Most of these Americans were strongly nationalistic and went through extreme hardship, sticking together, remaining loyal, and singing patriotic American songs. "England," Benjamin Franklin declared, "ought to be proud of having the descendants of such virtue."

One wonders what Franklin might have said about Iva Toguri, who fully supported the American cause and endeavored to entertain and encourage the American GIs, bravely sabotaging the Japanese propaganda broadcasts while living under oppressive military rule in Japan. She had demonstrated a full, undivided loyalty to the United States, even against Japan, from where her parents and brother emigrated.

American patriotism in the thirties, forties, and fifties, quite different from "patriotism" used in the current political and partisan debates and issues, was an ideology most Americans shared, and Iva's patriotism manifested itself differently at different times.

Iva Toguri grew up in a family in Southern California. Although there were a large number of Japanese in the area, Jun Toguri made every effort to bring up his family in the American way and wanted his children to be fully Americanized. Their contact with other Japanese was minimal, and they seldom participated in the Japanese American festivals, social gatherings, and events. The father was very careful to select predominantly white neighborhoods whenever the family moved so that his children would have Caucasian playmates and friends. By the time Iva went to UCLA, her family was a fully Americanized family, which subscribed to the American way of life and culture. Iva's desire to be a true, genuine American seemed to have made her actively despise everything Japanese, including Japanese foods.

In her college life, as her classmates and friends attested, Iva was "a lively and lighthearted person, no different from the other American girl students," who had "a good sense of humor" and did not have "any interest in Japan at all." She was "a completely average American girl" and "did not have anything particularly Japanese about her." She expressed her feeling more than once that she would go and fight for her country, the United States.

In Tokyo during the war, Iva was dedicated to supporting the American cause at all costs, and her patriotism took the form of strong pro-American, pro-Allies, and anti-Japanese attitudes. When the war started, the Japanese *kempei-tai* came to see her and pressed her to become a Japanese citizen. Iva flatly refused, saying that "a person born and raised in America doesn't give up his citizenship for a piece of paper." Despite repeated pressures exhorted on her, she refused to become a Japanese citizen, while desperately trying to get out of the country and return home.

Writing to her sisters in California, Iva advised them to "plan to live and die in the country which can give you so much." Her deep convictions about the American system and democracy and her strong patriotism were such that she was not intimidated by the threats of the police and *kempei-tai* even when they seemed immediate.

Iva's life in Tokyo was full of defiance and resistance in support of her country, all of which she did openly. One day, on her way to work on the bus, she refused to bow toward the emperor's palace as the bus passed in front of it. When another passenger told her to bow, she got off the bus, instead of obeying the order.

At work, all the Radio Tokyo workers realized that she was a pro-American patriot, and some of her coworkers (*nisei*) did not like her snobbish and critical attitude toward them for giving up their American citizenship. Also at Domei, Iva Toguri occasionally got involved in heated arguments with the workers who advocated a strong pro-Japanese position.

With Filipe d'Aquino, three-fourths Japanese but a Portuguese citizen, whom she met at Domei and eventually married, Iva shared the pro-American view. They both deeply hated Japanese militarism and disliked the suppressive atmosphere of wartime Japan. Iva, however, was a strong American patriot who refused to give up her American citizenship for Portuguese citizenship.

All through the war in Tokyo, Iva did not contribute to the Japanese war efforts. She never bought the Japanese war bonds and gave no clothing, old jewels, old metals, or food to the neighborhood organization collecting for the war effort.

Everyone who came in contact with Iva quickly recognized her unblemished love of America and loyalty to it. When Iva met and talked to Cousens and other POWs at NHK, they soon realized that she was a strong American patriot and thought that she could be trusted to assist in their efforts to sabotage the Japanese propaganda program. When she started to work as a Radio Japan announcer for the POWs in their attempt to subvert the Japanese program for the first time in the war, Iva felt useful, doing something for the American war effort under the very noses of the Japanese. She helped the POWs' effort courageously in every possible way.

Iva started to openly exhibit her firm pro-American attitude even to the military police as represented by Sergeant Okada, her surveillance officer. Okada soon began to admire her courageous adherence to the American cause and her outspoken expression of pro-American sentiment and patriotism. He said to her that he could arrest her at any time for many things she had been doing, but he simply cautioned her as a friend just to keep her mouth shut.

Not only to be loyal to America during the war but to serve the country by doing various things were her unquestionably patriotic duties. Even during her trial in San Francisco, Iva helped by cleaning up the dining room in the prison every day after dinner. Throughout her life until she died at age ninety, Iva continued to love her country and had abundantly revealed her patriotism in her attitude, conduct, and activities. Why, then, was such a loyal, patriotic American indicted, put on trial, and convicted of treason? Iva seems to have been manipulated and used by some political leaders to promote their own particular interests.

———

Over sixty years have passed since the conviction of Iva Toguri of treason and her sentence of ten years' imprisonment and a $10,000 fine. As earlier chapters have demonstrated, appeals to the Court of Appeals and the Supreme Court were rejected many times over, and her petitions for pardon (executive clemency) filed in 1954 and 1968 were not even answered.

It was not until 1977 that President Ford finally granted Iva a full and unconditional pardon. A pardon, it should be emphasized here again, restored her American citizenship but did not go far enough for her. It implied "guilt" and is thus only "forgiveness of guilt," not "an acknowledgment of innocence," and is granted to a felon who has suffered too much, to borrow Howe's words, not because society owes the victim "something for having her suffer unjustly." What Iva really needed, whether she realized it or not, was to void the conviction. Despite all the disgrace she had been unfairly forced to endure as the result of the key witnesses' false testimony and the government's misconduct, all the formal steps had already been exhausted. There seemed no recourse left to explore for Iva.

This book, however, is by no means the first one to expose the misconduct and abuses in the trial. Duus (1979) and Howe (1990) severely criticized the government's misconduct and all other irregularities, but they have found only deaf ears. Nor is my book the first one to advocate a rehabilitation of Iva. "Now the time has come to go further," Howe insisted, "and to acknowledge her innocence," and he suggested a joint resolution of Congress, offering Iva "a national apology." This and other suggestions notwithstanding, no action has yet been taken for Iva to rescind the miscarriage of justice.

After all these efforts, there is still one possible remedy available for Iva. It is a little-known "ancient writ" of English law, namely the writ of error coram nobis, a judicial ruling that the original verdict had been tainted by official misconduct. It was used by Peter Irons, constitutional scholar and lawyer, to challenge Fred Korematsu's 1944 conviction. Using the new Freedom of Information Act, Irons conducted his research on the Justice Department's file in the Hirabayashi, Yasui, and Korematsu cases. He discovered "several astonishing documents," vividly revealing "smoking guns" and other records of legal misconduct. He persuaded Gordon Hirabayashi, Min Yasui, and Fred Korematsu, all in their sixties then, to agree to join an effort to erase their criminal records.

Irons, who fully recognized the fact that criminal defendants normally cannot ask judges to reopen their cases after appeals have been exhausted and sentences completed, hit upon the only exception available to the "finality" rule. He decided to pursue the campaign to reverse the wartime convictions of these Japanese Americans using the writ of error coram nobis.

This term, as Professor Irons explains it, "is legal Latin for 'error before us,' referring to the trial judges, and this judicial relief is related to the better-known writ of habeas corpus," an order to bring the body of the defendant into court for a hearing on the legality of the detention. In coram nobis cases, Irons maintains, the former defendant must show that "prosecutorial misconduct" during the original trial deprived him or her of a fair trial.

Irons points out two grounds for coram nobis relief: (1) proof that government lawyers deliberately withheld "exculpatory" evidence that would show the defendant's innocence and (2) the government's introduction at trial of false evidence of the defendant's guilt. He also states that the burden of proof on defendants is extremely high and for that reason "coram nobis relief is rarely sought and even more rarely granted."

Irons recruited a team of young lawyers, most of whom were the children of internment camp survivors. The coram nobis legal team prepared a 150-page petition to be submitted in 1983 to federal district judges in San Francisco (for Korematsu), Portland (for Yasui), and Seattle (for Hirabayashi), in the same courts in which the defendants had been tried and convicted in 1942. The petitions urged the judges, based strictly on evidence from government files, "to carefully weigh the complete record of governmental abuses" in the wartime cases and "do justice where it was denied forty years ago."

Korematsu's petition came before federal judge Marilyn Hall Patel in November 1983. Ruling from the bench, she found "substantial support" in the petition that "the Government deliberately omitted relevant information and provided misleading information" to the Supreme Court in 1944. "The judicial process is seriously impaired," the judge concluded, "when the Government's law enforcement officers violate their ethical obligations to the court." The *Korematsu* decision, she added, "remains on the pages of our legal and political history" as a "constant caution that in times of war or declared military necessity our institutions must be vigilant in protecting constitutional guarantees." Accordingly, federal judges in Portland and Seattle similarly vacated the wartime convictions of Min Yasui and Gordon Hirabayashi, respectively. Yasui, who died November 12, 1986, could thus have witnessed the very court that convicted him forty years earlier dismiss the original indictment and conviction against him nearly three years before his death.

These successful cases that voided the earlier convictions of Korematsu, Hirabayashi, and Yasui are certainly a useful suggestion that Iva Toguri could somehow follow. Iva died on September 26, 2006, and with her all her legal rights and duties died. The conviction (and dishonor) that had stigmatized her as a traitor, however, could never be erased but would persist beyond her death. It is, therefore, still necessary for her close relatives to clear her name and wipe out the disgrace that was forced on her unjustly. Following the footsteps of Peter Irons and his legal team, it is imperative, posthumously, even this late in time, to seek for Iva the coram nobis relief to void her conviction from the original trial court, the Federal district court in San Francisco.

In fact, Iva's trial record contains a host of prosecutorial misconducts, not to mention the judge's misconduct and discriminatory treatment against the defense. In every step of the trial, we have found abundant evidence of prosecutorial misconduct; the Justice Department had undermined the judicial system by ruthlessly prosecuting the case as if it were their sole, absolute objective and by abusing and manipulating the rules and regulations, which had been designed to guarantee the proper, smooth operation of the administration of justice.

Specifically, the most conspicuous ones are the move to re-indict Iva, after the case was dropped in Tokyo, without any new information to justify it; a highly problematic "confession" as evidence; two questionable, unreliable witnesses for the constitutional requirement; false statements by the key witnesses; a long detention preventing a speedy trial; and withholding and suppressing perjured prosecution evidence instead of moving to drop the case entirely. Most of these misconducts would fall into two categories, which, Professor Irons argues, are grounds for coram nobis relief: withholding of evidence showing the defendant's innocence and introduction of false evidence of the defendant's guilt.

If such a legal action is not at all possible to correct the record of the court that tried the case, should the motion of coram nobis be used as merely a metaphor to correct the record of history?

———

The Tokyo Rose case has clearly demonstrated that the American law of treason has come full circle. The law of treason as established by the U.S. Constitution was to reform the English law of treason, eliminating all kinds of abuses for political purposes. The Aaron Burr treason trials vividly reveal that John Marshall strictly adhered to the constitutional provisions and declared that the conviction for treason was based upon actual waging of the war or adhering to the enemy with the clear intention to betray the country, testified to by two witnesses to the same overt act.

In *Cramer v. United States* (1945), as discussed at the outset, Justice Robert Jackson of the Supreme Court, who wrote the opinion for the court, stated that the framers of the Constitution not only intended the charge of treason "as an effective instrument of the new nation's security against treachery that would aid external enemies" but were also "aware of the misuse that a partisan executive might make of treason and impose 'every limitation' possible. Overt acts must be so visible that two witnesses to each act could clearly testify to the nature of the act as well as the participants in it."

"Jackson's reading of these limitations," Peter Hoffer points out, "came directly out of Marshall's earlier opinion." Justice Jackson further maintained that the court had to define the treason offense "as narrowly as possible and limit what juries might hear" in order to prevent (1) treason prosecutions "by established authority to repress peaceful political opposition" and (2) convictions of the innocent "as a result of perjury, passion, or inadequate evidence." "A citizen intellectually or emotionally," Jackson continued, "may favor the enemy and harbor sympathies or convictions disloyal to this country's policy or interest," but there is no treason "so long as he committed no act of aid and comfort to the enemy." Jackson concluded: "On the other hand, a citizen may take actions which do aid and comfort the enemy—making a speech critical of the government or opposing its measures, profiteering, striking in defense plants or essential work, and the hundred other things which impair our cohesion and diminish our strength — but if there is no adherence to the enemy in this, if there is no intent to betray, there is no treason."

These lines written by Jackson, which "Marshall himself," Hoffer insists, "would be proud to have written," are the essential element of the law of treason. It was, however, only three years after this landmark case was decided that Iva Toguri d'Aquino was tried. This case, in which the defendant was declared guilty, even though it had never been proven that she had had a definite intention to betray her country, clearly deviated from the seemingly well-established law of treason, vividly demonstrating the fact that the treason law came once again to be used to serve political purposes.

July 4, 1916	Iva Ikuko Toguri born in Watts in South Central Los Angeles. Two months after her birth, her father entered her name in the genealogical registry at the family's ancestral village in Japan (the procedure, customary among Japanese Americans at the time, gave her citizenship rights in Japan), but her father canceled the registration in 1932 when she had nearly reached sixteen.
1933	Graduated from Compton Union High School.
Fall–Winter 1934	Attended Compton Junior College for a half a year.
Fall 1935	Transferred to UCLA.
June 1941	Graduated from UCLA with a bachelor of science in zoology.
July 5, 1941	Sailed from San Pedro, California, to Japan.
July 24, 1941	Arrived in Yokohama Port. She stayed with relatives in Tokyo for a little over ten months, attending her sick aunt.
December 8, 1941	Left stranded in Japan when war broke out following the Pearl Harbor attack by the Japanese.
July 1942	Obtained employment with the Japanese Domei News Agency as a typist.
August 23, 1943	Started to work as a part-time typist at Radio Tokyo.
November 13, 1943– August 13, 1945	Became a regular announcer on Radio Tokyo's program "Zero Hour."
December 1943	Started to work as a part-time secretary at the Danish legation in Tokyo and quit her job at Domei.
April 19, 1945	Married Filipe J. d'Aquino.

May 1945	Lost her job at the Danish legation when it closed and the Danish minister, Lars Tillitse, left as Denmark broke off relations with Japan.
August 15, 1945	World War II in the Pacific ended.
September 1, 1945	Signed the one-page contract with Harry Brundidge and Charles Lee for her exclusive story as "the one and only Tokyo Rose" for $2,000.
October 17, 1945	Arrested as being "suspected of treason" and imprisoned at Yokohama Military Stockade. The picture on the front cover was taken then.
November 1945	Transferred to Sugamo Prison in Tokyo.
October 25, 1946	Released from Sugamo Prison.
November 1946	Applied for readmission to the United States.
October 1947	Renewed her effort to return to the United States.
January 5, 1948	Her baby died at birth.
March 26, 1948	Met with Brundidge and John B. Hogan, the FBI special agent, and signed her "confession."
May 2, 1948	Brundidge published his sensational article on Tokyo Rose in *Nashville Tennessean*.
May 25, 1948	Tom DeWolfe recommended the case against Iva Toguri d'Aquino be dropped.
August 16, 1948	U.S. Attorney General Tom Clark announced that Iva Toguri d'Aquino would be tried for treason in the federal district court in San Francisco.
August 26, 1948	Rearrested and imprisoned in Sugamo Prison.
September 3, 1948	Left Yokohama for San Francisco under guard of military police on board the U.S. Army Transport *General H. F. Hodges*.
September 25, 1948	Arrived in San Francisco.
October 8, 1948	Indictment returned by the federal grand jury.

October 9, 1948	Iva Toguri d'Aquino's press release on her reaction to the indictment.
October 11, 1948	Iva's request to be released on bail denied.
January 4, 1949	Iva Toguri pleaded not guilty to all counts.
January 25, 1949	Mildred "Axis Sally" Gillars's trial began in Washington, D.C.
March 10, 1949	Gillars was convicted of treason, and she was sentenced on March 16 to a term of ten to thirty years' imprisonment.
July 5, 1949	Iva's trial began in the federal district court in San Francisco with Judge Roche presiding. All-white jury selected.
September 20, 1949	The closing arguments for the prosecution and the defense began.
September 26, 1949	Judge Roche gave his final instructions to the jury.
September 27, 1949	The jury went into deliberation.
September 29, 1949	The jury rendered its verdict: guilty on one count, and not guilty on seven counts.
October 6, 1949	Sentenced to ten years in prison and a $10,000 fine.
November 15, 1949	Left San Francisco for the Federal Reformatory for Women at Alderson, West Virginia.
October 10, 1951	The U.S. Court of Appeals for the Ninth Circuit ruled that her original conviction had been proper.
December 17, 1951	Petition for rehearing denied by the U.S. Court of Appeals for the Ninth Circuit.
April 28, 1952	Certiorari denied.
May 26, 1952	Petition for rehearing denied.
April 6, 1953	Petition for rehearing denied.
June 7, 1954	Attorney Theodore Tamba filed a petition for executive clemency (pardon) with President Dwight D. Eisenhower, but his petition was not answered.
January 28, 1956	Released from the Federal Reformatory for Women at Alderson after serving six years and two months, with reduced time for good

	behavior. The Immigration and Naturalization Service immediately began deportation proceedings, claiming Iva was an "undesirable alien." Went to live at the home of her lawyer, Wayne M. Collins, in San Francisco.
July 10, 1958	Deportation order was dropped.
November 4, 1968	Wayne Merritt Collins filed a second petition for presidential pardon (Lyndon B. Johnson was president; Richard M. Nixon was elected one day later), but Collins's petition was not answered by either. A petition for presidential pardon can be filed only once during a six-year period.
January 18, 1977	After six years and two months of imprisonment and after decades of debate over the fairness of her trial, President Gerald R. Ford granted Iva Toguri a pardon. It was the first time in American history that a person convicted of treason was pardoned. Toguri was thus officially forgiven, and her U.S. citizenship was finally restored. Toguri's trial was one of only seven American treason trials following World War II.
September 1978	The rumor that Iva would visit Tokyo for the first time in twenty-nine years for a "joyful reunion" with her Portuguese husband, who lived in Yokohama then, did not materialize. She and her husband were divorced later in the year.
September 26, 2006	Died in Chicago at age ninety.

BIBLIOGRAPHICAL ESSAY

Note from the Series Editors: The following bibliographic essay contains the major primary and secondary sources the author consulted for this volume. We have asked all authors in the series to omit formal citations in order to make our volumes more readable, inexpensive, and appealing for students and general readers. In adopting this format, Landmark Law Cases and American Society follows the precedent of a number of highly regarded and widely consulted series.

The most important primary materials for this book are legal sources. One of the Founding Fathers and one of the first justices of the Supreme Court was James Wilson. His views on treason, originally expressed in his law lectures, can be found in Kermit L. Hall and Mark David Hall, eds., *Collected Works of James Wilson*, 2 vols. (Indianapolis, 2007), especially in the chapter "Of Crimes Immediately against the Community." For all the modern laws and annotated federal and state court cases on treason, see *U.S. Code Annotated*, Title 18: *Crimes and Criminal Procedure*, 582–628 (18 U.S.C.A. 582). Treason and misprision of treason are defined and the punishment set for death or no less than five years, and a fine no less than $10,000, in *U.S. Statutes at Large*, vol. 35 (1909), 1088–1089 (35 *Stat* 1088); 62 *Stat* 807 (1948). See also 76 *ALR* 2nd (*American Law Reports Annotated*, 2nd Series) 262–263 and 18 *U.S.C.S.* (*U.S. Code Service*, Lawyers Edition) 494–506; 70 *American Jurisprudence*, 3rd ed. (Thomson/West, 2005), "Treason," 53–76.

The manuscript trial records of Iva Toguri d'Aquino are located at the Federal Records Center in San Bruno, CA. They have been fully mined by some historians, especially John J. Hada and Masayo Duus. All of Iva Toguri's five appeals (an appeal, three petitions for rehearing, and a motion for a writ of certiorari) were denied: 192 F 2nd (*Federal Reporters*, Second Series) 338–377; 203 F 2nd 391; 343 U.S. 935; 343 U.S. 958; 345 U.S. 931. Iva's application for bail was denied by the Court of Appeals for the Ninth Circuit, but William O. Douglas reversed the decision, holding that the question of the guilt or the innocence of the defendant was not an issue on application for bail: 180 F 2nd 271–272 (1950); 192 F 2nd 338; 203 F 2nd 391.

A brief survey of all treason cases from the *Burr* case to the treason by radio cases arising out of World War II is included in Arthur M. Stillman and Frederick R. Arner, *Federal Case Law Concerning the Security of the United States* (83rd Congress, 2nd Session. Printed for the Use of the Senate Committee on Foreign Relations. Government Printing Office, Washington, 1954), 3–21. For similar treason cases decided during and after World War II, see the *Quirin* case (1942), 317 U.S. 1; the *Cramer* case (1943–1944), 137 F 2nd 888; 325 U.S. 1; the *Haupt* case (1946), 330 U.S. 631; the *Chandler* case (1948), 171 F 2nd 921, cert. den. 336 U.S. 918; the *Best* case (1950), 76 F Supp. 138-184 F 2nd 131, cert. den. 340 U.S. 939; the *Gillars* case (1950), 182 F 2nd 962;

the *Burgman* case (1951), 188 F 2nd 637, cert. den. 342 U.S. 838; the *Kawakita* case (1952) 343 U.S. 717, 741; and the *Provoo* case (1954), 215 F 2nd 531, 124 F Supp. 185.

Reliable contemporary accounts useful for my study are very few. Rare exceptions are Master Sergeant Katsuo Okada's report on Iva's daily life, an English translation of which is fully discussed in Rex B. Gunn's work (see below) and Namikawa Ryo's activities at Radio Tokyo in "Japanese Overseas Broadcasting: A Personal View," L. R. M. Short, *Film and Radio Propaganda in World War II* (Knoxville, TN, 1983), 319–333. Clark Lee, "Her Neck in a Noose," in *One Last Look Around* (New York, 1947), 84–91, and Harry T. Brundidge, "America's First Woman Traitor," in *The American Mercury* (January 1954), 37–41, are too one-sided and distorted to be reliable.

In addition to the primary materials above, my study heavily depends upon many secondary works. In fact, all the historians build on the work of others who precede them, and I would like to fully acknowledge my indebtedness to the following studies, both books and articles.

On the general topic of treason in American history, some significant studies have been made. Bradley Chapin, in his *American Law of Treason: Revolutionary and Early National Origins* (Seattle, 1964), briefly surveys the colonial developments and then devotes the rest of the book to the American Revolution and the New Nation through the trial of Aaron Burr. James Willard Hurst, *The Law of Treason in the United States: Collected Essays* (Westport, CT, 1971) is more comprehensive in scope. It is the definitive study of the historical growth of treason law in England and the United States. See Chapter 6 for post–World War II developments. Lawrence M. Friedman treats the law of treason succinctly in various phases of American history in his *Crime and Punishment in American History* (New York, 1993). In his recent work, *The Treason Trials of Aaron Burr* (Lawrence, KS, 2008), a concise analysis of the American law of treason, Peter C. Hoffer treats the *Burr* case in a broad context of American legal history, including the World War II treason cases. Useful for the general history of treason is Alfred H. Kelly, Winfred A. Harbison, and Herman Belz, *The American Constitution: Its Origins and Development*, 7th ed., 2 vols. (New York, 1991)

More specifically, the Tokyo Rose case has attracted the close attention of the American reading public, both general and scholarly, and the story has become a very familiar one as many books and articles have been published. John Juji Hada's study, "The Indictment and Trial of Iva Ikuko Toguri D'Aquino—'Tokyo Rose,' September 1948–September 1949" (MA thesis, University of San Francisco, 1973), is the first extensive study on the trial itself, concentrating on meticulous analysis of the indictment, the trial, and the abortive attempts at appeal. Fully utilizing various court and other records, Hada points out many irregularities in the trial. The Japanese American Citizens League, which had been fainthearted, afraid of being involved in the Tokyo Rose trial at the end of World War II, later strongly supported Iva's cause. The organization played a major role in the movement to win a pardon for Iva. Its National Committee for Iva Toguri prepared a useful booklet, *Iva Toguri (d'Aquino): Victim of a Legend* (May, 1976). Through the life of Iva from her early years to her retirement in Chicago, the pamphlet depicts a number of abuses of her rights, injustice in her trial and sentence, and deportation threat, mainly from the legal point of view.

Indispensable for my study is a brief yet thorough work by Rex B. Gunn, *They Called Her Tokyo Rose* (Santa Monica, CA, 1977), which provided the basic framework of Iva's story but also an eyewitness account of the trial. Gunn was war correspondent in the South Pacific and was in Saipan in 1944. In 1949, he reported on the trial as an Associated Press radio editor. He later interviewed Iva Toguri and the judge and the jurors. The book included some materials that could be found nowhere else, such as Tokyo Rose's broadcast scripts, personal memos within the Justice Department, and Master Sergeant Okada's account on Iva's daily life in Tokyo during the war.

Fuyuko Kamisaka's *Pardon: The Myth and Reality of Tokyo Rose (Tokusho: Tokyo Rosu no Kyozo to Jitsuzo)* (Tokyo, 1978), written in Japanese, is a detailed account of Iva Toguri until 1978.

A year later, a more comprehensive work, Masayo Duus, *Tokyo Rose: Orphan of the Pacific* (Tokyo, 1979), appeared. This book, originally written in Japanese but superbly translated into English by the author's historian husband, Peter Duus, has laid the foundation for the subject. It still remains the standard, general work on Tokyo Rose. Especially valuable are her interviews with many participants.

Another work that was essential for this study is Stanley I. Kutler, "Forging a Legend: The Treason of 'Tokyo Rose,'" *Wisconsin Law Review* 1980, no. 6, 1341–1382 (reprinted as Chapter 1 of his *The American Inquisition: Justice and Injustice in the Old War* [New York, 1982], 3–32, 243–250). It is brief but touches on key aspects of the legal history of Tokyo Rose, written by one of the leading American legal historians. The article contains superb legal analysis and also makes use of some new, crucial documents, only made public since 1975.

Ten years later, Russell W. Howe, in his *The Hunt for "Tokyo Rose"* (Lanham, MD, 1990), tried to elaborate on many aspects of the story thus far treated lightly through extensive interviews of surviving participants in the trial. Frederick P. Close, *Tokyo Rose/An American Patriot: A Dual Biography* (Lanham, MD: Scarecrow, 2010) includes all kinds of useful but familiar documents; however, it appeared too late for me to utilize for my book.

On the presidential power of appointment to the Supreme Court, Henry J. Abraham, *Justices and Presidents: A Political History of Appointments to the Supreme Court*, 2nd ed. (New York, 1985), is a valuable work that fully analyzes the presidential appointments and examines in detail the relations between Harry Truman and Tom Clark. Peter Irons, *Justice at War: The Story of the Japanese Internment Cases* (New York, 1983) and his *People's History of the Supreme Court: The Men and Women Whose Cases and Decisions Have Shaped Our Constitution* (New York, 2006) discuss the

Japanese internment cases, including the dramatic reopening of these cases in the 1980s and their reversal on grounds of governmental misconduct through the writ of error coram nobis.

For more general treatments of the Japanese American internment camps, see Roger Daniels, *Concentration Camps USA* (New York, 1970), revised as *Concentration Camps, North America: Japanese in the United States and Canada during World War II* (Malabar, FL, 1989), and *Prisoners without Trial: Japanese Americans in World War II*, rev. ed. (New York, 1993), and Peter Irons, *Justice at War: The Story of the Japanese American Internment Cases* (New York, 1983).

There is a large body of literature on the Japanese Americans in California and the other Pacific states, but the most useful studies are by the leading authority on the subject, Roger Daniels. See especially *The Politics of Prejudice* (Berkeley, CA, 1962) and *Asian America: Chinese and Japanese in the United States since 1850* (Seattle, 1988). Also important are Yuji Ichioka, *The Issei: The World of First Generation Japanese Immigrants, 1885–1924* (New York, 1988), and Mae M. Ngai, *Impossible Subjects: Illegal Aliens and the Making of Modern America* (Princeton, NJ, 2004).

I have read numerous articles on treason and other related subjects in law reviews and legal journals and other scholarly periodicals. They cover a wide range of topics. The following are selected ones indispensable for my work. Articles dealing with the history of treason are "Historical Concept of Treason: English, American," *Indiana Law Journal* 35: 70–80 (1959); "Treason: Observations on the Law of Treason in the United States, as Applicable to the Case of Colonel Aaron Burr, Written before the Trial at Richmond," *American Law Journal* 1808: 344–360; Gordon S. Wood, "The Real Treason of Aaron Burr," *Proceedings of the American Philosophical Society* 143: 280–293 (June 1999); R. Z. Steinhaus, "Treason, a Brief History with Some Modern Applications," *Brooklyn Law Review* 22: 254 (1956); W. G. Simon, "The Evolution of Treason," *Tulane Law Review* 35: 667–704 (1961). James W. Hurst's three-part essay, "Treason in the United States," in *Harvard Law Review* 58: 226–272, 395–444, 806–857 (1944–1945), his "English Sources of the American Law of Treason," *Wisconsin Law Review* 1945: 315–356, and his "The Historic Background of the Treason Clause of the United States Constitution," *The Federal Bar Journal* 6: 305–313 (Westport, CT, 1945) were all prepared for the defense in *Cramer v. U.S.* and eventually became part of his *The Law of Treason in the United States* (1971).

Some special topics of treason are discussed in Horace J. Bridges, "A Suggestion toward a New Definition of Treason," *Journal of Criminal Law and Criminology* 30: 470–484 (1939); G. P. Fletcher, "Case for Treason," *Maryland Law Review* 41: 193–208 (1982); Herbert N. Rosenberg, "Constitutional Law—Treason, Recent Decisions," *University of Pittsburgh Law Review* 11: 700–703 (1950); Simon Greenleaf, "The Law of Treason," *Monthly Law Reporter* 14: 409–416 (1851); W. T. Brotherton, Jr., "A Case of Treasonous Interpretation," *West Virginia Law Review* 90: 3–16 (1987); "Treason—Overt Acts—Elements of Offense," *Virginia Law Review* 30: 183–184 (1943); Charles Warren, "What Is Giving Aid and Comfort to the Enemy?" *Yale*

Law Journal 27: 331–347 (1918); J. G. Wilson, "Chaining the Leviathan: The Constitutionality of Executing Those Convicted of Treason," *University of Pittsburgh Law Review* 45: 99–179 (1983).

The *Quirin* and *Cramer* cases are analyzed in Trevor Rapke, "A Trial for Treason in the United States," *Australia Law Journal* 19: 210–212 (1946), on traitorous intent; Michael R. Belknap, "The Supreme Court Goes to War: The Meaning and Implications of the *Nazi Saboteur* Case," *Military Law Review* 89: 59 (1980), on *Ex parte* Quirin; James M. Marsh, "The Supreme Court Debates the Law of Treason: Article III, Section 3 of the Constitution (the *Cramer* Case)," *Temple Law Quarterly* 19: 306–317 (1946), on intent; Richard M. Achey, "The Law of Treason in the United States: A Sequel to the *Cramer* Case," *Temple Law Quarterly* 20: 475–482 (1947). J. Woodford Howard, Jr., "Advocacy in Constitutional Choice: The *Cramer* Treason Case, 1942–1945," *American Bar Foundation Research Journal* 1986: 375–413 is an extensive and superb analysis of the Cramer treason case. Hoffer discusses the importance of Justice Robert Jackson's opinion in the *Cramer* case in his *The Treason Trials of Aaron Burr.* More generally, on the eight German saboteurs convicted in the United States during World War II, see Louis Fisher, *Nazi Saboteurs on Trial: A Military Tribunal and American Law,* 2nd ed. (Lawrence, KS, 2005).

Several articles specifically examine the Tokyo Rose case. David Holmstrom, "By Any Other Name: The Trial of 'Tokyo Rose,'" *California Lawyer* 5: 45–48 (1985); Stephan G. Christianson, "Tokyo Rose Trial: 1949," Edward W. Knappman, ed., *Great American Trials* (Detroit, 1994), 450–451; George G. Olshausen, "*D'Aquino v. United States,* the So-Called 'Tokyo Rose' Case," *Lawyers Guild Review* 15: 6–10 (1955), which is a severe criticism of the circuit court opinion, 192 F 2nd 338 (1951) by one of Iva's defense attorneys.

Yuma Totani, the author of *The Tokyo War Crimes Trial: The Pursuit of Justice in the Wake of World War II* (2008), reviewed my manuscript and offered many comments throughout, including the legal effect of the United States/Japan notes on the prisoners of war and interned civilians in Chapter 10.

"The *Shinohara* Case (1948)," *George Washington Law Review* 17: 283–285 (1949), is an analysis of one of the important treason cases, *U.S. v. Shinohara* (1948), treason against the United States by an alien enemy. The case would have had a significant implication in the Tokyo Rose trial regarding the defendant's allegiance.

World War II in the Pacific has attracted the attention of many first-rate historians, who have produced significant works. The following are indispensable works, which I have heavily relied on for my book: Samuel E. Morison, *History of U.S. Naval Operations in World War II,* 15 vols. (Boston, 1947–1962); A. Russell Buchanan, *The United States in World War II,* 2 vols. (New York, 1964); Walter Lord, *Incredible Victory: The Battle of Midway* (New York, 1967); John W. Dower, *War without Mercy: Race and Power in the Pacific War* (New York, 1986); and, most recently, David M. Kennedy, *The American People in World War II* (New York, 1999).

INDEX

DeWolfe, Thomas (Tom), Special Assistant
    Attorney General, 153
  during trial, 87–90, 106–107, 119–122, 124–125
  life of, 82, 87, 153
  and other treason trials, 65, 68–69, 74,
    80–81
  view of trial, 51, 58–59, 72, 89, 113, 115, 144
  See also Clark, Tom C.; United States
    Justice Department
dismissal, motion for, 91
directed verdict of acquittal, 59, 91, 122
"dogs to please their masters," 124
Domei News Agency (Domei Tsushin
    Sha), 50, 37, 38
  Iva at, 22, 24, 25, 162
Douglas, William, U.S. Court of Appeals,
    136, 140
Duckett, Earl M., 81, 131
duress, 92, 123
  defense plea of, 105–106
  definition of the Court of Appeals,
    Ninth Circuit, 141
  Judge Roche on, 128–129
  problem of, 92, 123
  in wartime Japan, 128–129
Dutch East Indies, 16. See also Japan
Duus, Masayo U., 1, 7, 49, 65, 105, 112, 114, 129,
    150, 163

East Asia, 91
eastern California, as relocation site, 23
Eichelberger, General Robert, the Eighth
    Army Commander, 45
Eisenhart, J. Richard, 90
Eisenhower, President Dwight D., 80,
    155–156
Eliff, Nathan, T., 49
emperor's palace, 37, 161
Endo, Mitsuye, 75, 85–87
"enemy race," Japanese Americans as, 21, 23
Enoshima, 51
equal protection, 140–141
evidence, scripts, and records, destruction
    of, 139, 145
"exculpatory" evidence, 164
executive clemency. See Pardon (executive
    clemency)

ex-GIs, 100. See also jury (petit jury);
    witnesses, in Tokyo Rose trial
Exhibits, at Tokyo Rose trial
  15: 119–120
  24: 143–144
  52: 146–147
Ex Parte Endo (1944), 87. See also Endo,
    Mitsuye
Ex Parte Milligan (1866), 86
ex post facto, 152

Fairman, Charles, 86
fair trial, 75, 160, 164
Federal Bureau of Investigation (FBI), 48,
    59, 70, 72, 78
  and Japanese defense witnesses, 77
  New York Times article by, 54–55, 100
Federal Communications Commission
    records59, 124
Federal Court Building, San Francisco, 84
federal criminal cases, 78
Federal District Courts, 154, 164, 165
federal liquor tax laws, 138
Federal Reformatory for Women at
    Alderson, West Virginia, 2, 135, 137, 138,
    155
  Iva at, 149, 150
food-ration card, 129
football, 30
Ford, President Gerald R., 158, 163
Ford, Payton, 73
Foster, Stephen, 34
Founding Fathers, 87
4Fs, 42, 116
Fox, Francis S. J., 64
Freedom of Information Act, 164
Friedman, Lawrence M., 3
Fujiwara (kempei-tai officer), 19, 20
Furuya, Mieko, 31, 35, 39. See also Radio
    Tokyo
futons, 29

General Headquarters of General Douglas
    MacArthur, 45, 75, 78
  Legal Section, 48
Geneva Convention, 29, 140, 142. See also
    Prisoners of War

{ *Index* }

Orphan Ann, 32–34, 39, 91, 99, 100–102, 107–108, 116, 121. *See also* Cousins, Major Charles H.; Toguri, Iva Ikuko d'Aquino
Orphans of the Pacific, 120, 121
Osaka Shipping Company, 13
"overt acts of treason," 5, 72
Overt Acts I-VII, 69–70
  Overt Act 5, 146
  Overt Act 6, "the loss of ships," 84, 134, 140, 146
  See also Toguri, Iva Ikuko d'Aquino
Ozasa, George Teruo, 133, 157

Pacific, 101, 103, 108, 114
Pacific Coast, as "military area," 23, 86
Pacific War, 80, 145
Page, Sergeant Merrit, 45. *See also* Counter Intelligence Corps, Eighth Army (CIC)
Pardon (executive clemency), 139, 155
  granting of, 158, 163
  and innocence, 158–159
  petition for, 156
  versus acquittal, 157
pari material, 142
Parkyns, Kenneth, 78
Patel, Judge Marilyn Hall, 164–165
Pearl Harbor, 1, 18, 87. *See also* Japan
pellagra, 36, 107. *See also* Prisoners of War; Tokyo
peremptory challenges, 81–83
  in *Batson v. Kentucky* (1986), 82–83
perjury, 67, 74, 96, 100, 134
  as a cause for dismissal, 139–140
  perjured evidence, 124, 165
  subornation of perjury, 96, 115
petitions
  for certiorari, 147
  for habeas corpus, 74–75, 85, 160, 164
  for rehearing, 143
  for pardon, 163
petit (trial) jury. *See* jury (petit jury)
Phelan, James D., 23. *See also* Japanese Americans
Philippine Sea, Battle of, 88
Pope, Walter L, 140, 144. *See also* Court of Appeals

Posse Comitatus Act of 1878: 145
  use of the army as *posse comitatus,* 143
  violation of, 139
Presidential election of 1948: 54. *See also* Clark, Tom; Truman, President Harry S
press corps, 125
presumption of innocence, 79, 105, 132
prima facie, 50, 58, 68, 83
Prisoners of War, 19, 29, 89, 107, 109, 128–129, 142, 147, 160
  during American Revolution, 160
  at Bunka Camp, 27, 33, 61, 92, 93, 107, 109, 127, 147
  in Burma, 27
  conditions of, in Tokyo, 128–129
  at Radio Tokyo ("Zero Hour"), 26, 37, 42, 92, 105, 111, 118, 122, 127
  See also Cousins, Major Charles H.; Toguri, Iva Ikuko d'Aquino
"probable cause," 66
Prosnak, Captain John, of the U.S. Army, 63
Provoo, John David, 113–114, 147
PT (motor torpedo) boats, 101
Purcell, James, 85–86

Radio Berlin, 137
Radio Japan. *See* Radio Tokyo
Radio Tokyo, 26–28, 36–38, 57, 74, 94, 121, 124–134, 162
  building, 67, 107
  employees of, 76–77, 162
  Overseas Section, 19
  propaganda or entertainment programs, 83, 91, 135
  "Zero Hour" program, 35, 123
Raufu Shinpo, the, 19
reasonable doubt, 122
  in trial, 79, 102, 105, 122, 124
  versus "a demonstration of innocence" 146
recross-examination, 109
redirect-examination, 116
re-entry to the United States, 64
"relocation centers," 23, 60. *See also* Japanese Americans
Republicans (the Republican party), 54

White House, 156
Whiting, Frances, 43–44, 55, 57
Wilkinson, General James, 4
Williams, George, 92
Willoughby, Major General Charles A., 56
Winchell, Walter, 19, 54–57, 79
wipe (erasure), 107–108
witnesses, in Tokyo Rose trial, 66, 119–120, 122
  ex-GIs as, 100–104, 112–114, 128
  from Japan, 74–77, 90–104, 120, 127–128
  Lee as, 93–96
  Oki and Mitsushio, 127–128, 165
  racial segregation of, 125
WAC (Women's Army Corps), 32
World War I, and treason, 4
World War II, and treason, 70, 75
writ of certiorari. *See* certiorari
writ of error coram nobis. *See* coram nobis
  relief
writ of habeas corpus. *See* habeas corpus
Wurts, Babette, 81
Wyoming, 23

Yagi, Hiromu, 74
  and Brundidge, 73, 115
  testimony of, 71
  as witness, 66–68, 134
  Yagi-Kodaira matter, 95–96, 155
  See also Kodaira, Toshikatsu
Yamaguchi, Jiro, 154
Yamaguchi, Shirley Yoshiko, 56
Yamamoto, Admiral Isoroku, 102
Yasui, Min (Minnoru), 164–165
Yates, Richard, 157
Yerbie, Matthew J., 81
Yokohama, 13, 63
Yokohama Military Stockade, 46

"Zero Hour," 27, 31–33, 35, 39, 42, 44, 76, 89,
  91, 101, 107, 124, 134
  scripts of, 56–57
  former POWs from, as defense
    witnesses, 105, 108, 111
  broadcasts of, 118, 120
Zirpoli, Alfonso, 86, 109–110. *See also* Ince,
  Captain Wallace E. (Ted)